'*It's Terrible the Things I Have to Do to Be Me* lives up to its fabulous, improbable name. It's a long-overdue ode to female creative genius, in all its messy, disturbing, ecstatic and wildly entertaining complexity. This book will make you feel things; it's sparkling and dark and utterly addictive. It *needed* to exist, and Snow has precisely the right blend of narrative elegance and irreverence, coupled with genius-level pop culture knowledge, to bring these stories to life'
Roisin Kiberd, author of *The Disconnect*

'A book of essays that deconstructs received notions of femininity, and obliterates those defunct categories of high and low culture by treating its celebrity subjects first and foremost as artists. Written in prose that glimmers with energy, wisdom and delectable turns-of-phrase, *It's Terrible the Things I Have to Do to Be Me* confirms Philippa Snow's place as the country's most exciting, talented and forward-thinking cultural critic: a writer who has turned criticism into her own form of art'
Ralf Webb, author of *Strange Relations*

'Philippa Snow's strength lies not only in her ability to diagnose why these women continue to captivate us, but why they move us; it is this ability, not just to examine her subjects but to weave them so deeply into the very fabric of our emotional lives, that makes her our most vital cultural critic'
Hannah Regel, author of *The Last Sane Woman*

'Threads together fame's complex relationship with femininity, agency, and beauty. With acoustic brilliance, Snow navigates the often-overlooked spiritual and physical labour the most iconic women of our time have endured, exposing something maniacal about our society's celebrity bloodlust – not just with its demands for perfection, but the gleeful schadenfreude that hits the tabloids when these icons inevitably crack. Like the women in these essays, Snow's work is intoxicating and glossily smooth. Put it up on the biggest billboards immediately'
Elle Nash, author of *Deliver Me*

'Philippa Snow is an incisive composer of criticism whose prose is always both muscular and musical. *It's Terrible the Things I Have to Do to Be Me* is at once a symphony and a manifesto, a virtuoso performance of feminist criticism. This rigorous, elegiac examination of women destroyed by stardom, desire, and the violent demands of femininity is not to be missed'
Emmeline Clein, author of *Dead Weight*

'What Philippa Snow does as one of the finest critics of our time is what I imagine the finest diamond-cutters do: they spend years honing their blade's edge with precision and skill, they train their gaze to go unwaveringly deep into the raw lump of material in front of them, and, from this sustained prowess, they shape a thing of decisive, staggering brilliance. Wherever Philippa directs her instruments of perception, clarity, and acumen is where we, her readers, are left with invaluable gifts. I trust to follow her wherever she chooses to go and, in this book, she takes me into new territories of insight about the punishing price of femininity – that no one can resist and very few can afford – with a wisdom that is as shimmering as it is sharp'
Johanna Hedva, author of *How to Tell When We Will Die*

'An instant classic from the sharpest cultural critic working today. Philippa Snow is witty, entertaining, and intellectually unmatched, a writer with a singular talent for showing us ourselves in the funhouse mirror of celebrity femininity. *It's Terrible the Things I Have to Do to Be Me* is a historical corrective, a loving sendup, and a serious exploration of iconic women too often passed off as unserious. I couldn't put it down'
Allie Rowbottom, author of *Aesthetica*

it's terrible the things i have to do to be me

ON FEMININITY AND FAME

philippa snow

virago

VIRAGO

First published in Great Britain in 2025 by Virago Press

1 3 5 7 9 10 8 6 4 2

Copyright © Philippa Snow 2025
Material from 'It's Terrible the Things I Have to Do to Be Me:
On Anna Nicole Smith and Marilyn Monroe' previously
published by the *White Review* in 2021
'On One Side of the Magic, or the Other: On Pamela Anderson and Tula'
was adapted from the essay 'Blonde Ambition', first published by the
Baffler as part of issue 69 in July 2023
Extract from *L.A. Woman* by Eve Babitz reproduced
with permission from Canongate Books

The moral right of the author has been asserted.

All rights reserved.
No part of this publication may be reproduced, stored in a
retrieval system, or transmitted, in any form or by any means, without
the prior permission in writing of the publisher, nor be otherwise circulated
in any form of binding or cover other than that in which it is published
and without a similar condition including this condition being
imposed on the subsequent purchaser.

A CIP catalogue record for this book
is available from the British Library.

ISBN 978-0-349-01771-6

Typeset in Caslon by M Rules
Printed and bound in Great Britain by
Clays Ltd, Elcograf S.p.A.

Papers used by Virago are from well-managed forests
and other responsible sources.

Virago Press
An imprint of
Little, Brown Book Group
Carmelite House
50 Victoria Embankment
London EC4Y 0DZ

The authorised representative
in the EEA is
Hachette Ireland
8 Castlecourt Centre
Dublin 15, D15 XTP3, Ireland
(email: info@hbgi.ie)

An Hachette UK Company
www.hachette.co.uk

www.virago.co.uk

For my mother, Angela

ALSO BY PHILIPPA SNOW

Which As You Know Means Violence
Trophy Lives

Contents

Introduction   1

1. It's Terrible the Things I Have to Do to Be Me:
   On Anna Nicole Smith and Marilyn Monroe   7

2. I Am the American Dream:
   On Aaliyah and Britney Spears   42

3. Movements of Thought and Soul:
   On Louise Brooks and Kristen Stewart   87

4. They Want a Woman, and I'm Good at That:
   On Joan Crawford and Jane Fonda   130

5. On One Side of the Magic, or the Other:
   On Pamela Anderson and Tula   173

6. Less an Actress Than a Great Natural Wonder:
   On Lindsay Lohan and Elizabeth Taylor   207

7. Some Damnbody Is Always Trying to
   Embalm Me:
   On Amy Winehouse and Billie Holiday   250

   Acknowledgements   291
   Credits   293

'I used to wander down Hollywood Boulevard hoping that Georgia O'Keeffe wasn't really just a man by accident because she was the only woman artist, period, but then [my mother] told me Marilyn Monroe was an artist and not to worry. And so I realized she was right, and I didn't.'

—EVE BABITZ, *L.A. Woman*

Introduction

'I went to the Metropolitan Museum of Art and just sat there, but [the paparazzi] didn't take pictures of that,' the actress, sometime-hellion and tabloid fixture Lindsay Lohan griped to *Elle* in 2006, 'which sucks, because that would have been more interesting than pictures of me coming out of a club.' Lohan's frustration was eminently understandable, even if she herself was also a frustrating figure at that time: a preternaturally gifted performer who quite often spent her downtime acting like a drunken brat, she was right to suggest that her desire to be seen as an appreciator of art was not quite as interesting to the media as her desire to be seen at Le Bain, or, for that matter, her desire for an enviable string of A-List men.

Just like Lindsay Lohan, I came of age in the noughties, in an era characterised by an aggressive style of paparazzi coverage that was largely aimed at women, and particularly aimed at documenting women's failures – their supposed lapses of decorum, of sobriety, of sex appeal, of taste. Watching this panoptic coverage, I became fascinated by the frequent and apparent gaps between person and persona that often resulted from such scrutiny, especially from the media deciding that a woman should be one thing (say, a virgin) and then capturing her behaving like another (say, an adult who has sex). For years, as a writer, I have found myself circling more or less continually around the subject of the things that women do to themselves – physically, psychologically, conceptually – in order to better adapt to fame.

More recently, I have come to believe that my eternal return to this topic is related to the fact that these transformations mirror the innumerable smaller, more mundane alterations of the self that characterise 'normal' feminine life. The female celebrity acts, in effect, as a metonym for womanhood, with her experiences and attributes being much like those of her civilian counterparts, but magnified into something stranger, more bombastic, and far easier to see from a distance, as if on a billboard rather than the screen of an iPhone. I am not a historian, nor am I a biographer. I am not an academic, either. What I am is an *interested party*, and my interest is in the repeated patterns that emerge across the stories of these high-profile women, like the dizzying refractions produced by a hall of mirrors, or by turning the lens of a video camera back towards a live-streaming monitor.

Since the Hollywood machine first whirred into action, a strong, saleable persona has been one of the most valuable assets for anyone who desires to be a star, and for women who are chasing stardom in particular: if we are already often categorised in everyday life – as prudes, feminists, sluts, nags, mothers, wives, girlfriends, femcels, daughters, virgins, socialites, crones, workaholic bitches, ingénues or bimbos, for example – then that categorisation is even more strict for those of us who occupy the public eye. Sometimes, these women's images are workshopped by their agents and their managers; sometimes, they are foisted on them by the press; sometimes, if they are particularly lucky and determined, they are permitted to design them for themselves. An iron-clad persona can be advantageous, acting as a mask, or it can calcify into a prison, stifling any chance of evolution or personal development for the individual trapped inside it.

In *It's Terrible the Things I Have to Do to Be Me*, fourteen famous women are contextualised in pairs, sometimes echoing each other across many decades. There are doomed, sensual blondes with Daddy issues (Marilyn Monroe and Anna Nicole Smith), and literally self-made women whose tireless embodiment of beauty standards drags them into unwarranted scandal (Pamela Anderson and Caroline 'Tula' Cossey), and naturalistic queer thespians with futuristic acting styles (Louise Brooks and Kristen Stewart). In some cases, initial similarities give way to a divergence in their fortunes, with one woman suffering under the immovable weight of her image, and the other finding a way to subvert it: Jane Fonda and Joan Crawford, for example, both made famous initially by their ultra-strict adherence to conventional femininity, or Lindsay Lohan and Elizabeth Taylor, both unusually talented child stars who grew into desirable adult actresses with tumultuous personal lives.

The book's title is a drawn from a statement made in court by Anna Nicole Smith, during a failed attempt to legally inherit her late husband's massive fortune. 'It's very expensive to be me,' she insisted. 'It's terrible the things I have to do to be me.' What she was saying was that she deserved all that money as repayment for the effort that it took to be Anna Nicole, a job that looked like hell from the outside. She put that work in for her husband, yes, but she also put it in for us, and it seemed only right that she was fairly compensated for her trouble. The things that well-known women do to advance themselves, sometimes by choice and sometimes by necessity, are not uniformly terrible; sometimes they are canny, or creative, or strategic, or a little odd. There is, though, always graft involved: sacrifices; heavy nights; late rehearsals; early mornings; major and minor surgeries; crash diets; hours spent in make-up chairs and PR crisis talks and advantageous couplings. 'Everyone is female,' the Pulitzer-Prize-winning critic Andrea Long Chu writes, in her provocative and often very funny 2019 book *Females*, 'and everyone hates it.' She goes on to explain that her definition of 'female', in this context, refers to somebody who has undergone 'any psychic operation in which the self is sacrificed to make room for the desires of another ... [where] the self is hollowed out, made into an incubator for an alien force'. Applying this truncated, somewhat simplified overview of Chu's book-length thesis to the famous woman as an archetype is interesting, since it is difficult to think of a figure who is more routinely subjected to the hollowing out of her interior in favour of the insertion of desire than a female celebrity. Does this, perhaps, make famous women the most female of us all?

One last note: it ought to go without saying, I hope, that 'male' and 'female' alone do not cover the full spectrum of gender, but my focus here is narrow for a reason. The classic tale of discovery, manufacture and ascent that is so often behind the creation of a major female star within a patriarchally driven system is by now as close to a contemporary myth as it is to a publicity yarn, helping to explain why Hollywood, in another bit of mirroring, loves recreating it onscreen. Myths are full of broad archetypes – with no pun intended – because they are designed, however obliquely, to explain us to ourselves. I think these women's stories might help to do this, too. I could not tell you for certain when I first came across that quote from Anna Nicole Smith's ill-fated trial, but I can tell you that, many times since, I have found myself performing some ritual or other for the sake of self-improvement – dieting, depilation, dyeing, dermatological enhancement, whatever – and her words have come unbidden into my mind: *It's expensive to be me! It's terrible the things I have to do to be me!* Funny, though – I still end up doing all of them regardless.

I

It's Terrible the Things I Have to Do to Be Me

On Anna Nicole Smith and Marilyn Monroe

Here was a woman who had modelled her life so closely on Marilyn Monroe's that it eventually killed her – the blonde waves and the fake breasts; the pill addictions and mock-airheaded pronouncements about men and sex and diamonds; all the years spent tumbling down the rabbit-hole in search of somebody with cash willing to play at being Daddy; the *Playboy* spreads, and the unwise sexual exhibitionism, and the occasional moments of bleak honesty that nodded at some formative abuse – and yet still she achieved twice the thing that Marilyn did not: for three days, from 7 September 2006 to 10 September 2006, Anna Nicole Smith was a mother to two living children. As it had for Marilyn, who confessed in her final year that she ached for it 'more than anything', motherhood held as much significance for

Smith as big-time fame did, her desire to be the world's hottest chick only commensurate with her certainty that she should procreate. 'I'm either going to be a very good, very famous movie star and model,' Smith told *Entertainment Weekly* at the height of her success, in 1994, 'or I'm going to have a bunch of kids.' She did not become a great actor, even if for a short time she was one of the most successful models on the planet, with or without her clothes on. She did not make it to forty, either, even though she outlived Marilyn by three sad, medicated years, dying at the Hard Rock Hotel in Florida at thirty-nine years old.

One thing she did make was herself. Vickie Lynn Hogan, born 28 November 1967, was a flat-chested brunette. At the age of five, she announced her intention to become a supermodel; shortly after this, she revised her previous statement and suggested that, in fact, the thing she wanted to be was the reincarnation of Marilyn Monroe. (Not an impersonator, note, or an entirely different starlet who took Marilyn as her inspiration: *the same woman*, occupying the same body, not to mention the same obviously troubled mental space.) A deadening, potentially damaging childhood and adolescence followed, culminating in her growing up too fast; on summer nights, she walked or drove the town's main drag, drinking cheap beer and hollering at boys. 'I thought, well, if I was to have a baby, I would never be lonely,' she said of her impoverished, tedious early life in Mexia, Texas, married to a man she barely knew who had worn blue jeans to their wedding. She gave birth in 1986, at nineteen, and in 1991 she split, leaving behind a husband she described as 'really physically abusive', a job as a waitress at a chicken joint, and a tumble-down childhood home whose windows – proving that life can be heavier handed, even, than bad fiction – overlooked a rubbish heap. In her yearbook photograph, she looks more like an actress from a Bergman movie than a bombshell. She has dolent eyes, an air of hunger; a gaze not quite focused on the here and now.

Later in life, she often claimed to be Marilyn Monroe's long-lost daughter, and although this was entirely impossible in any real or literal sense, in the abstract the statement carried within it a spooky, diamantine ring of truth. Her bimbo-baby mannerisms and her Coke-bottle curves were not Smith's only inheritance from her idol: like Monroe, she was the daughter of an absent daddy, the product of an unhappy home, and the alleged victim of sexual, emotional and physical abuse. 'You want to hear all the things [my mother] did to me?' Smith once asked a television interviewer. 'All the things she let my [stepfather] do to me, or let my brother do to me or my sister? All the beatings and the whippings and rape? That's my mother.' 'From the moment Anna Nicole got famous,' one reporter wrote in *Texas Monthly*, 'she told the world that her role model was Marilyn Monroe. It was a shrewd move, as it linked her image with one of the greatest American icons of all time, and it had a neat logic: one platinum-haired sex symbol taking after another, one poor, deprived child latching onto the success of another.' In the nineties, she ended up renting 12305 5th Helena Drive in LA, where Marilyn had died. 'I'd love to play a psychotic woman, like Marilyn Monroe in *Don't Bother to Knock*,' Smith told *The Morning Call* in 1994. 'She was so good in it, and I just know I could play it. I can just see [it in] her eyes. I know I could get into it.' She carried VHS tapes of Marilyn Monroe movies with her at all times in her purse, as if to do so might attract some of her glamour. If Hugh Hefner had not already bought the burial plot next to Marilyn's grave, Smith often said she would have purchased it herself.

Given that Monroe had not been especially fond of him in life, claiming that she had been stiffed financially when he republished nude photographs of her without her consent in *Playboy*'s inaugural issue in the fifties, Hefner's sinister decision to encroach on her in death had seemed at best like an egregious show of ownership over the woman he had used to help define the slick, all-American vision of his magazine, and at worst like a violation. Had Anna Nicole Smith occupied the space instead, the implication might have been a little different: certainly, Smith was bisexual, and there may have been a part of her that longed to sleep with Marilyn, but the impression left by her desire to do so for an eternity is that of a young woman who is well aware that she is on the same trajectory as her long-dead, luckless heroine. In 1993, Smith briefly signed on for a remake of the Monroe-starring noir *Niagara* whose screenplay '[played] up the sexual undercurrents that, because of the times, were [subtler] in the original', according to *Variety*. In the 1953 film, released in the same year Hefner published Monroe's naked photographs in *Playboy*, a young couple on their honeymoon at the titular landmark meet another married pair named Rose and George, who are both volatile and wild. Rose is having an affair, and because she is played by Marilyn Monroe, the movie paints her as the physical embodiment of Eros, as untameable and dangerous as the Falls. A promotion for *Niagara* boasted that the movie had the 'longest walk' in cinematic history, with 116 feet of film devoted to one shot of Monroe's undulating form in a tight skirt and high heels; it failed to mention that the shot was of Rose trying to flee her murderous husband, and that it ended with her being strangled, casually and in cold blood, in a bell tower.

When it came to Marilyn Monroe, Anna Nicole Smith herself was a remake who played up sexual undercurrents that had been far subtler in the original version, and Smith's recreation of *Niagara*'s 'longest walk' would no doubt also have made subtext into something more like text, the resulting scene imbued with a more obvious commingling of the deathly and the pornographic thanks to our knowledge of both actresses' biographies. 'I can just relate to [Marilyn],' Smith said, in an interview that addressed her speculative casting in the project – adding, as if she had not taken fully corporeal form until her transformation into America's newest and most naked sweetheart, 'especially after I got my body.' Because it was 1993, what she meant when she said 'my body' was the body that had made her the new Guess girl, i.e. one of stacked, Amazonian improbability. She would have many bodies over the ensuing decade: fat and thin, a desirable body and a goofy slapstick body, a drug addict's body and a junk food addict's body and the body of a girl who owed it all to *TrimSpa, baby!* By 2006, photographed holding her brand-new daughter Dannielynn in a hospital in Nassau, she looked ruddily tanned, blonde enough that her hair seemed to glow, and sweetly, strikingly vacant, as if once she had fulfilled what she believed to be the true destiny of her ever-changing physicality not just once, but twice, there was little left for her to think, or say.

Marilyn herself miscarried twice, and also suffered an ectopic pregnancy, her longing for a child only increasing as she moved into her thirties. She may have been the sex symbol to end all sex symbols – 'if I'm going to be a symbol of something, I'd rather have it be sex than some other things they've got symbols of,' she once said, ruefully – but for her the act itself was purely recreational, never procreative. 'I used to think if I ever had a child, I would have wanted only a son,' she wrote, in a letter to the poet Norman Rosten. 'But... I know I would have loved a little girl as much – maybe the former feeling was only Freudian, anyway.' A long-time advocate of psychoanalysis, Marilyn knew her Freudian from her Jungian, and when she began to undertake more therapy than ever in the last year of her life, she often circled back to the same topics: her ultimate goal of pregnancy; her mother, Gladys Baker; men she'd fucked and men she'd wished had been her father, and the way that those two groups had overlapped. Her increased interest in the workings of the mind had sprung from her connection to a Los Angeles psychotherapist, Dr Ralph Greenson, who met her in 1960 and was soon seeing her for four hours a day, and sometimes also in the evenings. Concurrently, she started to record her own stream-of-consciousness monologues about her familial, sexual and professional history, inspired by her love of

Ulysses, which she read several times and preferred to dip into out of order to preserve its tangled, offbeat mystery. 'This damn free association,' she said on one of those tapes, 'could drive somebody crazy. Oh, oh – "crazy" makes me think about my mother.' As a schizophrenic's child, the terror Marilyn felt when she thought about ageing into her mother was acute – both more rational and more extreme than the equivalent fear experienced by most middle-aged women, having far less to do with the loss of her youth than it did with the potentially catastrophic loss, or the splintering, of her self. At all times, she kept a letter sent to her by Gladys in her pocket which read, 'I'd like to have a child that loves me, not hates me', as if she were carrying a protective spell – her own version, in a sense, of Smith's superstitiously held copy of *Don't Bother to Knock*.

Greenson's relationship with his famous patient was both thoroughly unorthodox, and terribly unethical: 'She had become my child, my pain, my madness,' he observed after she died, noting that she rarely appeared to be suffering from any kind of psychic pain herself, even when the things she talked about were unbearably bleak. He seemed to muddle sexual and paternal feeling just as much as she did, in spite of the fact that, at just fifty-one, he was not old enough to be her actual father. That he thought of Marilyn as a 'child' – albeit an 'abandoned, masochistic' one – in light of the apt, sophisticated pronouncements she so often made about her image and her sex life suggests that even if Greenson believed himself to be a brilliant therapist, he was not much of a listener. Perhaps he was simply far too much of a man to be impartial in the presence of a self-styled sexual phantom. 'Too many questions, doctor,' Marilyn chastised him, once, when he suggested that her continuing nervousness vis-à-vis appearing on film had something to do with a phobia of her soul being stolen, and with her idea that each new movie allowed Marilyn Monroe to chisel away at Norma Jean, killing her slowly. 'I don't know. What I *do* know is that men don't see me. They just lay their eyes on me.' When she first began her sessions, she confessed she was surprised that he had not asked her to lie down on the couch, reasoning that most men would not pass up an obvious opportunity to see what Marilyn Monroe might look like in bed: open, unguarded, and recumbent. As it happened, she rarely lay down in front of men at all – frightened of the dark, and of leaving herself vulnerable to judgement, she told Greenson that she only ever had sex standing up, and in daylight. He claimed that she discussed having one-off encounters in extremely public places, being more used to performing for an audience than she was to playing a sex kitten in private. She frequently gave out the number of the LA morgue to her dalliances in lieu of her actual digits, telegraphing her closeness to the void ahead of time.

When her then-husband Arthur Miller wrote *The Misfits*, the 1961 film in which she played a beautiful, morose divorcee who is romanced by two tough cowboys, he intended to provide her with the big, serious role she had long dreamed of being able to inhabit. Her combination of sultriness and sadness had been what drew the playwright to his wife, and it thrilled him to believe that only he could see how miserable she was. 'As he describes it,' she once said, either wittingly or unwittingly seeding the idea that there was sometimes a divergence between what Miller described, and what had actually happened, 'I was crying when he met me.' In *The Misfits*, the ageing and rumpled Gay, played by Clark Gable, tells Monroe's luminous Roslyn that she is the saddest girl he's ever met. 'You're the first man that ever said that,' she replies – a little private joke from Arthur Miller, since he'd said those words to Marilyn himself, boasting that 'a smile touched her lips' as he had done so. Not long after *The Misfits* was released, she told her therapist that she longed to 'disappear, onscreen or offscreen, I don't care', and to watch her in that movie is to see it happening in real time: one last burst of creative, kinetic energy from a brilliant performer who was fast becoming too strung-out and melancholy to go on. Miller, pulling away from his wife, began an affair with the stills photographer on-set, and in response, Marilyn began her fatalistic disappearing act in earnest. 'Reading Freud,' she told Greenson, with a touch of the unhappy pragmatism often seen in depressed individuals as they slip into complete, starless darkness, 'taught me that failures are often desired by the subconscious.'

Whether she was talking to her therapist or, in one of her stream-of-consciousness recordings, to herself, Marilyn Monroe spent the last year of her life extremely interested in teasing out, and then dissecting, her unconscious urges. 'I would have liked him to be my father,' she said dreamily of Clark Gable in one of her sessions, 'and call me his little girl.' In *The Misfits*, she had pushed to have a nude scene opposite him, and a bit of unused footage shows her naked back, a sheet covering her breasts, as Gable leans in and tenderly puts his lips on her bare shoulder. The shot, risqué by the standards of the time, makes evident both the great difference in their ages – Marilyn's smooth buttermilk skin brushing against her co-star's tanned and weathered face – and the unbridled lust shared by their characters. When Gable invited Marilyn to his son's christening in 1961, she attended in a black veil looking as if she were going to a funeral instead, and it seemed possible, if a touch deranged, that she was mourning two things simultaneously: the fact that she wasn't the mother of the baby, and the fact that she was not the baby, either. Both roles were desirable to her for the access they would offer to what she saw as the ultimate in love – the warmth and care that Gable radiated in her presence, the stout-hearted quality that made her see him as an ideal partner and an ideal parent all in one. As a child, Marilyn had believed her mother, who worked as a film-cutter at a Hollywood studio, when she'd told her that Gable was her biological father; his casting in *The Misfits* was therefore both the inevitable culmination of her lifelong Electral fixation on the actor, and an unintended confirmation of her belief that nobody made a better husband than one's daddy. Ultimately, however familiar a girl gets with her paterfamilias, his influence on her taste in partners is obvious, even if that influence springs from his not being there at all. Anna Nicole Smith and Marilyn Monroe both yearned for masculine protection, and did not much care how strikingly uncanny their young bodies looked beside the bodies of much older men. Both of them, too, would eventually arrive at a similar idea about what real fathers and sexual father figures had in common: that they screwed you up or screwed you, and then left you, and then either way you'd end up alone unless you'd made yourself a baby to spend time with in their absence.

♦

Anna Nicole Smith had a son in 1986, and then a daughter in 2006, her attitude to the former proving to be just as Freudian as Marilyn Monroe had imagined hers might be: having lustily said that her favourite thing was 'cowboys' in her *Playboy* questionnaire, Smith would often describe Daniel as her 'favourite' or 'number-one' cowboy, as if his having being made within her perfect body made him automatically her perfect man. ('Daniel is truly the love of my life,' she said once, beaming.) There are no images of her with other men as easy and as full of un-faked happiness as those of her with Daniel as a boy, her body language often almost adolescently giddy in spite of the adult-with-a-capital-A shape of her distinctive anatomy. 'People ask me about my childhood,' she monologues wearily in the opening of an episode of her reality TV show, *The Anna Nicole Smith Show*. 'Well, I didn't have a childhood, so I'm having one now.' Like Marilyn, she operated on a continuum between mother and baby, one moment expressing her fervent desire to have further children, and the next behaving like a child herself. Both women seemed to want to procreate because of the unspoken implication that to do so meant being loved and loving limitlessly, in stark contrast to the changeable and brief encounters that they'd had with adult men. Whether or not it occurred to Smith that this was one way in which she had managed to outdo her idol, it would not be possible to say. What it is possible to say is that for three days in 2006 – in spite of everything else that had happened that year, and the year before that, and the year before *that* – she got everything she had really wanted – more than the fame or the money or the implants or the mansion – two times over. Her faraway, vacant look in that hospital photograph with Dannielynn is not the distant glaze of dopedness, or of put-on dumbness, but a look of being emptied out by tenderness: she is beatific, a Madonna with a dye job.

On 10 September 2006, seventy-two hours after she had given birth, she would awake in hospital to find her son dead in his chair, killed by an overdose of Lexapro and Zoloft and his mother's methadone. Reports suggest that he was sitting at her bedside, that the overdose had been an accident, and that he had been trying to get over a badly broken heart. 'I want another baby,' Smith had written in her diary before Dannielynn had been conceived, 'before my Daniel leaves me.' This apparent moment of clairvoyance did not do much to prepare her for the intensity of her grief: in the immediate aftermath of Daniel's death, she lost her grip on reality enough to ask that someone photograph her with the body, so that there remains a mirror for the image of her with her newborn daughter – a Pietà to that earlier Madonna. She claims to have suffered memory loss from the trauma, resulting in a temporary but total mental blackout;

the hospital later said that they sedated her and forcibly removed her from the room, taking four full hours to pry her from her son. 'It was necessary,' her attorney Michael Scott informed the press, 'for Howard [K. Stern, her lawyer and lover] to tell Anna again that Daniel had passed away.' 'Daniel was on TV and they were showing all the footage,' her friend Patrick Simpson said, per an unauthorised Anna Nicole Smith biography, 'and she was saying, "see, he's here, Daniel's here, he's coming home".'

It became necessary to tell Smith a lot of things over and over; robbed of Daniel, she transformed, finally and irrevocably, into a stunted child herself. 'Anna Nicole Smith spent the last days of her life drifting in and out of consciousness under the pale-blue comforter of a king-sized hotel bed,' the *Los Angeles Times* reported in 2009, 'too weak to walk, sit up or drink from anything other than a baby bottle.' Like Marilyn, she had been taking chloral hydrate, a sedative that did not mix well with her usual meds; she had developed abscesses on both her buttocks from injecting slimming drugs, and she had been obtaining medication from at least three unscrupulous doctors under numerous false names. Her 63-year-old psychiatrist, Dr Khristine Eroshevich, was photographed sharing a bath with her, which did not bespeak a great interest in upholding the Hippocratic oath, nor a particularly fervent wish to aid in her patient's recovery from an alleged sex addiction. (Anna Nicole Smith, it seemed, had also taken after Marilyn Monroe when it came to a weakness for medical professionals with questionable methods.) Her room at the Hard Rock Hotel and Casino in Hollywood, Florida, with its white four-poster bed and marble tub, ended up strewn with her detritus: SlimFast cans, nicotine patches, pill bottles and junk food wrappers. She remained in it, decaying, as if lying in a tomb. 'If Daniel has to be buried,' she had said at her son's funeral, trying to climb into his coffin, 'I want to be buried with him.' 'She was having nightmares,' one of her legal team later recalled, detailing her insomnia. 'She was having hallucinations.'

On 5 February 2007, Smith had flown to Florida to buy a yacht, complaining on the flight that she was suffering from pain in her left buttock from injections, and announcing on her limousine ride to the Hard Rock Hotel that she had chills, a cold sensation running up and down her body. When she arrived at the hotel, she had a temperature of 105 degrees Fahrenheit; choosing to treat herself with drugs rather than call an ambulance, she dosed herself to sleep, and woke up drenched in stinking sweat. She did not stir until the morning of the seventh, getting up to eat an egg-white spinach omelette, and then climbing into the hotel room's empty tub, bewildered and afraid. At dinner time, she ordered room service, and at around ten, she watched TV and took more chloral hydrate. By the following afternoon, she was found dead, as pale and frigid to the touch as a statue. Just as Marilyn had been, she was naked, with her nakedness serving as a stark, sad reminder of the significance of her unclothed body – of the way that maintaining it, to say nothing of actually inhabiting it, cost her far more, in the end, than she could reasonably pay.

Because both women were superlatively famous, we have

the dubious honour of being able to compare images of them not only in life, but as they looked in death. When the two are placed side-by-side, Smith's mortuary photograph serves as an uncanny mirror for Monroe's, as if it were a recreation made for an evil magazine editorial: here the same dirty, swept-back platinum hair, seen in profile; there the same bluish lips and thin, black brows. When in 2008, the artist Marlene Dumas showed a new painting called 'Dead Marilyn', she cited as inspiration not only her mother's death in 2007, but a longing to express what she perceived as the 'end of a certain era' in the States. 'In a sense, it is a portrait of death,' she told the MoMA. 'But it is also a portrait of Marilyn Monroe. It is a portrait of a period. It is a portrait of one's own potential death.' ('I believe a little bit in voodoo also, you know?' she added, as if her intention with the painting had been to produce an object whose effect was closer to an invocation or an exorcism than that of a work of art.) Marilyn's death has long been talked about by conspiracy theorists as a possible murder, usually pinning it on the involvement of the FBI after her long-rumoured affair with JFK. More likely, if more mundane, was that she took forty barbiturates on purpose in order to escape an existence that felt, increasingly, murderous in and of itself.

Anna Nicole's autopsy suggested she had died as a result of ingesting a mix of medications – chloral hydrate, diphenhydramine, clonazepam, diazepam, nordiazepam, temazepam, oxazepam, lorazepam, atropine, acetaminophen, topiramate and ciprofloxacin – in amounts that were not large enough to kill her by themselves, meaning that the overdose had been an accident, and that like Daniel, she had probably been trying to recover from a badly broken heart. There was a parity with Marilyn here, too, even if Smith had not meant to take her own life: a longing to escape, or to withdraw from, a world in which the grasping attention of the public had begun to feel like violence. 'Covering a cluster of small scars on her right leg and ankle was an icon medley [tattoo],' the Broward County medical examiner observes in his summary of identifying features: 'Christ's head, Our Lady of Guadalupe, the Holy Bible, the naked torso of a woman, the smiling face of Marilyn Monroe, a heart, shooting flames, and a cross.' 'Vickie Lynn Marshall was a thirty-nine-year-old white female who died of acute combined drug intoxication,' the autopsy concluded. 'Abscesses of buttocks and viral enteritis were contributory causes of death.' Minus her liveliness, her sex appeal, she had returned to being Vickie Lynn, a fact that might be an indignity if it did not mean that 'Anna Nicole Smith' managed in some way to escape death.

♦

Officially, Anna Nicole Smith might be said to have been born in 1993, when she was christened by Paul Marciano, the then-President of Guess. (Vickie Lynn, he later said, had been 'too cheap'.) Still, there was an extended period of gestation: the addition of her married surname, Smith, marked the first stage of her development; the bleaching of her hair defined the next. Her first strip club job, on the day-shift at a place with the business-minded name of The

Executive Suite near Houston International Airport, proved that Vickie Lynn – even with hair the colour of Marilyn Monroe's – had not yet convincingly become a sex symbol: she was flat-chested, and broad-shouldered, and reportedly an awful dancer, off-beat and uncertain. She toyed with being called 'Nikki,' and then with being called 'Robin,' neither alias quite seeming like the right fit. The addition of her breast implants made her, in form if not necessarily in name, into the woman who would eventually make it as a centrefold, and then as a different breed of consumable image altogether. Rumoured to have been created by Dr Gerald Johnson, the rich Texan doctor who had made so many millions of dollars out of breast implants that he had built a breast-shaped hot tub in his yard as a boast, they contained 400cc of silicone apiece. She was an American DD, like women tend to be in porn, or in teenage fantasies – this being, indisputably, the platinum blonde of cup sizes.

It did not take Anna Nicole Smith long after the finalisation of her new identity to become an icon of sex; then, after a few years at the top, one of extreme, near-pornographic camp. As with the actress Joan Crawford, who had experienced a similarly ignominious upbringing and then used her rare beauty to escape it, rumours swirled that Smith made a kind of actual love to the camera, often visibly turned-on by the act of being photographed. 'She gets into a sexual trance,' one photographer panted in a *Texas Monthly* profile. Often, this sexual trance expressed itself as a curious cycle of repeated faces: pursed lips, wide eyes, pursed lips, narrowed eyes, as if the same five or six memories of sexual encounters were replaying on a loop inside her head. Those faces, unnatural in motion, work like magic on the page: she is gloriously striking in her Guess ads, not quite Monroe or Jayne Mansfield or Brigitte Bardot, but sharper, diamond-hard. Her bone structure was naturally more elegant than that of the pre-Monroe Norma Jean, so that even if she *was* poor 'white trash', she still passed for a deb in dark green taffeta in *Playboy*. Like Monroe or Mansfield, too, she was blonde in a way that signified not just desirability, but a desirability that was meticulous in its design, as hard-won as it was perfect. This was blondeness as a bona fide achievement; blondeness as a form of sacrifice in favour of capitulating to the male gaze, marrying the abstract idea of heterosexual masculinity the way a nun might be said to marry Christ.

When Marlene Dumas talked about her Marilyn Monroe portrait marking the end of an era in America in 2008, she was referring to the same age defined by the souped-up retrosexuality of women like Anna Nicole – like burlesque, which made a comeback in the nineties to mid-noughties, Smith embodied what the trend forecaster Gerald Celente called in 1995 'a doomed attempt to return to the '50s – updated with a computer'. If other Guess girls, including Drew Barrymore and Eva Herzigová, were similarly styled to imitate Monroe, Anna Nicole Smith drew more plausible comparisons by dint of dressing like her in her private life, as well. Merging the silicone-centric thrust of nineties-era porn with the attire and ambitions of an MGM gold-digger, Smith fulfilled the expectations of a generation in which women were being told that it was possible to reclaim, and then modernise, an old-school brand of femininity, wearing tired gender roles as ironically as a backwards Von Dutch trucker cap. 'Nostalgia is a distorted view of history,' Celente also said, helping to explain why being Marilyn Monroe might have looked tempting to a stone-broke, desperate girl from Mexia, Texas. 'People look at the '50s as a simpler, better time, and it really wasn't. Remember, the people of the '60s rebelled ... against a phony society [and] false expectations.' Danger, already a mainstay of her early life, hummed like electricity beneath Anna Nicole Smith's smile, in the same frightening way it hummed beneath the supposed morality of the fifties, or in almost every cultural artefact produced in America in the wake of 9/11.

Surprisingly, one of Anna Nicole Smith's biggest fans was the director Werner Herzog, who said in an onstage interview in 2009 that he was 'fascinated by poets who have gone to the very limits of language,' and then went on to imply that she was one of them. 'I am fascinated by *The Anna Nicole Smith Show*,' he continued with genuine awe. 'I mean, [she is] the most vulgar blonde with [huge breasts], but [she] is important; there is something big going on [in her show]. And the big thing going on, of course, was the vulgarity on one side – but it was also that there was some sort of a new image, a new prototype of so-called "beauty" out there. A comic-strip beauty of utter vulgarity. And it's very strange how the collective mind creates these kinds of fantasies.' 'The Mexicans,' he added, 'have a very nice [term] for it: *pura vida*. It doesn't mean just purity of life, but the raw, stark-naked quality of life.' Few stars appreciated the raw and stark-naked quality of life like Anna Nicole Smith. Her attitude to sexuality was ludic, all-encompassing. Her drugs of choice – among them Imipramine, Temazepam, Aldactazide, cocaine, Decadron, speed, Methocarbamol, ecstasy, Prilosec, Paxil, Seldane, Synthroid, Vicodin, and Xanax – reflected an equally unfiltered attitude to getting high. In New Orleans, once, she had fucked another woman in a hotel's clear glass elevator, and at the dizzying pinnacle of her modelling career, she had insisted that all household visitors paid appropriate tribute to her breasts. 'They were more pleasing to the eye than the touch ... but Anna felt she owed everything to [them],' a piece in the *Houston Chronicle* observed, 'and everyone in the house was expected to pay their respects.' She was an exhibitionist, fond of insisting that she would not have spent fourteen thousand dollars on her breast implants if she did not intend them to be seen, or firmly grabbed.

In the 2002–2004 reality show Herzog liked so much, she is a sex symbol exploded frighteningly outwards, destroyed by her own aggressive, lascivious commitment to consumption. She belches, falls down, and gets stuck inside a chair; she reads aloud from Henry Miller. ('I've got her!' she yells delightedly, clutching a copy of *Opus Pistorum*. 'I've got her good! And she's taking a fucking that whoever made her never intended her to have.') In one episode, she challenges her lawyer-cum-lover Howard K. Stern and her personal assistant to an eating contest, leading to one of the most Herzogian, haunting moments in her onscreen history: dressed in a t-shirt bearing a bedazzled screen-print of Marilyn Monroe's signature, slurring as if she is drunk or high, she sits in an Italian restaurant shovelling food into her mouth, sweating and dribbling marinara sauce down her chin. 'This is one of the seven deadly sins, you know,' her purple-haired assistant Kim says, sombrely. 'Gluttony. That's what it says in the Bible.' When Smith retires to the bathroom, the show amplifies the audio of her vomiting into the toilet; Stern, an obvious snake, forces her son to listen in. 'As a matter of fact,' she snarls when she returns, 'I took a shit. How about that?' Herzog's belief in the idea that 'the common denominator of the universe is not harmony, but chaos, hostility, and murder' makes it easier to understand why *The Anna Nicole Smith Show* appealed to him – not just for its vulgarity, but for its abject brutality. Reviews universally referenced Smith's stupidity, her cupidity, and her restive sexual obsessiveness, as if the public had not asked her to play up these traits specifically in order to retain their attention. 'It's not supposed to be funny,' E! shrugged in their promotional tagline. 'It just is.'

Smith's biography might also be said to at least partially resemble that of the titular character in Herzog's 1974 film, *The Enigma of Kaspar Hauser*: the tale of a feral foundling, with no means or education, who ends up enlisted by a travelling circus, rescued by a rich older man, made into a celebrity, and then eventually destroyed. In 1991 she met J. Howard Marshall, her octogenarian husband and her would-be benefactor, while employed at Gigi's Cabaret in Houston; notably, she danced to Chris de Burgh's 'The Lady in Red', a song as cheesy-sweet and schlocky as the buxom, grinning girl performing to it. He was eighty-six, and she was twenty-six, and where she still remembered being poor enough to steal her family's toilet paper from the bathroom of a nearby restaurant, his net worth approached 100 million dollars. The widely publicised details of their affair – that he referred to her as Lady Love, and she referred to him as Paw-Paw; that he bought her an enormous Houston ranch, several Arabian horses, and a house in Brentwood; that she danced with him by circling his wheelchair on their wedding day in 1994 – are rote enough for the relationship between a sugar baby and a very old, extremely wealthy sugar daddy that it does not seem particularly important to examine them up close. J. Howard Marshall, a man with everything who nevertheless had a taste for things other people might call 'cheap', described Red Lobster as his favourite restaurant. Anna Nicole, desperate for cash, had previously worked at Red Lobster, waitressing. It was destiny, a mutually beneficial *coup de foudre*.

The marriage lasted fourteen months, after which time J. Howard Marshall succumbed to pneumonia, and a new hell began for Anna Nicole Smith. In 1995, at one of the late oil tycoon's two funerals, she sang 'Wind Beneath My Wings' wearing her wedding dress and looking every bit as demented as Marilyn had looked wearing a black veil to a christening; afterwards, she tried to take his coffin home in order to display his body on the patio. ('I had to talk her out of it,' a staffer at the funeral home told *People* magazine. 'I could just see him sliding into the swimming pool.') Making matters worse, in 1994 one of her breast implants had ruptured, leaking saline and deflating, and forcing her to endure a three-hour surgery that left her with a painkiller addiction. 'She had a little black bag, like a medicine bag,' the photographer Eric Redding recalled, 'and once, when [my wife and I] looked in it, there were about twenty different medications. There was no way to keep her straight.' By the time her husband died, she was less ditzy than disorientated, and her life was no longer harmonious, but chaotic, hostile, and impossible to watch without a sense of anticipatory terror. Her every televised appearance had the air of something posthumous, profoundly cursed; a gruesomely erotic version of the video from *The Ring*. 'You know those bumper stickers that say "Shit Happens, And Then You Die"?' she once said on her MTV reality show, clear-eyed and frightened and sincere. 'Well, they should make one that says "Shit Happens, And Then You Live". Because that's the truth of it.'

The following decade was spent in a legal battle to inherit what she believed to be her share of her former husband's fortune, which it turned out she was not entitled to as a result of being omitted from his will. The case ran so long that in courtroom images, she appears to be several different women, although a photograph of her waiting to testify in October 2002 remains, it must be said, one of the most beautiful shots of her in public record – in a red suit, her small upturned nose in profile and her sad eyes making her resemble a life-sized, disconsolate doll, she looks breathtaking enough that it is suddenly easy to believe she is worth millions of dollars. It is difficult, too, not to take in this scene and think about her Monroe-starring favourite movie, *Don't Bother to Knock*, with its too-familiar plot: a small-town girl-hick born from nothing, so pleasing to look at that her loveliness can scarcely be believed, is eager to escape her former life. She ends up slipping on the diamonds and fine clothing of a richer, married woman, playing at having a new identity. Obsessed with finding the right man to save her, she eventually goes mad – the seeds of this madness having already been buried deep inside her, apt to bloom. 'If I liked a boy,' she says, 'my folks would whip me. When I went away from them, I didn't cry.' When Marilyn's character, Nell, is caught wearing the other woman's clothes by her dubious uncle Eddie, they discuss her one way out:

EDDIE: You could have kimonos, and rings, and toilet water with Italian names. A handsome girl like you.
NELL: No, I can't! I can't!
EDDIE: Give yourself a little time.
NELL: [Those women] are married. That's what you have to be.

Nell ends up sectioned, dragged away to an indefinite, unhappy future as – presumably – a stunning, lonely mental patient. We assume she never marries. Would her life have been better if she did? 'I'm not happy,' Smith wrote to her mother in a letter in 2000, several years into her raging court case. 'Never have been really. Very lonely mom. I no [sic] how you've felt with men!! ... I don't love anyone but I'll find someone just to get preg and not let him no [sic]. Is that so bad? I don't think so. Men are pigs.'

♦

'My sex life, my life in general, I see as a series of mismatches,' Marilyn Monroe told Dr Greenson in one of her final sessions. 'A man enters, takes me, loses me. In the next frame we see the same man after a second time, only he doesn't have the same smile. His gestures are different ... maybe that's the truth to relations between men and women.' What she meant was: men were mostly pigs, made hungry by her image but disgusted by her damage, her humanity, her agonising periods and her infertility and her sexual neuroses and her need, above all else, to be enveloped by desire at all times. The mismatches between Monroe and her various men were ultimately a result of the mismatch between her physical presentation and her psyche, so that each of them pursued and wooed an empty-headed sexpot, and ended up with a mournful, thoughtful girl who wasn't all that fond of sex at all. 'My only way of being someone,' she once said, 'is by being someone else. That's why I wanted to be an actress.' Before Hollywood came calling, she had posed nude for a calendar, and when the shot eventually resurfaced she surprised both fans and tabloids by appearing not remorseful or embarrassed, but pragmatic. 'I was broke and needed the money,' she informed a female interviewer, brightly. 'Why deny it? You can get one any place. Besides, I'm not ashamed of it. I've done nothing wrong.' From the start, she'd learned to separate her body from her mind, intuiting that both the men who ran the world and the men who ran after her to get her number might see one of these things as having more value than the other. Once, she might have made a pornographic picture, although whether or not the young woman who appears in the clip that was circulated is in fact a pre-surgery, pre-bleach Norma Jean is unconfirmed. If it is, it marks the first time she appeared on film, meaning that her legacy is bookmarked by two instances of onscreen nakedness. When she died, she had been working on a movie called *Something's Gotta Give*, in which she would play a man's ex-wife, lost at sea and presumed dead, who returns to claim her now-remarried husband; in one of the few scenes she actually filmed, she appeared naked in a swimming pool, hitching one leg up on the poolside as if inviting the audience to think about what lay beneath the water. Had it been released, it would have been the first nude scene by a major American actress. It is indicative of her mindset in the last year of her life that rather than accepting the flesh-coloured bodysuit she was supposed to wear in order to look naked, she refused, going topless in a beige bikini bottom and appearing to be almost as undressed as she was in those pin-up shots, that rumoured pornographic movie, or her cut scene in *The Misfits*. Her suddenly cavalier attitude to exposure in this moment could be interpreted either as defeat, or as defiance: the fact that the part was, in effect, one that required her to occupy two states, and two divergent roles, at once – dead and alive; a wife who is also a mistress – suited Marilyn's singular superposition of light and darkness so well at that point in time that it seems criminal the film was never finished. When her character, Ellen, first appears giggling in that pool, her husband Nick genuinely believes, at first, that he is witnessing a ghost – a reminder of the possibility of death, wrapped in a shape so alive as to seem obscene, extravagant, borderline unreal.

In 1962, George Barris photographed Marilyn Monroe for the last time over several weeks, showing her leaping on the beach, climbing a chain-link fence in heels, and wearing seaweed like a barely there bikini: where we typically remember her as being quintessentially and obviously of the fifties, here she is a sixties girl with the bright smile and easy moves of liberation. She is thirty-six and looks a decade younger; hot as LA sand. Two months later, she was dead, ensuring that her image in the public consciousness remained aspic-neat and alluring, and allowing her to be the focus of a new feminine cult of beauty: sentenced to a lifetime of being depicted not just on the silver screen, but in screen-prints on t-shirts like the one worn by Anna Nicole Smith during her televised eating contest; on lampshades and votive candles; on compacts and waste-paper bins and postcards. If Marilyn had lived to be old or become ugly, she would not have been reanimated via CGI for a Dior ad in 2011, looking like a Frankensteinian sex monster in a gilded dress. It is interesting, if a little sad, to think about what a circa-2011 Marilyn Monroe might actually have been like, at the age of eighty-five, and more interesting still – if even sadder – to imagine her as a version of Marilyn Monroe who had achieved the things she'd dreamed of at the pinnacle of her fame: Marilyn Monroe the mother; Marilyn Monroe the grandmother; Marilyn Monroe the Broadway actress, and the Oscar winner, and the public intellectual who talked about James Joyce and Sigmund Freud at dinner parties in New York instead of trotting out one-liners about Chanel No. 5 and diamond necklaces for LA journalists and studio men. The degradation of her perfect mask, with its ever-present smile and its attendant promise of easily malleable stupidity and sex, might have set her free, allowing her to transform into something onscreen husbands and Hollywood producers and executives alike would have doubtless found even more frightening than a ghostly apparition: an undesirable woman, first middle-aged and then elderly, the dream of Marilyn dissolving into ash and champagne bubbles as the clock struck midnight on her youth, and she turned back to Norma Jean.

◆

If Marilyn believed that her life might have been set on a smoother, less calamitous course by a successful pregnancy, this was not what could be said to have happened for Anna Nicole Smith. Her love for Daniel, at first offering her a lifeline, ended up becoming the thing that destroyed her, the loss of him proving to be more than she could bear. Some vital thing in her switched off, as though her soul had for some reason inhabited her son's body, and not hers – as if *her* body, having been reshaped in order to be looked at, was to be kept empty, like a show-home, for display. The most traditionally feminine of her life achievements were, on balance, the most damaging, like the result of wishes on a curling monkey's paw. Her marriage to a rich man, thanks to her omission from his will, bankrupted her; the savage engineering of her body left her too reliant on painkillers to feel much of anything at all. There are photographs from 2006, taken about five months before she died and roughly three weeks after Daniel's sudden death, of her commitment ceremony with Howard K. Stern: she is wearing a white wedding dress flecked with gold, as full-skirted as the gown of a princess in a children's illustration, and yet the prevailing mood is nothing like that of a fairy tale. When the two lovers jump into the sea after exchanging their vows, it looks as much like a suicide pact as it does like spontaneous romance; afterwards, sitting on the beach and squinting, she suggests a woman stranded on a desert island. Earlier that year, while she was still heavily pregnant, Stern had filmed her in full clown make-up, drugged, confusing a plastic baby doll for her own unborn daughter: 'I didn't lose my mind,' she slurs in the clip, 'my baby's over there sleeping.'

In her final months, Smith got thin again, but also became dangerously manic, so that while the public no doubt thrilled to learn that half her weight had disappeared, it could not have escaped their notice that her attachment to the earthly, concrete world had followed suit. 'She would say, "I want to die naked under the covers just like Marilyn Monroe,"' Eric Redding claimed, "and die from an overdose of sleeping pills".' As if to highlight her previous closeness to the superhuman, and to underscore how far she'd fallen as a consequence, the suite she died in at the Hard Rock Hotel in Florida was the Apollo Suite – Apollo, the Sun God, being the most beautiful of all of Zeus' children, a symbolic representative in myth of both tenderness and terror, medicine and punishing disease. ('Although Apollo had many love affairs,' an entry in the *Encyclopaedia Britannica* notes, drily, 'they were mostly unfortunate.') Anna Nicole had been called 'goddess' – usually with the modifier 'sex' – for most of her career, first lovingly and then ironically. What once marked her out as more-than now became an impossible standard to live up to; a perversion of the natural, un-augmented order.

In *Illegal Aliens*, a film she made not long before her death, she played a different kind of superhuman or celestial being – one from outer space, posing as a sometime-reality-star named Anna Nicole. Released posthumously, the movie is a (space)shipwreck; Smith rarely finishes her lines, and often appears to be reading, squinting, from a cue-card. Still, there are moments of accidental poignancy: when the opening voiceover informs us that the aliens chose to inhabit these bodies 'because super-hot chicks have it really easy', it does not seem to know that it is making an unforgivably ironic joke. Likewise, when Smith's lingerie-clad earth visitor walks into a rough redneck bar and simply stands there, looking at her fingernails as if she's high as shit and has forgotten what a fingernail is for, it feels like an unintended piece of commentary when two slavering men – choosing to overlook the fact that she is barely sentient, barely conscious – rush up to her to exclaim how *hot hot hot* she is. 'Anna Nicole Smith, [*Illegal Aliens*] star and one of its producers, [fought] to get through a speech that she herself wrote. Her idea [was] for her to break character and launch into a fit of comic rage about the sloppy script, an explosion that builds to her shouting: "Who do I have to fuck to get out of this movie?" In response, male crew members raise their hands into the shot. It's a dark joke,' *The Village Voice* observed, 'and it's the film's best.'

'Help, help, help,' Marilyn once wrote in her diary, 'I feel life coming closer, when all I want is to die!' To be Marilyn Monroe or Anna Nicole Smith was to be asked to embody the opposite of death – the promise of an orgasm, of twenty-four-hour fun; of a pretty blonde head so thoroughly empty inside that no serious thought could survive in the hollow of its well-formed skull. The problem for them both was precisely this intense rush of life, this *un*deathliness, that rose up inside them; the way that it built into a suffocating wave, the need for drugs or sex or babies or jewellery or pure, unalloyed, devastating love subsuming them entirely. The fact that Marilyn Monroe ultimately died in the 'real' Hollywood in California, and Anna Nicole Smith died in Hollywood, Florida, is – like the view of the trash heap from Vickie Lynn's shack – such a melodramatic, almost tragicomic narrative detail that it feels as if it should be a mean-spirited invention of the press, and yet somehow none of the barbative obituaries written about Smith seemed to come up with anything half as inventive in their efforts to belittle her. 'All the attempts to justify her fame that have flowed in since her death on Thursday are hollow. She was not Marilyn Monroe,' the critic Caryn James wrote, a few days after Smith's death, 'and she was not a cautionary tale, [because] she courted attention too relentlessly to seem innocent or deluded.'

Born in dirt, shaped by violence, and convinced that her one asset was her body, Anna Nicole Smith was undoubtedly determined to be rich and famous, but her desperation to succeed did not necessarily negate her legitimate victimhood, nor did it save her from implosion. In a clip from the Billboard Awards in 2004, about three years before her death, she can be seen stepping on-stage to introduce the rapper Kanye West. Dressed like a porno-lite flamenco dancer, she throws up her slender arms and then runs them down her body, grinning in a way that starts out looking wolfishly sexy, and then suddenly becomes more like the grimace of a beast that is cornered in a zoo. She rolls her eyes, and bares her orderly white teeth. She looks incredible, this terrifying and post-human woman with her supernatural outline, her face like a Patrick Nagel drawing of a female face. 'You like my body?' she asks in a doped, molasses voice, running a long, red fingernail across her ample breasts and sounding like a slowed-down recording of herself. 'Ah was honoured tew . . . be on awr . . . next purformer's new videowwww. An if I evuuuuuur record an allllbum . . . I want thiiis guy to produce mah . . . me . . . make me beeeauuuuutiffuuuul dueeeeets . . . cause he's freeeeaaakiiiin jeeeenyuuuuuuus!'

And then what Anna Nicole Smith does is throw up her manicured hands once again, and begin clapping them, repeatedly and rhythmically, in the air, as if she is an amateur magician trying to perform a misdirection. What she presumably does not want us to be looking at, in that humiliating moment, is her face: her bowed blonde head, the tight mouth and the downturned eyes that suggest that she might be trying not to cry; that she has only now realised just how very high she is. *Help, help, help,* the face says to us for a fleeting instant, before the camera cuts and she disappears off-screen. *I feel life coming closer, when all I want is to die!*

As conflagrant and hard to look away from as a car crash, what this clip most calls to mind is a video of Marilyn Monroe – who never arrived at anything with time to spare except, perhaps, her death – running late to breathily sing 'Happy Birthday' to President Kennedy. In the footage, it is 1962, and the rumour is that Marilyn and Kennedy have slept together, but the President has iced her out for being needy, making her unwillingness to be on time for the engagement feel like yet another bit of sexual strategy – a chance to make him wait for her, and only her, and thus prove her irreplaceability as a woman and a star. When she rushes out into the black velvet vacuum of the stage, glowing like a silver spectre, the compere announces her as 'the *late* Marilyn Monroe': a frightening example of predestination, or else of the kind of coincidence that cannot help but feel like destiny in the life of a girl who was apparently built to die, a sacrifice to the machine. The feminist writer Gloria Steinem used to say that she did not believe in walking out of movies, but that she had done so twice, and that one of those times had been during a screening of the 1953 film *Gentlemen Prefer Blondes*, in which Marilyn had played a showgirl and aspiring sugar baby named Lorelei Lee. 'I was embarrassed by her,' Steinem told a PBS documentarian in 2006. 'She was a joke, she was vulnerable, she was so eager for approval. She was all the things that I feared most being as a teenage girl. It wasn't until the women's movement came along much later in my life that I realised that we had to look at the *why* of those feelings.' What she'd come to realise was that Marilyn Monroe, in taking on the mantle of the ur-sex-goddess, the ur-woman who was designed to please men and men alone, had also taken on and amplified all of the most embarrassing qualities of female heterosexuality, reflecting them back at her audience. 'When I was a model,' Marilyn Monroe told Dr Greenson, 'I looked in mirrors or to other people to find out who I was.' If women were embarrassed by the sight of Marilyn Monroe or Anna Nicole Smith performing their bottle-blonde burlesques of femininity, Steinem posited, it may be because they are the mirrors *we* look into to discover things about our sexual or gendered selves.

'I was walking in a little Spanish town,' Truman Capote wrote in a diary entry about Marilyn Monroe's death, '[and] I saw these headlines saying: "Marilyn Monroe, *Morte*", I was shocked, even though you knew she was the kind of person this might happen to.' Anna Nicole Smith was this kind of person, too, and we know by now that a woman in this mould – an allegedly abused child who had grown into a sex symbol, an erotic cartoon fated to be underestimated and exploited – might at first appear to lead a charmed life, but is in fact often burdened by the weight of expectation. When Anna Nicole Smith appeared in court to argue that she ought to be entitled to the money she'd expected to receive from her late husband, one of the points she made was that the cost of being Anna Nicole Smith, in contrast to the cost of being Vickie Lynn Hogan, was untenable, financially but also spiritually and emotionally. 'It's very expensive to be me,' she appealed to the jury, adding with deliberate emphasis: 'It's *terrible* the things I have to do to be me.' For years the public watched her do them, on their televisions and in magazines, just as their predecessors had watched Marilyn Monroe. She was not lying.

2

I Am the American Dream

On Aaliyah and Britney Spears

'It is dark in my favourite dream,' she told a journalist for the German newspaper *Die Zeit* in 2001, sitting in a hotel room in Paris. 'Someone is following me. I don't know why. I'm scared. Then suddenly I lift off. Far away. How do I feel? As if I am swimming in the air. Free. Weightless. Nobody can reach me. Nobody can touch me. It's a wonderful feeling. Still, the dream worries me a little.' That this conversation occurred not merely in 2001, but in July of that year, is significant – it makes her dark dream into something like a premonition. The clipped, formal diction of this quote – 'I am' rather than 'I'm', for example, or the severing of several of its statements into small, gnomic fragments – might be attributed to its being doubly translated, first into German for the paper, and then back into English to be circulated on various English-language blogs. It seems fitting, though, for the subject at hand, as if its message were beyond considerations of space and geography, or as if the person speaking might be thousands of years old. What is age, anyway, in the context of our dreams? It is nothing but a number.

Aaliyah Dana Haughton was twenty-two when she gave this interview, and if this answer to a question about dreams seems particularly sombre and poetic for a young, hip pop star, it is also not entirely out of character for *her*. Aaliyah, to use the mononym she became famous under, always had a certain preternatural air of maturity – a characteristic that was used against her, cruelly, in the industry, but which also lent a rare lustre to her voice. She did not write her own songs, she explained to the music critic Jon Caramanica in another 2001 interview, but she had 'always been the interpreter'. 'I act it out,' she added, noting that there were 'obviously' reasons she was drawn to certain tracks. 'The scars are there,' Caramanica writes. 'In an era of unchecked frivolity, Aaliyah is the last of the torch singers.' In other words, Aaliyah knew how to touch things that other people could not see; how to access places and ideas that one might not have expected such a young and radiant girl to have been able to access. Partly, this might have been because she was also tasked with learning to interpret the rules of adulthood long before she had been an adult, in all of the usual ways that a teenager who becomes famous has to, and in some more alarming and unusual ways, as well. But in her early poise, this quality also seemed innate, and it was easy to imagine that her dreams might be more serious, more portentous, than those of many of her peers. The producer

Mark Ronson once described the teenage Aaliyah, lovingly, as being possessed of an 'almost grandmotherly grace'.

At ten, in 1989, Aaliyah appeared on the TV competition series *Star Search*, an occurrence that would go on to be something of a rite of passage for the icons of the future in the nineties. Dressed like a woman of forty, her white clothes – pale stockings, a long, ruffled skirt, and a broad-shouldered jacket like a matador's – make her look almost ghostly in the low-res VHS rip that exists online. Rather than a contemporary song, or even a recently vintage one, she sings 'My Funny Valentine', a show-tune from the 1937 musical *Babes in Arms* famously covered by Ella Fitzgerald. It is this version of the song – soulful, swooping, vaguely mournful and molasses-slow – that has inspired her vocal style in this performance. Still, in spite of her miniature-adult bearing and her miniature-adult clothes, she is obviously a child in the clip, and there is something sweetly mannered about her delivery and inflection, as if she is trying to convince us of her depth and seriousness by literally deepening her voice and exaggerating her enunciation. Underneath it all, there is that nascently grand talent – if this is a preteen's impersonation of wisdom beyond age, it is a convincing enough one that we have to guess that something in it is authentic. In 2021, the acclaimed music journalist Kathy Iandoli published a biography entitled *Baby Girl: Better Known as Aaliyah*, and her descriptions of the singer reveal both the touching intensity of Iandoli's fandom, and the degree to which those who loved Aaliyah saw something in her that they found hard to describe without resorting to extreme and almost spiritual language.

'This mythical creature,' Iandoli calls her: 'A goddess, whose art transformed into this fantastical silhouette that hangs over her music.' 'It's apparent she was otherworldly,' she insists elsewhere, 'even when she walked this earth ... she felt abstract, and yet tangible at the same time.'

As if pointing out Aaliyah's natural suitedness for stardom, Iandoli also notes that her name is the feminine form of 'Ali', which means 'the highest, the most exalted one', or alternately 'the champion, the greatest, king of kings' when translated from its original Arabic roots. All of this effusiveness might have seemed othering or patronising if it had not so obviously been rooted in great love, and in boundless admiration. Iandoli, in committing this vision of Aaliyah to the page, is issuing a corrective – making up for lost time. It is poignant that, as she notes, one of the most common descriptors applied to the pop star when she interviewed her friends, her family and her peers was 'angel'. On 25 August 2001, mere weeks after she had described her 'dark dream' about flying to the journalist from *Die Zeit*, Aaliyah was killed in a plane crash over the Bahamas. As this happened, she was caught up in two things: an unthinkable tragedy, and an uninspired metaphor about the risks of fame. We could no longer follow her, or reach her, or touch her, only mourn her; the least painful way to think about it was for us to imagine her being weightless, being free. Of course it had taken something huge, almost mythic, to put an end to her life – the life that seemed to vibrate out of her whenever she appeared on camera, and that seemed so rich and deep. Forever, she would be preserved as a woman who was barely old enough – in her native America, at least – to legally order a drink.

This preservation was a tasteless joke on the universe's part for several reasons, only one of which was the fact it denied audiences the chance to see the full maturation of her talent. Another was that her professional nickname, Baby Girl, would stay appropriate forever. A third was that, as alluded to in the opening paragraphs of this essay, she had already lived through an ordeal in her teens that might have broken her, and she had flourished in the wake of it instead: her early success had been bound up with the older man who'd discovered her, the predatory singer, songwriter and Svengali Robert Sylvester Kelly, who began a 'relationship' with her when she was somewhere around fourteen, and then falsified her documents in order to illegally marry her at fifteen. It is difficult to know whether the things done to vulnerable women by those in positions of authority should be allowed to dominate our accounts of their lives, and that question is a double-bind of sorts: if we ignore their work in favour of their abuse, we diminish them as artists, but if we do not acknowledge that some of this work was made under duress, or in spite of it, we are stripping them of a notable achievement – denying their ability to still be brilliant and productive in the face of cruelty, or failing to commemorate their bravery. 'When I first began working on *Baby Girl*, I decided not to write about the circumstances surrounding her involvement with R. Kelly, and how it unfolded over time,' Iandoli says in her author's note. 'Mentioning him within [an account of] Aaliyah's life cheapened the narrative, in my opinion.' Later, however, Iandoli reached a different conclusion, understanding that there was more than one way to honour a girl who had endured all the things that Aaliyah had endured in her teens: 'I realise[d] that disregarding R. Kelly's chapter in her life would be denying Aaliyah another title she so greatly deserved: "survivor".'

In the final years of the twentieth century, two very young women became world renowned, and their lives and their careers became helplessly, inextricably muddled with the actions of unethical older men in such a way that, in spite of their great success, some of their work has been tainted by the intervention of this dark male power. Taken together, their stories have something significant to say about the music industry, and about who gets to survive in it; who gets used, and how; who gets to become, and to remain, a role model; who is forced to grow up far too fast. One of these women was, of course, Aaliyah. The other was another former *Star Search* contestant by the name of Britney Spears. Spears also appeared on the show at ten years old, in 1992, and she also sang like an uncanny little adult, full of fire and determination. Where Aaliyah's impression of a grown-up had been smooth and smoky, hers carried the suggestion that she might have spent some time on the beauty pageant circuit, where made-up adolescents are encouraged to imitate cruise-ship divas. Also wearing black and white, in the same white stockings, she performed 'Love Can Build a Bridge', hitting the most intimidating notes with perfect, thundering clarity – a V12 engine of a voice in a Mini Cooper body. Aaliyah's ten-year-old face, like that of a beautiful college student who had been miniaturised with a science-fiction shrink ray, could not have been more different from the face of this blonde, Southern white girl who looked like an American Girl doll, or like a cherub from a Botticelli painting if that cherub were a little, as she herself later put it, 'country'. Afterwards, *Star Search* host Ed McMahon asked her if she had a boyfriend, and when she demurred, saying that boys were mean, he countered: 'How about me?' The audience did not find this odd, merely funny, and if she found it odd, she didn't say.

After losing *Star Search* and declining Ed McMahon, Britney Spears spent two years on *The Mickey Mouse Club*. Once the show went off the air in 1994, she began thinking about entering the music industry, and by 1998, she had burst into the charts with a single written by the Swedish pop maestro Max Martin. Where Aaliyah had been remarkable for her adult affect as a teenager, Spears' self-presentation underscored her adolescent status to the point of either camp or perversion, depending who you asked. She recorded '... Baby One More Time' when she was just fifteen, its lyrics either requesting one final fuck or one final act of violence from an ex, also depending who you asked: 'Hit me, baby, one more time.' Her PR team were quick to brand her as a virgin, and the resonant voice that she had displayed as a child was replaced by one that sounded, paradoxically, more infantile than ever: playful and distinctive, yes, but with a fried, babyish cadence. At sixteen, she appeared in a music video for the track that took place in a high school, wearing, in one memorable scene, a Catholic schoolgirl's uniform to gyrate in the halls. The setting for the video for '... Baby One More Time' had been Spears' own idea, one imagines because it was her milieu;

some adult male viewers saw it differently, as a reflection not of the experiences of a normal girl who simply wanted to look cool and foxy for the cameras, but of the familiar tropes of barely legal porn. This plausible deniability – a marketing gimmick that read as innocent to underage girls, but which could be interpreted as something more provocative by certain interested adults – helped to make Spears a star, and it also helped to set her off on a trajectory that has ensured that much of her life has been spent in a state of suspended animation as far as her agency and psyche are concerned. She *is* a Baby Girl who got to grow out of the title, in a sense – and yet not really, given that she spent many years being subjected to attention in the most unhealthy, topsy-turvy way: sexualised as a child, and then infantilised as an adult, the resulting pressure squeezing her conception of herself into something fundamentally misshapen.

In 2001, two weeks after Aaliyah's death, Britney Spears performed at the VMAs with a phallic snake wrapped around her shoulders, a tanned and toned Louisiana white chick singing about wanting to be treated like a slave. If the message of the song struck anyone back then as tasteless, its insensitivity went unremarked upon, and the jumbled pop-exoticism of her stage set and her costume likewise went uncountered. A beautiful blonde with newly full breasts and an abdomen so chiselled it looked more like something out of a depiction of the crucifixion than a young girl's belly, Spears was just the kind of woman one might guess would have the world on a string; and in this moment, as far as fame and money were concerned, she certainly did appear to. Her involvement in her own branding, too, was at this point still reportedly considerable, and by all accounts Spears was an enthusiastic, talented performer with opinions about almost every aspect of her stagecraft, from her costumes to her choreography. She was at her gleaming peak: so slick, so taut and so golden that it was easier to think of her as a piece of iconography than as a twenty-year-old girl. Seeing her as an abstracted symbol also made it easier to swallow the strange line in the track where she pleads with the listener to leave behind her name and age, letting us re-contextualise what might otherwise have been an unpleasant bit of creepiness into a nod to her post-human pop significance. Onstage at the VMAs, she was no longer merely Britney Jean Spears from Kentwood, aged twenty, but America itself.*

---

* It would be odd, I think, not to mention here the fact that just two days after Spears' performance at the VMAs, 9/11 happened. Obviously, there is no literal connection between Britney Spears' ensuing mid-00s breakdown and this famous act of terrorism, and to convincingly suggest that there might be would require a truly Didionesque knack for doomy free-association. Nonetheless, it is widely understood that America's culture entered a far darker period in the aftermath of that terrible event, and that it felt as if some form of madness – a greater interest in both cruelty and surveillance – took over mainstream culture, birthing everything from torture porn to invasive 24/7 paparazzi coverage. If Spears' subsequent downfall did not actually have anything to do with 9/11, it certainly felt as if it fit comfortably into the prevailing mood of the decade that succeeded the collapse of the Twin Towers. Promoting his 2017 film *Vox Lux*, a horror-satire about a teen pop sensation who survives a school shooting and then sells her soul to the devil for success, the director Brady Corbet put it thus in an interview with *The Scotsman*: 'When people talk about the early part of the new century, I think that they are going to talk about school shootings, terrorism, 9/11 and, in equal measure, they will talk about Britney Spears.'

Reducing a woman to a symbol, however, leaves her at risk of not being treated like a person. Spears' status as a star who was expected to be pure *and* playfully naughty led to a contradiction of persona that unmoored her. As the world's sexiest so-called virgin, she was in effect being sold to her audience as the ultimate exclusive product, a commodity a little like a brand-new sports car, especially when one considers how the value of a brand-new sports car depreciates once it is driven off the forecourt. In 2000, an anonymous multimillionaire contacted Jive, Spears' record label, offering the precise sum of 7.5 million dollars in exchange for her virginity. 'It's a disgusting offer,' Spears spat, rightly furious. 'It's outrageous how a man like that can offer something which is totally unacceptable.' Spears undoubtedly meant it was outrageous for a man to attempt to buy her body without its having been explicitly advertised for sale, but the offer was outrageous, too, in the sense that it was something of a lowball when it came to the value of her dirty-saintly image. A year later, Spears was paid ten million dollars in exchange for her endorsement of Pepsi alone, and she appeared in an ad that depicted her dancing with furious precision in a mocked-up Pepsi factory, the spot dedicating just as much airtime to her smile and her navel as it did to the soda company's logo. Intercut with her routine were shots of a teenage burger-flipper in a diner, watching her on television open-mouthed as a stove caught fire in the background, threatening to reduce the whole place to ash. The implication was that Spears was so molten-hot that her desirability was almost dangerous, but also that her sex appeal was a force that she exerted at a distance – like the influence of the moon on the tides – and only ever through the prophylactic medium of the screen. 'It is not that Britney Spears denies that she is a sexual icon, or that she disputes that American men are fascinated with the concept of the wet-hot virgin, or that she feels her success says nothing about what our society fantasises about,' Chuck Klosterman wrote, profiling Spears for *Esquire* in 2003. 'She doesn't disagree with any of that stuff, because she swears she has never even thought about it.' Of course, Spears was no fool, and thus must have thought about 'that stuff' in private – but the careful projection of her sexless sexuality was a lucrative business for both her and her team, and it was necessary for her to adopt an almost Zen-like state of blank denial to maintain the status quo. The public's belief in her virginity became, for a time, more of a matter of faith than of logic, perhaps helping to explain why her fans have long referred to her as 'The Holy Spearit', or as 'Godney Spears'.

In 1999, she began a relationship with *NSYNC's Justin Timberlake, and the two of them became pop music's version of a dignified royal family; on the red carpet for the American Music Awards in 2001, they both wore pale blue denim head-to-toe. If Spears had already seemed like an all-American fantasy by herself, here they looked like somebody had plugged the prompt 'pretty white Americans' into an AI generator, at once tasteful in the sense of 'chaste' and tasteless in the sense of 'tacky'. While they were together, Spears' team made the executive decision to suggest that she was continuing to save herself for marriage, and so although by her own later admission she had already had sex with her older brother's friend at just fourteen, the party line was that these two people were so pure of heart that they were above temptation. (In their fans' defence, these denim outfits did not do much to suggest a couple who were having sex. Side-by-side, beaming, they looked clean, covered-up and – crucially – woefully un-horny.) The trouble began when they broke up the following year, in 2002. Timberlake, appearing on *The Howard Stern Show*, admitted they'd had sex; he also implied that her cheating was behind the breakup. Suddenly, Spears was not only a non-virgin, but a whore, and all of the girls who had believed they could relate to her because they, too, were *not* fucking Justin Timberlake – to say nothing of the middle-aged men who'd felt that their own failure to have sex with Britney Spears was fine, provided no one else was doing it, either – rioted. Diane Sawyer, comporting herself like a disappointed mother, invited Spears onto her show and then laid into her, reducing her to tears. Taking on the role of judge, jury and executioner, Sawyer read aloud from a statement made by the then-wife of the Governor of Maryland. 'Really,' the politician's wife had said, 'if I had an opportunity to shoot Britney Spears, I think I would.' Spears would later say that she felt 'something dark come over [her] body' immediately following this interview, as if Sawyer merely invoking the idea of her death secondhand had been enough to set her on the road to ruin. It was the beginning of her own dark dream, and of a period of her life in which she frequently behaved as if being shot by the wife of the former Governor of Maryland would have been not a threat, but a relief.

At the age of twenty-two, the same age Aaliyah had been when she died, Spears co-wrote and recorded a song called 'Everytime', a plaintive ballad about her unfaithfulness to Timberlake which began with the phrase 'notice me'. Working with the fashion photographer David LaChapelle on a concept for the video, she had one specification, and that specification made the opening of the track seem less like a command than a threat. 'The only direction Britney gave me,' LaChapelle wrote on Instagram in 2019, 'was that she wanted to die in the video.' 'Everytime' depicts Spears being grabbed and shoved by both fans and paparazzi with nightmarish faces; violently fighting with her boyfriend, who is played by the actor Stephen Dorff; drowning in the bath after sustaining a mysterious head injury; being pronounced dead in a hospital, and then apparently being reborn as an infant in the neighbouring bed. 'It's dark,' Spears told TRL, in a phone-in timed to the video's release, 'and it shows me in a different light.' She is not wrong: if the vague outline of the clip is horrifying, the specifics are more haunting still. At one point, LaChapelle shoots her standing directly in front of her own corpse, the scene behind her white and sterile and unnerving, and Spears looks directly into the camera as she sings, as if we are being implicated in the image. *Here is my body*, Spears had said in that performance of 'I'm a Slave 4 U', and that body had been vital beyond measure, perfect and athletic, and we had been glad to see it; *here is my body*, Spears is saying to us again in this video, and the mood and the message this time are flipped, horribly, into something ghoulish and unnerving. Watching her at the 2001 VMAs, it had seemed impossible to imagine a version of Britney Spears that could die, just as the same had once seemed impossible of Aaliyah. In 'Everytime', Spears seemed keen to tell us that any illusions we might have about her mortality were just that, and that if we pricked her, she would bleed – and bleed, and bleed, and perhaps drown.

Spears chose to die in the video, in other words, to prove to us that she could do so, and one has to guess that if she had any input on the rest of the plot, she chose to be reborn for the same purpose. Recently, since her admission in her 2023 memoir *The Woman in Me* that she had become pregnant while with Timberlake and then had an abortion, there has been a tendency for fans to reframe the reincarnation scene at the end of 'Everytime' as an expression of her longing for that infant, and to see the 'baby' of the song's repeated chorus line as a reference to the termination, rather than a term of endearment for a lover. To view it in this context strips the video of Spears' message about her connection to her inner child, and about wanting a fresh start, a new life; a chance to be a version of herself who had not yet been shaped by marketing, cleansed of all her media-appointed sins. What happened over the next six years of both her life and her career, rather than a rebirth or a death, was a kind of reputational downhill motor race, characterised by bursts of controversy and embarrassment. Spears partied, hard, and was photographed getting in and out of cars without her knickers on, and wandering into public bathrooms barefoot, and exiting a car with her bloodied menstrual pad on display. Of course, many of the stupid things she did – the drugs, the bad relationships, the reckless living – were merely the stupid things that many young women do, amplified by the addition of fame and cash, and by the malevolent pressure being exerted on her by the media and the paparazzi.

In 2004, she got wasted and got married to a childhood friend in Vegas, after the two of them watched *The Texas Chainsaw Massacre* in her hotel room and, as one does, gave in to the romantic mood. Fifty-five hours later the marriage was annulled, on the grounds that Spears had 'lacked understanding of her actions' when, drunk and high on ecstasy, she'd hired a lime green limousine to drive them to a twenty-four-hour wedding chapel whose website encouraged you to tip the minister. This seemed fair; it also seemed, given that this man had been her friend since before she had become a star, that she might have been trying to reconnect with her past – to *marry* herself to her past, the pre-recorded bells at the Little White Wedding Chapel ringing out her intention to return to Kentwood, and to a time long before she'd slipped into that fateful Catholic schoolgirl uniform.

Her second shot at marriage in 2004 was to Kevin Federline, a back-up dancer with a proudly 'white trash' aesthetic. They had two beautiful children, then divorced, and a custody battle sent Spears further into meltdown. A fiercely devoted parent who once described taking a nap with her sons as being the closest she had ever felt to God, she was also a hedonist who routinely used the phrase 'blowing off steam' to excuse the wild behaviour that led

Paris Hilton to admiringly nickname her 'The Animal'. She was, in other words, a young single mother under great duress, surrounded by opportunities to self-medicate her trauma with both legal and illegal substances. In February 2007, Spears walked into a salon, picked up a pair of clippers and calmly shaved her head. She unsexed herself, as Lady Macbeth once hoped to, for self-protection and for courage. Her desire to sever herself from the sexy, girlish Britney who sold soda and pink Skechers could not have been clearer if she'd cut off her own breasts, or in some way scarified her perfect, all-American face.

'I'm tired of people touching me,' she kept saying as she did it, and although no doubt she meant this literally, she was also figuratively sick of the touch of the paparazzi lens on her skin, and of the fingers of so many typing bloggers tapping on the inside of her skull. She was Joan of Arc, burning on a pyre; she was a shaven-headed prisoner-or-patient attempting a jail break. 'I don't know who you think I am,' a *Rolling Stone* reporter recorded her snarling at a fan in the mall the following year, 'but I'm not that person.' There was a sense by then that Britney Spears, the pop star, was a cultural hallucination entirely separate from Britney Spears, the person, and that the latter felt herself to have been caught up in a case of mistaken identity. 'I honestly believe Britney Spears was so insulated from the public (and so exhaustively governed by the people trying to control her image) that she became unable to differentiate between (a) the person who was famous and (b) the person she actually was,' the critic Chuck Klosterman wrote in 2010, in a new introduction to his interview with Spears. Perhaps – or perhaps she could differentiate all too well, and her terror came from not knowing how to make that separation obvious except by acting out. Fame, on this scale, is almost unsurvivable, and there are no normal icons; as Don DeLillo writes in the opening lines of his 1973 novel *Great Jones Street*, it 'requires every kind of excess' to achieve 'true fame, a devouring neon ... Understand the [wo]man who must inhabit these extreme regions,' he continues. 'Even if half-mad [s]he is absorbed into the public's total madness; even if fully rational, a bureaucrat in hell, a secret genius of survival, [s]he is sure to be destroyed by the public's contempt for survivors.' The public's contempt was certainly directed full-force at Spears at that time, to such a degree that her persecution did not feel contemporary, but Biblical: an MTV-age stoning in the square.

That she would remain a survivor was not certain. In the video for 'Everytime' there is a scene where her corpse is extracted from the hotel on a gurney, and as if she were alive, it is swarmed by paparazzi, their flashes further illuminating her lifeless face. In 2008, life almost mirrored art, with photographers surrounding her, strapped to one for real, as she was removed from her home in a psychiatric hold after locking herself in the bathroom with her youngest son for three hours. She had been driven to distraction by what she saw as her ex-husband's attempts to separate her from their children, and her relatives' obsession with using her as a cash cow, and by the media's failure to permit her any privacy at all. When she emerged from the hospital a few days later, she would discover that while she had been detained, drugged, and drifting in and out of consciousness, she had been placed under a medical conservatorship by her father Jamie, and that she no longer had the right to spend her own money; to get an IUD; to date a man without his being vetted by her family; to get married; to drive her own car; to spend time alone with her children; to decide how to run her own career. She would go on, more than a decade later, to appear on a video-screen in court and deliver a lucid and perfervid twenty-minute monologue about her family's legal control of her life, finances and body, in which she would say that her parents and her management 'should be in jail', and that her requests for basic dignity had been ignored for so long that she had begun to feel 'like [she] was dead, like [she] didn't matter'. By the time she was hauled out on that gurney in 2008, the Associated Press had pre-written her obituary – a sign that the media itself already felt on some level as if she was dead and didn't matter, or that if she did, it was for clicks and sales and ratings. Per a 2021 article in *The New Yorker*, one paparazzo 'posted a photo of Spears on the gurney to his MySpace account with the caption "Cha-ching! Cha-ching!!"' She was twenty-six years old.

Like Britney Spears, Aaliyah had also been roughly fifteen when she'd recorded her first album, although there was a deliberate vagueness around her exact age in the press, and she would often demur in an interview if asked. 'It's a secret,'

she whispered to Leslie Segar, the co-host of *Video Soul* on BET, in 1994, holding up her finger to her mouth to pantomime a hush. Sitting next to her was twenty-seven-year-old R. Kelly, and the two were wearing matching outfits, as they often did: outsized plaid shirts in blue and green, blue sweatpants, white sneakers. The one point of difference was Aaliyah's baseball cap, which she wore low over her eyes like a visor, as if trying to hide her identity or her mood. In lieu of being dressed like a schoolgirl à la Britney Spears, Aaliyah was styled in loose, large streetwear that only served to enhance her smallness, like a child dressed up to sneak into a movie for adults. She wore sunglasses so often that at one time, she was rumoured to be either half or fully blind. Later, she allowed her long, sleek hair to fall over one of her eyes: an affectation that, combined with her almost ethereal air of mystery and her symmetrical beauty, led some critics to compare her to the Golden Age movie star Veronica Lake. 'With the sunglasses, I think it was just persona,' her eventual mentor and songwriter Missy Elliott once observed. 'I mean, she was always a star, but when people can't see your eyes, they really don't know how you looking.' They were less a disguise, then, than a tool, permitting her to assess others in a manner that was deeply necessary for a child in a grown woman's job, and also allowing her to play her cards close to her small, delicate chest. Either that, or she was trying to hide her feelings – to play it cooler than she really felt.

Aaliyah hid under her hat a little more when Leslie Segar asked her what her relationship was with Kelly, before answering shyly that the two of them were close. 'He's my very best friend,' she said, before adding for emphasis: 'He's my very best friend in the whole world.' It is an affecting statement, since nobody but a child would describe another person in this manner, and no child should be using the phrase 'very best friend in the whole world' to describe an adult. Rather than an entire publicity department pretending that their young star was saving herself for marriage, here was a fully grown man hanging out one-on-one with a teenager, and matching outfits with a teenager – writing sexual songs for a teenager, with lyrics that implied *she* was seducing *him* – without apology or restraint. Aaliyah had been twelve when she first met Kelly, after being introduced to him by her uncle, who was also Kelly's manager. Any questions we might have about what kind of man would meet a child of twelve and decide to enter into a relationship with her only two or three years later are answered by a few more recent revelations about *what kind of man* R. Kelly is. He is currently serving a combined thirty-one-year sentence for racketeering, sex trafficking and the manufacture of child pornography; of the three victims in the latter case, one is his own goddaughter, who was fourteen at the time he made the tape. 'The government called forty-five witnesses, including eleven victims who painstakingly recounted Mr Kelly's brutality,' *The New York Times* reported in 2022, covering his first conviction. 'Jurors were also confronted with hours of jarring audio and video recordings, including one in which, at the singer's behest, a woman sullied herself with her own waste.'

Kelly's defence team pointed out that he himself had

been abused as a child, and while this is tragic, it does not do much to cancel out the harm that he did to his 'protégés', all of whom would have initially felt special as a result of being singled out by someone they had heard on the radio and seen on the TV, and who would have later endured terrible things because they felt that doing so would somehow act as further proof of their specialness, their readiness for adult life. Many of these girls, some of whom no doubt had teenagers of their own by the time Kelly stood trial, had wanted to be singers, and it is undeniable that R. Kelly could make or break a career. His crimes were so extensive that they have been covered in a three-season, fifteen-hour documentary for the Lifetime channel, entitled *Surviving R. Kelly*. In the show, a common theme is the victims' longing, in their teens, to transcend their ordinary, unaffluent family lives. Kelly frequently hung around Kenwood High School in Chicago, and one talking head describes him testing out his powers, scoping out underage girls by seeing who would hold eye contact with him for the longest time. What he was looking for was not fearlessness, exactly, but a lack of guile, and in particular a lack of guile that came twinned with desperation. Many of the women who bravely describe their abuse at his hands share a common air of bewilderment, as if they had suddenly been placed back in their teenage selves, and as if they still could not be certain how the situation had arisen: a subtle manipulation of their minds, of their bodies, with the result being an act that, decades later, they still cannot bring themselves to describe. It is a relief to us, the viewer, when they fail to articulate exactly what befell them, even if being relieved in this context is both selfish and naive. There are, after all, 'hours of jarring audio and video recordings' that reveal Kelly's barbarism in great detail, and the fact that these women have no words for what happened does not mean that they do not have private memories, or nightmares, to remind them.

Aaliyah was also a child who had dreams of being a star. More than this, she was a child who believed that being a star was her birthright, not because she was arrogant or spoilt, but because it was not clear what else a girl with her talents might have done for a job. In the laundry list of things to hate R. Kelly for, one should surely be, in a perverse sense, the fact he was the one who delivered her to us, and in doing so rubber-stamped his influence all over her debut album. *Age Ain't Nothing but a Number*, a record with a name so farcically, openly paedophilic that you do not even have to listen to its title track to feel a chill, was released in 1994, and its cover featured an image of Aaliyah in her trademark shades leaning almost listlessly against a wall, with the out-of-focus figure of R. Kelly in the background. Just as that title is a ludicrously obvious nod, in retrospect, to his many crimes, this picture is an uncanny depiction of his role in her legacy: that of a shadowy figure we are powerless to unsee, even if we try to unfocus our eyes and only look at her. One of Kelly's other victims testified that she had witnessed Kelly and Aaliyah in what she gently described as 'a sexual situation' when Aaliyah had been fourteen or fifteen; she also claimed during the trial that Kelly would refer to his sexual assignations as these girls 'paying their dues', further underscoring the degree to which their future livelihoods were linked to the things that they were willing to do for him, with him, or in front of his ever-present video camera. What might Aaliyah have felt that she needed to do in order to guarantee her destiny? Maybe when she sang, and when the two of them were in a setting in which they were artistic collaborators, and not 'lovers', such things were easier to forget. Perhaps Aaliyah could live, then, only in her talent – only in her lovely voice, and not in the body that had caused her so much trouble, even as it sometimes moved so gorgeously in time to the music that she seemed to levitate, even fly.

In 1994, Kelly bribed a government official to falsify paperwork that declared that Aaliyah was not fifteen, but eighteen, and the two of them married in a quick, secret ceremony witnessed only by Kelly's manager Demetrius Smith. 'I was in the room when they got married,' Smith admits, in *Surviving R. Kelly*. 'I'm not proud of that ... It was just a quick little ceremony. She didn't have on a white dress, and he didn't have on a tux. Just everyday wear. She looked worried and scared.' The mind strains trying to imagine the nuptial scene as it's described. You see her hiding her eyes behind her signature glasses, but how can she have been if it was so obvious to Smith that she was frightened? A short, slight girl in casual clothes, standing next to this adult man and agreeing to let him have her life. How could Smith, or anybody for that matter, simply let it happen? The answer is, of course, fame, and its terrifying, aphrodisiacal power, capable of turning a gifted man who had been abused as a child into a god, infallible and enviable, and then finally into a monster. Rather than Aaliyah's whole life, in the end R. Kelly only got two further months: the marriage was swiftly annulled by her parents, and Kelly made Aaliyah sign an NDA. On *The New York Times* podcast The Popcast in 2018, the Chicagoan music journalist Jim DeRogatis detailed his years-long attempts to bring Kelly to justice, and he also described being shown a copy of this 'harrowing document – a non-disclosure agreement on both her part and Kelly's, vowing not to pursue further legal claims for physical abuse'. 'So, it wasn't just an underage sexual relationship,' he clarified. 'He hit her, allegedly, according to that court document.' The sheer length of his sentence means that in all likelihood if he is ever freed, it will be when he is frail and broken, in his eighties. Still, it is astounding now to think of how long it took for him to be convicted in the first place, given that his marriage to Aaliyah was common music industry knowledge even as it happened. It is difficult, too, to imagine that if Kelly had been serially targeting girls who were upper middle class and white rather than Black and often relatively poor, we would have had to wait so long. 'I want to emphasise that when I've said that nobody in our society matters less than young Black women,' DeRogatis also said on The Popcast, 'I'm just repeating [the words of] young Black women.'

Kelly's influence over Aaliyah lasted only for a handful of years, but these years were formative ones for the teenage singer, and the fact that she ended up with relatively little time on earth to express herself without him lingering, out-of-focus but still threatening, in the background of her life, makes that influence grimmer still. 'Look at Jerry Lee Lewis,' Kelly is alleged to have said, per the testimony of a witness at his trial, in reference to Lewis' marriage to his own thirteen-year-old cousin. 'He's a genius and I'm a genius. We should be allowed to do what we want – look at what we give to the world.' In his callous worldview, there was no consideration of what it might mean if his victim were a brilliant innovator, too, and no consideration, either, of what they themselves might go on to produce. Here it seems prudent to push R. Kelly aside altogether, and to look at some of the ways in which Aaliyah herself was a genius. Look at what she gave to the world: a sound that seemed flung from outer space, and which achieved perfect synergy with her stage presence by rendering sonic the distinctive blend of twitchy syncopation and chill, circumfluent smoothness she employed when she danced. There is something out-of-time about her best tracks, almost metallic-sounding and a little alien; her voice, with its crystalline beauty and its fluttering falsetto, often sat in thrilling opposition to the ticks and thumps of the arrangement underneath it. On 'One in a Million', recorded when she was just seventeen, some of that skittering percussion comes from the sound of crickets – an innovative choice made by her visionary writer-producers, Missy Elliott and Timbaland, but presumably also signed off by Aaliyah herself, who always wanted what was next. 'She grabbed onto the same mentality that we [her producers] had: be risky,' Elliott said, in a posthumous tribute in *The Fader* in 2011.

'We always said we don't want somebody else to do it before we do it, so let's just take it there.'

'She [was] killin' it on some real warrior shit,' the rapper Method Man remarked in that same piece. 'I didn't see anyone doing what she did. I mean, Britney Spears tried but I laughed at that fuckin' video ... [As far as rappers go] she was *our* pop princess.' The video he is referring to is the one of that performance at the VMAs with the snake, and when he says that Spears was trying to be like Aaliyah, he does not just mean her attempt to be sexier and more 'street' than she had been on '... Baby One More Time', he also means the snake itself. In the music video for Aaliyah's 2000 single 'We Need a Resolution', she appears with one wrapped around her torso, the snake and the singer both appearing sinuous and coiled: gothic rather than exotic. In a sense, it hardly matters who deployed a reptile first, as both women's sensibilities could not have been more different. In Aaliyah's later style, there was often a note of the tastefully fetishistic, more alt-domme than sweet baby diva. She wore spiked heels; long leather trenches; oil-slick make-up; an expression of such deep solemnity that she sometimes evoked a silent movie actress rather than a pop star. 'There was an edgier side to her that people didn't know,' her friend Kidada Jones, an actress and designer, has suggested. 'She was more forward thinking than most people. Deeper. She was fine spending time alone. She was a thinker.'

She loved Nine Inch Nails, and noted several times in profiles and on camera that she saw parities between the band's production, and that of some of the tracks on *Aaliyah*.

She was not wrong, even if there were some fundamental differences in play. '[Nine Inch Nails' music is] about juxtaposing human imperfections against very rigid, sterile, cold arrangements,' Trent Reznor told an interviewer at *Spin* in 1996. 'If the music is very precise, [I] make a vocal tape that's less perfect, so you've got this meshing of man versus machine.' A track like 'Try Again' from *Aaliyah* is about the collision of (wo)man and machine, too, but the startling contrast at its centre is not between a cold, sterile arrangement and an imperfect vocal track, but between a cold, sterile arrangement and a vocal track that is perfectly soulful in a way that indicates it could not have been made by a computer – listen, for example, to the way Aaliyah's voice takes flight on the second syllable of 'suc*ceed*' in the chorus, reaching antigravity somewhere impossibly high above the syncopated squelch and fuzz of the accompanying music. Somehow, the most accurate description of Aaliyah's singing voice does not come from a review of her music, but from the 1962 novel *A Clockwork Orange*, in a paragraph where its teenage antihero is describing what Beethoven's Ninth feels like as it plays in his bedroom: 'Like a bird of rarest-spun heaven metal, or like silvery wine flowing in a spaceship.' 'Silvery wine flowing in a spaceship' is an image fit for a Hype Williams music video; it is also a fine allegory for the sound that emerged from Aaliyah's mouth, something gleaming and entirely situated in the future or in space.

For a while, Aaliyah herself ascended like a bird of rarest-spun heaven metal, and her flight from R. Kelly marked the start of a brief but fecund period of musical experimentation that produced two iconic, much-loved albums, 1997's *One in a Million* and 2001's *Aaliyah*. 'Thanks... to the management of her protective family, and more importantly, to a fine sophomore opus, the new *One in a Million*, Aaliyah may not only have survived her melodramas but might just become our next princess superstar,' dream hampton wrote in 1997, reviewing the album for *Vibe* and pointedly reminding male readers that although Aaliyah certainly possessed, as all teenagers inevitably do, a distinct sexuality, it was very much 'still illegal to act on the thought' of her appeal if you yourself were an adult. Her collaborations with Missy Elliott in particular felt meaningful because of the things the two women had in common. Elliott, another musical maverick who had been a serious, clever child, not only understood Aaliyah's desire to be better and more interesting than the average pop star, she also understood her pain: in 2011, she revealed that she herself had been abused growing up. 'Being molested,' Elliott told *Spin* magazine. 'It don't disappear. You remember it as if it was yesterday.' Knowing what she must have about Aaliyah's 'relationship' with Kelly, it is plausible that for Missy Elliott, time collapsed when the two began to work together, and that she saw herself in her teenage protégé. What Elliott remembered as if it was yesterday had, in a sense, truly been yesterday for Aaliyah, and the ease with which she must have been able to reach out and touch Aaliyah's hurt must have contributed in some way to their closeness. Two Black geniuses, two shy artists, two women who had pulled themselves through something terrible in order to excel. It was a match made in heaven, and the music that they made together was at times transcendent, too.

'Aaliyah has ... a truly staggering charisma-to-force ratio,' the music critic Rob Harvilla writes in his 2024 book, *60 Songs That Explain the '90s*. 'Maximum charisma, minimum force.' Effort was not something one associated with her, even though as she grew older she would often work impossibly long hours: for a time in 2001, she routinely spent her days filming the Anne Rice adaptation *Queen of the Damned*, and then travelled to the studio to record *Aaliyah* after dark. There was something featherlight about the way she wore her power, as if exerting it took nothing. Part of this was because in spite of everything she'd lived through and in spite of her 'edgier side', she seemed so outwardly sunny, so sure that she'd course-corrected in such a way as to fulfil her destiny on schedule. Her dark, adumbrative recurring dream, however, suggested a rushing undercurrent of trauma that was being repressed during her hyper-productive working hours. It is not Kelly's fault that Aaliyah died young; it is his fault that, during her short life, she was forced to contend with his damage, his manipulation, his abuse. It is impossible to know how many of the twenty-two years she spent on earth were genuinely happy, but more of them might have been without his influence, and although he made her a star, it's also true that those around her had been telling her that she was born to be one more or less since she was four. Might she not have got there on her own? After she failed to win *Star Search* – just as one Beyoncé Knowles had in 1992; just as Spears had, too – her mother says that the ten-year-old

Aaliyah asked her every day: has a record label called yet? She felt certain that somebody would have seen her on the show and realised her potential. She knew that she was hard to miss, even harder to forget.

Years later, at twenty, she appeared on a late-night talk show with the interviewer Craig Kilborn, and when he asked her about *Star Search*, she suggested that the footage – because this was the year 2000, pre-YouTube, and pre-almost everything from a star's early life being searchable – was lost. 'What did it sound like?' he prompts, and she sings the first line, her voice having turned into that of the grown-up, sophisticated woman she was pretending to be when she was ten. Unaccompanied, it's gorgeous, light and sultry. Something about this snatch of a cappella song is reminiscent of a video Britney Spears posted on her Instagram in 2022, where she performs her own personal arrangement of '... Baby One More Time'. She sings in a lower register; the nasal quality of her voice, as it sometimes appears on record, has been thoroughly excised. She finally sounds like an adult, and it is clear that whoever was responsible for keeping her from doing the song her way had been making a mistake. Picturing an alternate history of Britney Spears in which she has full agency is difficult because of the restrictive nature of her actual working life, but in her 2023 autobiography *The Woman in Me*, there are many indications of her genuine interest in music – she describes staying up all night before recording '... Baby One More Time', for instance, to ensure that her voice would come across as 'fried and gravelly' on the record, lending it a little edge. Her 2007 album *Blackout* is brilliantly eccentric, and its best tracks recall the syncopated tenebrosity of certain songs from the much earlier *Aaliyah*. Some of its lyrics also nod at her breakdown, as when she insists that she's crazy as a motherfucker, bet it on your man, in 'Get Naked (I Got a Plan)' – a line that is made more interesting by the fact it very much sounds as if she says, à la Leonard Cohen, *'I'm* your man,' as though Spears is acknowledging the mutability of her own identity circa 2007, or as if she is attempting to repeat the defeminising trick she first performed by shaving off her long blonde hair.

In a 2007 piece for *Pitchfork* that compares Britney Spears to the ill-fated *Twin Peaks* character Laura Palmer, the critic Tom Ewing points out that it's likely Spears had some hand in *Blackout*'s strangeness. 'You might still look at the public [mid-breakdown] Britney and see someone who can barely string a sentence together,' he suggested, 'but even so that sentence could have been "I want an album that doesn't sound like anyone else's". Or "I want an album that's basically untourable".' Just as Aaliyah said of herself, Spears is an interpreter of music that is written for her, and on *Blackout* what she channels is the sickness of the industry itself, her delivery sometimes reminiscent of a woman in a horror film who has been possessed: mocking, scratchy, elastic with distortion. *I don't know who you think I am, but I'm not that person.* When the album opens with a sample of her saying 'it's Britney, bitch', it ought to feel like a battle cry. Instead, she sounds low in the mix, almost anaesthetised, and it is tempting to wonder why exactly she has felt the need to remind us who she is in the first place. As when she left the house in 2004, the year of her ill-fated fifty-five-hour marriage, in a hot pink t-shirt emblazoned with the phrase I AM THE AMERICAN DREAM, there is a sense that the meaning of the words is being undermined by their delivery: a bit of subversion that, like her original marketing as a schoolgirl who was sexy but did not have sex, carried with it a familiar air of plausible deniability. Listeners who were not aware of the drama playing out in Spears' private life could hear the words 'it's Britney, bitch' and imagine they were tuning in for an empowerment anthem. Likewise, the song 'Gimme More' itself, with its chorus that sounds more like a roar than a purr, could be read two ways – as a party hit about being crazy-horny, or as a song about being actually crazy and insatiable, and about the fact that when you are that kind of person, other people like to watch. 'They want more?' Spears asks, mumbling, almost slurring. 'Well, I'll give them more.' 'Gimme More' is an incredible pop song, grimy and black-hearted, but there is no doubt that it was made at a time when Spears had very little left to offer us that we had not already tried to ruin, however much we wanted her to give, and give. 'Entertainers [like Spears] make so much revenue but are still wildly underpaid [because we] use them for things that are worth more than money,' Chuck Klosterman also wrote, as early as 2003. 'It's a new kind of dehumanising slavery – not as awful as the literal variety, but dehumanising nonetheless.'

'Not as awful' is a rather mild way to mark out the distinction between slavery proper and the sale of an artist's soul, but Klosterman's point is not an incorrect one. It became more correct still once Spears entered into her conservatorship, and found herself in a situation where she 'earned' an allowance of $2,000 every month in spite of theoretically being paid $300,000 *a night* for her eventual shows in Vegas. As passé as it is to describe a legal or administrative situation as 'Kafkaesque', it is difficult to know what other word to use to describe the conditions of Spears' conservatorship, which considered her at once too incompetent and weak to drive a car, and mentally and physically robust enough to release her sixth studio album, promote it with a tour that grossed just shy of 132 million dollars, and sign on for the aforementioned residency in Las Vegas where she worked, by her own estimation, 'seven days a week, 8 a.m. to 6 p.m., [with] no days off'. If she had once been the owner of Schrödinger's virginity, she was now judged to be in possession of Schrödinger's sanity, instead. The Hulu documentary *Framing Britney Spears*, which was released in 2021, and which was met with a firestorm of public outrage and retroactive horror, presented a harrowing account of her descent into total captivity and almost total helplessness immediately following her 2008 hospitalisation. Footage of her on that gurney bleeds into an overview of the effects of the conservatorship on her finances, her freedoms and her health: she loses the ability to decide who can visit her at home, and is kept under twenty-four-hour surveillance; Jamie Spears is given access to her credit cards and her medical records, and permitted to make tour and TV bookings for her at his own discretion. His status as his daughter's co-conservator, alongside a lawyer of his choice, makes very little sense in light of the testimonies of several of the interviewees in *Framing Britney Spears*, who paint a picture of him as an intermittent alcoholic, and as being so bad with money that he'd had to file for bankruptcy when Britney was a child. 'I'm Britney Spears now,' several sources – not least Spears, in her autobiography – record him saying during the conservatorship, to his daughter and to others. One has to wonder who, at that point in history, would want the job.

It is also pointed out more than once in *Framing Britney Spears* that Jamie was something of an absentee parent until Britney became rich. 'The only thing Jamie [Spears] ever said to me was "My daughter's gonna be so rich, she's gonna buy me a boat",' a Jive Records employee named Kim Kaiman tells the camera, barely hiding her disdain. 'And that's all I'm gonna say about Jamie.' A lawyer Britney met with claims that she had long had an issue with her father 'as a person', and not merely with his status as her court-appointed master. Already, by the time the documentary made the air, there was a burgeoning movement online that advocated for Spears' release from the conservatorship, with fans uniting under the battle cry 'Free Britney'. Once *Framing Britney Spears* was released, the general public began to understand what Spears' hardcore fans had been alleging all along, and the assembled evidence was not pretty. The chronological nature of the film allowed viewers to track not only Spears' time in the conservatorship, but her treatment in the media from day one, and to watch each stage of her development being met with some new challenge to her dignity and intellect – interviewers asking her about her breast implants or her virginity as casually as if the question were about her latest album, or interrogating her about her breakups as if they themselves were personally involved in her sex life. The dehumanisation that occurred under the conservatorship remained possible for as long as it did because Spears' personhood had already been separated from her public image by the coverage of her in the press, and we had been trained to see her first as a Lolita-sweet sex doll, then a target, then a joke, and then finally as a cautionary tale. Her flattening into a two-dimensional figure who did not deserve our sympathies occurred in such minor increments that we had barely been aware that it was happening at all, the heat being gradually turned up on the pot until she seemed in danger of being boiled alive.

All these uncomfortable realisations about our complicity in Spears' two-decade hell, along with the tireless efforts of the Free Britney movement, led to the moment in which Spears, via Zoom, refused to have her testimony sealed at the hearing for her case in June 2023. 'Somebody's done a good job at exploiting my life. I feel like it should be an open-court hearing,' she said. 'They should listen and hear what I have to say.' Along with detailing the various ways in which she felt she had been gaslit and controlled, she also took the time to rebuff any suggestion that she might be incapable of caring for herself, or even that she might be anything less than stellar at her job. 'I actually did most of the choreography and taught my dancers my new choreography myself. I take everything I do very seriously. There's tons of video with me at rehearsals,' she insisted before adding, thrillingly: 'I wasn't *good*, I was GREAT.' This assertion was an echo of one of the few positive snippets that appear in *Framing Britney Spears*, a brief shot of her rehearsing as a younger woman and saying, calmly but definitively, 'I am *not* a diva. I just know what I want.' This was what it sounded like when she said *it's Britney, bitch* for real, not low in the mix but certain and triumphant. Throughout her ordeal, Spears may have been driven crazy, but she still knew what she wanted, and she did not intend to take her punishment without a fight. She'd made numerous attempts to defy the legal boundaries of her ever-narrowing life: she arranged to meet a connection in the sauna of a gym to pick up a burner phone; she had a journalist she knew slide some paperwork under the door of a public toilet cubicle so that she could attempt to retain her own lawyer; at the announcement of her 2018 residency, she walked straight off the stage she was supposed to perform on and, without greeting her fans, headed straight to her car, a protest that some coverage misinterpreted as a mistake. 'Through [all] the fear,' she wrote in *The Woman in Me*, 'I remembered that there were still things I could hold on to: My desire for people to understand what I'd been through. My faith that all this could change. My belief that I had a right to experience joy. My knowledge that I deserved my freedom.' Now Spears had finally got her day in court, and she was going to use it. 'Ma'am,' she told the judge, firmly, 'I'm not here to be anyone's slave.'

As it had when she performed 'I'm a Slave 4 U', the word 'slave', even if the context here was closer to the true definition, continued to sound a little piquant in the mouth of a woman who looked like Britney Spears. Another thing that Jim DeRogatis said on The Popcast when discussing R. Kelly's crimes was that his friend, the African American music critic Mark Anthony Neal, had remarked to him some fifteen years earlier that if Kelly had victimised 'one white girl from Winnetka, it would have been a different story'. Here was one white girl from Kentwood, and it had still taken thirteen years for her allegations of a differing form of abuse to be heard, as opposed to some of Kelly's tens of victims having to wait decades, but at least she'd broken free. In November 2021, Spears' conservatorship was dissolved. 'I'm Miss American Dream ... Mrs Lifestyles of the Rich and Famous,' she had sneered in her self-lacerating, jaded single 'Piece of Me' all the way back in 2007. Clearly, Spears began early on to loathe her status as a blonde, bodacious representative of her nation – an impossible appointment at which anyone would fail. She had qualified for this position, in no small part, as a result of her race; such expectations had not been placed on Aaliyah, who by virtue of being a Black woman would never be seen as an everywoman on the same scale in an industry – in a wider Western world – that perceived her white peers instead as 'the highest, the most exalted'. The loss of Spears' virginity had mattered so much to the public because of the way her purity had been bound up with her image, and accordingly she was treated like a Barbie doll that had been played with too much: broken, then discarded. That said, it was also inescapable that she was very much like a Barbie doll in other ways. Black Americans have been dealing with the long and macabre reverberations of what Chuck Klosterman would call 'the literal variety' of slavery for centuries, and those reverberations have shaped almost every aspect of their lives. Spears, even stripped of her dignity and treated with such savagery, still theoretically retained the privilege of her whiteness, and some of the public interest in rescuing her was no doubt related to the fact that she resembled exactly the kinds of victims who receive the most press coverage, the most police interest, and the most mercy from the law. 'A lot of people ask, why didn't anyone notice?' one of Kelly's victims says in *Surviving R. Kelly*, with regards to his serial abuse of teenagers. 'The answer is, everyone noticed, and no one cared because we were all Black girls.'

Part of Aaliyah's early maturation had been a natural by-product of her development and her intelligence, but part of it had been a reaction both to her environment, and to the way young Black girls are perceived by the media and, for that matter, the white world: as little adults, somehow worldlier and less capable of feeling fear or pain than their white counterparts. She would have known that she always needed to be calmer, more impressive, more professional; she would have known, too, that because she was a young Black woman, she ran an especially high risk of being blamed for her own statutory rape. Intersectional feminism matters precisely because all women get fucked by the patriarchy to some degree or another, but Black women get fucked by the patriarchy *and* by white supremacy, and this double-fucking means that they are expected to comply with twice as many contradictory, patronising rules as white women in order to guarantee even the barest minimum of respect from society at large. Aaliyah's virtue, by virtue of not being that of a Caucasian teenager of the same age, was not seen as being particularly valuable, and accordingly its loss did not generate quite as many column inches as the loss of Spears' imaginary virginity did. Never mind that Spears had been having sex with an age-appropriate partner in the context of a romantic relationship – as close to pleasing Middle America as it was possible to get without a ring and a trip to the Little White Wedding Chapel. She was white, and a cute white girl with golden hair was worth getting all worked up for. Ultimately, both Aaliyah and Spears have been left with artistic legacies that have been tarnished by the touch of domineering older men in such a way that our appreciation of their work is muddied by our knowledge of the misery underpinning it. It is impossible to listen to *Age Ain't Nothing but a Number* and not hear the man who worked so slyly to convince Aaliyah that her age was immaterial, and you cannot hear Spears asking if we want a piece of her without remembering just how large a piece her father took by legal force.

'I defy any pretty girl who is rocketed to world stardom [as a teenager] in a sex-nymphet role to stay on a level path,' the actress Sue Lyon, who is best known for playing Lolita in Stanley Kubrick's 1962 film, told the *Sunday Times* in 1997, the year *One in a Million* hit double platinum, and the year Britney Spears first met with executives from Jive. It is a tragedy when girls are forced to grow up into women before they are ready, and it is an even greater tragedy when they do not get the chance to grow up at all. In Spears' case, her adult status – as one of her own early singles put it, before we had any idea how accurate an observation this would be – as neither a girl nor a woman was a direct result of her being placed under such baroque legal restraints that she found herself being infantilised even at thirty, thirty-five, thirty-nine. Unlike Aaliyah, with her love of Egyptian symbolism and her penchant for black leather, Spears has never employed particularly gothic imagery in her videos or her styling, in spite of her long-term suffering; she has, though, chosen to invoke the idea of her own death several times over the course of her career, as a way to communicate to us just how destroyed she has felt at various moments in her life. There was, of course, 'Everytime'; there was also her assertion in court that her family made her feel like she 'was dead'. In 2022, a year after that trial, she posted a twenty-two-minute-long voice note on her social media in which she used the phrase 'they literally killed me' to describe her experiences under the conservatorship. Reddit users seized on her use of 'literally' here, using its apparent grammatical incorrectness to suggest that she was stupid, or that she should get a grip. In fact, the statement made perfect sense if the death in question had not been the death of her body, but that of her earlier, more innocent self – the death of her hopes, or of her ability to live in the world without feeling constantly under surveillance and encroached upon, as if she were a spy or a prisoner. Two things can be true at once: that Spears feels she was 'killed' by the conservatorship, and that she still remains alive to tell the tale, and to decide on its ending for herself. The Associated Press has had no use for its prewritten obituary in spite of all her tribulations. She may yet be reconfigured as a new kind of star, if not literally reborn as she'd hoped to be when she made the video for 'Everytime'. At present, she insists that she will never perform on-stage or record new work again, as is her right. It is a pity, though, in light of the way she talks about her relationship with music in *The Woman in Me* – as a conduit for her relationship with a higher power, and as a saving grace. 'I [sing] for myself now,' she says. 'I feel God more when I'm alone.' 'Anything that gets your heart rate up is good,' she writes elsewhere. 'Music is that, plus a connection to God. That's where my heart is.' Regardless, now Spears can spend her money, drive her car, and spend her time doing what she wants to do, assuming that recording herself dancing barefoot in her house and then uploading the results to Instagram *is* genuinely what she wants to do, and not merely the result of a kind of muscle memory – an expression of a private, maybe subconscious conviction that her flesh and flexibility are the only things we want her for. At least she decides now when to jump, and how high, and when we are going to watch her. We do still watch her, obviously, as why would we stop watching Britney Spears?

Aaliyah, by contrast, is definitively lost, and with that loss comes the acknowledgement that there will be no further albums, no further movies, and no further interviews in which she makes expert use of her shy, lovely charisma. She was denied the chance to grow up by the most permanent tragedy of all, and although she, too, might have felt that she'd experienced a kind of soul-death during her abuse, the fact remains that the real thing trumps its metaphysical or metaphorical counterpart when it comes to shattering, irreversible cruelty every time. All that remains is for us to tell the story she has left behind for us differently, so that rather than a frightening cautionary tale about male domination, or a melodrama about a woman who was killed before she'd reached her professional and intellectual prime – or rather than just being these things – it becomes a sad, gorgeous fable about an unusually brilliant girl with unusual, brilliant powers. Too often in her lifetime, Aaliyah's persistent air of preternatural maturity was appreciated for its sexual qualities, when in fact the most interesting facet of her wise-beyond-her-years sophistication had been her immediate certainty about her taste as an artist: her skill when it came to anticipating, then directing, the developmental flow of contemporary music. The very last image we were gifted of Aaliyah is the one presented in the video for her 2001 single 'Rock the Boat', which was released posthumously on 9 October 2001, and which opens with a dedication: 'As we watch this video of an angel, we will remember her spirit flying free along with the eight others who were with her. They soar together with her eternal love.' There is that word again, 'angel', and this time it is serving double duty, both to commemorate her famous sweetness and to mourn her early death: Aaliyah's plane crashed on a return flight home from the Bahamas, where she had been filming this particular promo with Hype Williams.

'Rock the Boat' begins with a near-silent shot of Aaliyah walking by the sea, the sky so luminous behind her that she is almost an outline. It is often said of famous people that the mark of being an icon is being recognisable when you are reduced to a simple silhouette, and although this might be true of some celebrities – an Amy Winehouse, say, or an Elvis Presley – it was never really true of Aaliyah, whose distinctiveness had more to do with qualities that were not visible on camera except ambiently, abstractly, like the spooky and phantasmal aura that appears around the moon in a picture of it taken with an iPhone. How strange, then, and how terribly bittersweet, to see her barefoot, half-anonymous, and looking like a normal college-aged girl on the beach. In general, 'Rock the Boat' is far lighter and far brighter than Aaliyah's other music videos from the same period, from the all-white clothing that she and her dancers wear to the paradisiacal setting. 'Paradisiacal' is, of course, apt – there is a reason that the phrase 'island paradise' exists, and it is because a place like the Abaco Islands, where 'Rock the Boat' was filmed, looks like heaven. In one scene, created with the aid of a greenscreen, the ocean becomes so expansive that it fully surrounds both Aaliyah and her dancers, stretching out until there is no longer any line between the water and the sky. As an image, it suggests something cool and infinite – at once of nature, and impossible to realise except by computer trickery or magic. Knowing that she died in the process of producing this particular music video makes it impossible not to want to overanalyse its symbolism, and it makes its extreme peacefulness especially poignant, too. In Iandoli's book, it is alleged that she did not want to take the flight at all, as if she had sensed some trouble – another indication, perhaps, of her weird-in-the-original-sense connection with the fates, or with some other world. She was carried onboard, having popped a sleeping pill, unconscious, and one hopes she slept through the rest, even if that hope is woefully misguided.

The last two shots of the video show Aaliyah kneeling in the sand, laughing at something we can't see, and then her floating underwater, a gossamer-light black dress leaving a trail behind her body. *As if I am swimming in the air. Free. Weightless. Nobody can reach me. Nobody can touch me.* It is a pleasant way to remember her, though it does not feel like we are seeing the whole picture. This is the ethereal Aaliyah, the girl with the glassy voice. It is not Aaliyah the businesswoman, or Aaliyah the innovator, or Aaliyah the artist. Dame Dash, her onetime boyfriend, might have said it best when he offered up his own memorial to her in *The Fader*'s 2011 tribute, which he closed with a perfect observation. It was a reminder of how much we'd lost, and of how seriously she took her job; by extension, it was also a reminder of how seriously we ought to take her legacy. It wasn't another quote that positioned her as an angel, or a comment on her beauty or her kindness, or a paean to her voice, but a tribute to her drive. It conjured her at age ten, coming home every day after school and asking whether anyone from the industry had reached out about *Star Search* – knowing already that one day a call would come, whether figuratively or literally, and she would answer it in the affirmative. It conjured her at the start of her twenties, spending her days playing an immortal vampire, and her nights making an album that would one day guarantee her a degree of immortality in real life, too. 'She died working, you know?' Dash pointed out simply, his *you know* weighted with the private knowledge of her grit. 'She didn't die playing around.'

3

Movements of Thought and Soul

On Louise Brooks and Kristen Stewart

I. THE BEST-READ IDIOT IN THE WORLD

In her 1922 yearbook photograph, she is in pure, zoetic flow, turning to the camera; her aliveness makes a mockery of the photographic image, as if proving that a woman born to be in motion pictures could not possibly be captured in a still. Already, she is wearing her hair bobbed, as black as dominatrix leather or as death, and her fringe as straight as the incision from a razor. Her eyes – also black, also shining, also at once deathly and erotic – are so filled with wicked energy that we immediately recognise her destiny: she will either become very, very famous, or she'll plunge straight into hell. (As it happens, what transpires is an alternating sequence of these outcomes, so that she first becomes famous, then is damned, and then is famous once again, never truly hitting the dizziest height of stardom and never quite cowed entirely into destitution, either.) Next to all the other high-schoolers, one of the strangest things about her is the fact that she does not appear to belong to her decade, as if a contemporary actress with a too-contemporary face and affect had been cast in a period film. She is fifteen in this picture, and already some terrible things and some wonderful things have happened to her that have helped transform her into the devilish, sometimes temerarious adventuress she is when this particular photograph is taken, and will be until she dies. There was the violatory sexual incident in the house of a middle-aged neighbour at the age of nine, which she will later say instilled in her a desire for unkind and dominating men, and which transpired because he lured her there with candy; the influence of her mother, who admits that she is not an especially maternal woman, but who makes up for the shortfall by emphasising the value of great art and independence, libertinism and intellectual exploration; her first forays into dance, the discipline that will teach her how to move her face and body in a style that first confounds, then delights, critics; and the development of her beauty, which at once affords her the means to make herself into a star, and condemns her to being treated like a fool so frequently and fervently that she eventually – erroneously – mistakes the myth of her stupidity for truth.

'I'm probably one of the best-read idiots in the world,' she will go on to remark in her old age, speaking to a critic representing *The New Yorker* as he takes note of all the books stacked on her nightstand: Proust, Schopenhauer, Ruskin,

Samuel Johnson. 'I get some consolation from the fact that, as an idiot, I have provided delight in my time to a very select group of intellectuals.' In fact, her writing and her interviews and her performances and the physicality of her, her true essence, all conspire to make it obvious that she is brilliant; even in this yearbook photograph, she radiates a kind of quickness, the suggestion that her mind is as capable and fluid as her body will prove itself to be. The same year this photograph is taken, she leaves Kansas and joins a globally touring troupe of dancers – one of whom is Martha Graham – before being dismissed by the troupe's director on the grounds that she's a brat who wants life 'handed to [her] on a silver salver'. (Secretly, this accusation pleases her, and she records the phrase for future use, thinking it will make a perfect chapter title for a novel; she may be a dancer, and she may eventually want to be an actress, but she will always be just as thrilled by language as by movement.) Dusting herself off, she joins the showgirl group the Ziegfeld Follies, her life transitioning to technicolour as if she is Dorothy in *The Wizard of Oz*: she falls into New York's wildest crowds, runs with its fastest hedonists, fucks like a maniac, drinks like a fish, acts as a proto-sugar baby to a string of millionaires and Wall Street bankers, lives at the Algonquin and the Ritz, and discovers that she does not like being a cute and nearly naked bauble on the stage as much as she loves being the centre of attention off it. When she does not feel like dancing, she wires a notice of her nonattendance to the theatre, citing, vaguely, 'other commitments', and perhaps proving her old troupe director right about her bratty streak. In the Follies, all the girls refuse to share her dressing room, complaining that she is too mad, too mean, and too quick to share her thoughts. One day, looking at the other dancers straining to seem effortless and upbeat underneath their heavy feathered headdresses, it occurs to her that none of these beautiful women will ever be allowed to break character and show the audience an authentic feeling – irritation or discomfort, boredom or unhappiness – and she discovers that this realisation makes her angry, both on their behalf and on her own. 'I decided right then,' she writes, practically hissing, 'that on-stage I would never smile unless I felt like it.' When a powerful man sees her in the Follies and approaches her to tell her that she ought to be in motion pictures, it feels perfectly inevitable, fate offering up her destiny on the same silver salver she was fired for expecting. As it turns out, the main difference between her and her contemporaries is that although she will sometimes play the pretty little plaything on the screen, offscreen she maintains her earlier promise: she only smiles when she means to.

II. BLESSED WITH THAT UNHAPPY WISDOM

A girl, or is she, slopes into a cavernous New York house and begins to traverse it on her (very noughties) razor scooter. The chill, easy way she snaps it into action, opening the scooter and then boarding it as fluidly as James Dean flicks a Zippo, is suggestive of an unusual thing, a loose-limbed and confident attitude to the occupation of the body that can only be defined with one word: cool. For a ten-year-old to be 'cool' does not sound terribly likely, but then it is inescapable that this girl in particular does not seem like a child at all – she is adult not in the sexual, Lolita-ish manner that encourages grown men to use the sinister phrase 'mature for her age', but in a kind of existentially sophisticated fashion, every fibre of her being seeming to project a lived-in boredom. We intuit that she has already seen past the illusory veneer of smoothness which characterises childhood for the children of the wealthy, and when she directs her shaded, slightly downturned eyes towards the middle distance, she appears to glimpse some future life that tires her out already. This is Sarah, a fictional character in a 2002 film by David Fincher called *Panic Room*, and the young actress who plays her makes her hard to look away from. 'Blessed with that unhappy wisdom which clings to some girls on the brink of their teens,' the critic Anthony Lane observes, in a review in *The New Yorker*, '[Sarah] is cooler than her mother.' That her mother is played by Jodie Foster, nervy but commanding, makes this an impressive feat, since if Foster is not cool in the colloquial sense, she is all steel, her gaze cold enough to freeze a viewer to their seat. It is unclear in this family of two who is in charge, and the love between them flows freely and evenly but almost silently, a river under ice.

'The fact [Sarah] talks and dresses like a boy,' Lane also writes, 'only adds to her mild mystery.' Foster playing the mother of this androgynous preteen is interesting on another level, too – the actress, although not technically out at the time of the film's production, has been one of the few female stars in Hollywood to be aligned with queerness in the public consciousness for many decades, and in 2002 most media-savvy audience members know that she is rumoured to be gay. When Lane describes the character of Sarah as both talking and dressing as if she is a boy, and when he observes that this makes her mysterious, he is ascribing a fluidity to her presentation that will seem percipient in later years, when the actress who plays her goes on *Saturday Night Live*, all grown up, and comes out in her opening monologue. (Because this film is about Foster's character and her daughter being subject to a home invasion by three macho thugs, it is *also* fairly interesting that it is effectively a battle of the sexes, and that this is fundamentally a movie about two women played by actresses who are or who will eventually be openly queer hiding out in a bunker from a group of men.) When Fincher writes the character, he initially writes her as 'tomboyish, androgynous, dismissive, a teenager at ten years old', doing so to make her the diametric opposite of Nicole Kidman, who is his first choice for Sarah's mother; with the role later recast, he reworks Foster's character, instead, wanting her to more closely resemble the prodigal child he has effectively discovered, who has made only one previous appearance in a feature film. '[Sarah] has Foster's blue eyes, blonde hair and sturdy, no-nonsense beauty,' Manohla Dargis writes in *LA Weekly*, in her review of the film, 'and she comes across as one of those girls who has no patience for feminine rubbish.' There is a distinctive moment early on in Fincher's movie in which Sarah, in a t-shirt featuring Sid Vicious, offers a pronouncement on her father's unfaithfulness to her mother: 'Fuck him,' she says, airily, as if she's thought it many times, 'and fuck her too.' It is the instant in which it becomes immediately obvious that this particular young actress has a quality we rarely see onscreen. She invites the camera in with her charisma, and then rolls her eyes at its attention, saying: you may look at me, but do not expect me to hand you myself on a silver salver.

III. THE BRIGHT KILLING RAY OF HER BITCHINESS

When Louise Brooks appears in Howard Hawks' 1928 *A Girl in Every Port*, she creates a similar impression to the one made in 1951 when Marlon Brando plays Stanley Kowalski in *A Streetcar Named Desire*: there is a shifting to make room, a sense that something of the future has cut, bladelike, through the present in order to show itself. She is as sleek as a blade, too, and the way she moves her body makes her seem not merely futuristic, but a little Futurist, her limbs effortlessly sweeping through the air in a way that suggests Umberto Boccioni's striding sculptural figure of the early 1910s, *Unique Forms of Continuity in Space*. In her yearbook photograph, she was Mary Louise Brooks; now, she has dropped the 'Mary', a fitting decision given that nothing about her – not a single drop of her wild Kansas blood – reads as pious or maternal. Introduced as 'Mam'selle

Godiva, Neptune's bride and the sweetheart of the sea', she plays a circus diver, and when she removes her silken cloak it is to show the audience her entire body, tightly wrapped in a leotard that appears in black and white to be the colour of her skin. Hawks has selected her because her easy sexual energy is underpinned with an appealing seriousness, and he finds her careful, acrobatic balancing of these two modes not merely hot, but radical. Climbing an apparently sky-high ladder to the high dive, she is grace personified, her dancer's limberness making what might have appeared dangerous or reckless read as casual and balletic, and this transformation of the act is a useful demonstration of the blend of sensuality and skill Hawks recognises in his new discovery. Later, dripping quietly in her costume, she meets eyes with a man in the audience whom she has also drenched during her dive, and when she smiles at him the smile itself is somehow startling, travelling up into her eyes and making her totally lambent with delight; this is a silent movie, but this is not classic silent movie acting, and its subtlety is, paradoxically, the thing that makes it so high-wire, so high-wattage. In the intertitles, she speaks her first line, a near-double-entendre that carries an implicit wink: 'I'm sorry you're all wet.' She is all wet, too, and it is not for this poor man, but for his money.

Critics, sensing something terribly important is about to happen, comment almost uniformly on the unusual nature of this black-haired, black-eyed actress. 'Then comes THE woman,' the *New York American* raves. 'Louise Brooks has a way of making a junior vamp and infantile scarlet lady seem most attractive.' 'Nobody could be more charming than Louise Brooks,' *TIME* agrees, a sentiment echoed by the *English Kinematograph Weekly*, who insist that she makes 'a charmingly heartless vamp'. The consensus is that Brooks is very good at being bad, the kind of bitch who is so deeply charismatic that the bright killing ray of her bitchiness being directed at you feels exciting rather than emasculating. Her character might be known as Mam'selle Godiva on the diving board, but Godiva's personal history is decidedly un-ladylike – she is actually from Coney Island, a serial sexual conwoman with charm to spare and a rough tattoo of an anchor on her arm. Contra the myth, often perpetuated in cinema, of love happening at first sight, it is possible to see a person many times before one really *sees* them, and the camera – beginning what will turn out to be a short but frantic love affair – finally sees Brooks here. She has previously appeared in several films, most of which are lost to history, playing girls with names like 'Snuggles Joy' and 'Fox Trot', but it turns out that the thing she excels most at is inhabiting a character who beckons to her own destruction, or threatens a man with his, or does both simultaneously. *A Girl in Every Port* is where she cuts her teeth playing a kind of evil babe, or rather where she sharpens them into the irresistible and gleaming fangs of a sexual vampire, and it gets the world's attention. 'Vampire' is, after all, the root of 'vamp', and both terms will come to suit Louise Brooks to a tee, perpetually driven as she is to fasten her mouth on the silken throat of life.

IV. AND SO THE LION FELL IN LOVE WITH THE LAMB

Here is how Kristen Stewart, six years after playing Sarah in *Panic Room*, becomes not just a promising indie starlet, but the A-List Actress Kristen Stewart: she reacts to the seductive, glittering presence of a hundred-year-old vampire by appearing to be bored. *Twilight*, a 2008 film by Catherine Hardwicke, is intended to be an inconsequential trifle: a brief flash in the pan based on a series of young adult vampire romance novels with regressive sexual politics, directed by a woman whose more serious first film was a grimy mother-may-I-sleep-with-danger thriller about what happens to thirteen-year-olds who are left to their own atavistic, hormone-fuelled devices in LA. Instead, both the novels and the movies based upon them become frighteningly dominating global hits, both feminist discourse and the young-adult-novel economy expanding significantly as a result. The premise of the first film in the *Twilight* trilogy is simple, and a little worrying: Bella, a 'plain' girl who actually looks like Kristen Stewart, meets a vampire in a science class at her regular rural high school, and the two of them fall passionately, adolescently in love, even though one of them only *appears* to be an adolescent. Edward, the vampire, is a little over eighty years the clumsy schoolgirl's senior; played by Robert Pattinson, who swiftly becomes Stewart's boyfriend in real life, he is pretty to the point of the absurd, ruby-lipped and pouting, and given to sweeping, starry-eyed pronouncements. If they fuck, he may kill her, and so their relationship becomes a tense, ostensibly erotic *pas de deux* that muddles, S&M-like, sex and death. The idea is that the audience, mostly female, will identify with Bella, and that because Bella is intended to be unremarkable, they will find it easy to effortlessly insert themselves into the black hole of her presence in the story. Stewart, though, has other plans, and it quickly becomes obvious that if anything makes her like a black hole, it is her limitless and exceptional depth.

The film, as is fashionable in the noughties, is a muddied blue throughout – blue as a bad mood, or a love song full of wailing melodrama – and both leads accordingly look bluish, too, as if both of them were deathly, thus eternal. In the sense of being immortalised in the Hollywood firmament, both of them *will* be eternal by the time the *Twilight* sequel is released, this particular era in the careers of Robert Pattinson and Kristen Stewart at once formative and calcifying vis-à-vis their images as stars. This is the movie that definitively makes her, and it is also the movie that hangs like a millstone or an albatross around her neck forevermore, millions of eyes turning towards her and millions of mouths enquiring as to whether she would not prefer to *smile*. Like Louise Brooks, Stewart projects seriousness when she feels like projecting seriousness, and discomfort when she feels uncomfortable, and as was the case with Brooks, the media and the industry are baffled by her failure to behave as if being gawped at – being told to shut up and look grateful and accept her status as a sexy image with no evident opinions – is the greatest prize on earth. ('Now I feel like if I smiled for a paparazzi photo – not that I *ever* would – that's exactly what people would be desecrating me for,' she goes on to say in 2014, to a journalist from *ELLE*. 'They'd be like, "now you're going to give it up, now you're a sellout".') She is pilloried for looking inadequately elated to be walking the red carpet; she is repeatedly labelled a bad actress who can only play herself, a wet blanket and a wooden emo cliché. Because *Twilight* is for teens, and especially for teenage girls, it is presumed that her laid-back inertness onscreen is not subtlety, but inexperienced incompetence. Never mind that she has already successfully kept up with Jodie Foster at an age when most girl-children are still playing with Barbie dolls – to make work intended to please teenyboppers is, in the minds of those who care about the difference between 'cinema' and 'movies', to relinquish any right to being treated like an artist. 'KRISTEN STEWART', a popular meme from that year trumpets underneath a grid of images of Stewart's impassive face, her eyes in each screenshot very clearly conveying something subtly distinct in defiance of the joke: 'BECAUSE A DIFFERENT FACIAL EXPRESSION WOULD BE TOO HARD.'

'Blue is the colour of the mind in borrow of the body; it is the colour consciousness becomes when caressed,' William H. Gass wrote in *On Being Blue*. 'Blue is therefore most suitable as the colour of interior life.' Nobody expects much of a showing of interior life in *Twilight*, and yet Stewart, centred in the movie's cyanopsic gaze, manages to use her body to suggest a certain mental fortitude, as if her sylphlike girl's form were being borrowed by the mind of a brooding masculine archetype. Blue is, after all, supposedly the colour of boys, and Anthony Lane's earlier oblique suspicions about

Kristen Stewart's tomboy consciousness are given further weight here, Stewart obviously playing the hero rather than the heroine in the romance: she is stoic, strong-jawed, often blank, leaving room for the great beauty of the pairing to take ostentatious centre stage. Stewart is a cowboy, her mouth set into a straight and challengingly un-kissable line in order to invite her lover's – and perhaps the audience's – lips, and if either party appears destined to go swooning into their beloved's arms, it is the delicate male vamp. 'And so the lion fell in love with the lamb,' he sighs to Bella, forcing her to reply: 'What a stupid lamb.' 'What a sick, masochistic lion,' he shoots back. By 2008, Stewart's relationship with her public and the press is becoming sincerely masochistic, too, and it is unclear whether she's the lion, or the lamb. Fame is a monster capable of lavishing you with its love and killing you in increments at the same time; if Stewart has never been richer or better known, she has also never been more fundamentally misunderstood. The media and the paparazzi drink from her and drink from her, and the version of her that becomes immortal is, at this point, pale and not entirely herself.

V. DEATH BY A SEXUAL MANIAC

Another film that muddles sex and death – considerably more explicitly than *Twilight* – is G. W. Pabst's 1929 *Pandora's Box*, an adaptation of a pair of Frank Wedekind plays about a wild girl named Lulu who is utterly determined to make oblivion her *inamorato*. At first, Pabst considers Marlene Dietrich for the role, but at twenty-seven he fears she is too old, and he also fears that her characteristic frigidity and cynicism might prevent her from convincingly portraying an impulsive, thoughtless sex maniac with the proper demented élan; rumour has it, he sees Louise Brooks' animalistic smouldering in *A Girl in Every Port* and realises he's found his lead. Brooks, who believes that she might actually *be* Lulu in her heart, agrees entirely with him, knowing all too intimately the sensation of pursuing hurt and pleasure at the same time, the commingling of horror and ecstasy that can result from allowing the sex drive and the death drive to shake hands. Her performance in the movie certainly suggests a perfect synergy between the fictional character and her actress, the meeting of Lulu and Louise proving as explosive as the meeting between Lulu and the nameless serial killer who destroys her in the last reel of the film. Lulu is excessively sexual, excessively wicked, and apparently unjudged by the director and his picture in spite of the downward motion of the plot: she is indiscriminate in the untroubled, arguably aspirational mode of the true slut, amoral only in the way that things in nature are amoral when they fight and fuck and kill. She is a lamb throwing itself into the red mouth of a lion, a prey animal whose love of being preyed upon makes her seem, paradoxically, both powerful and predatorial. In an early scene, she meets an older, richer lover in her chambers, and when he insists that he cannot make love to her because he is engaged to someone else, the revelation does not hurt her or surprise her – it arouses her, instead. Stretching herself out across the daybed, Brooks allows the shortness of that famous hairstyle to draw emphasis to one of the most swanlike necks in cinematic history, and pouts playfully as if she already knows that she has won. 'You won't kiss me just because you're getting married?' she demands. The purr in the American honey of her voice is somehow audible in spite of the fact that there is no sound.

If audiences hate a woman who will not smile unless she feels that a smile is necessary, they are equally incensed by one who smiles at something they themselves do not find pleasant or amusing. Nothing makes the critics who review *Pandora's Box* more furious than the changeable and sometimes inscrutable moods that flicker, evanescent, across Brooks' perfect face. She has a strong nose, slender brows that augur mischief, and eyes that look beetle-black in monochrome, and the combination of these features makes it difficult for her to seem straightforwardly unhappy or delighted, radiating instead a persistent air of irony that feels as if it belongs to the twenty-first century rather than the first years of the twentieth. This irony is the quality that allows her to suggest injury is an awfully big adventure, or to project 'true love' as a raffish mockery of itself; it is the attribute that keeps her Lulu from ever appearing cowed or chastened, and which makes this particular telling of the Lulu fable less of a morality tale than many of the moralists watching hoped it might have been. 'Miss Brooks is attractive and she moves her head and eyes at the proper moment,' Mordaunt Hall sniffs in *The New York Times*, 'but whether she is endeavouring to express joy, woe, anger or satisfaction is often difficult to decide.' 'Louise Brooks cannot act,' a viewer is purported to have said on leaving a screening. 'She does not suffer. She does nothing.' Lulu's lack of evident suffering appears to be a sticking point; likewise her unusually childlike prizing of sensation and immediate gratification over caution. One might think an actress who had been inducted forcibly into the world of sex at nine years old might know a little more about the ways women behave when faced with sexual violence than a snide male critic, but at this point in history, Brooks' depiction of a character who has an unusual relationship with degradation is so ahead of its time that her unwillingness to appear broken is confused with 'doing nothing'. Lulu may end up being murdered, but she is no victim in the strictest sense: how can a violation be a true crime if it ends up giving the one being violated everything she's ever wanted?

Notice, as Lulu careens from fuck to fuck, disaster to disaster, the way men she meets describe her. 'One doesn't marry such women,' one of her lovers insists. 'It would be suicide!' At first, one wonders if this is a mistranslation of the German, and that what he means is 'social suicide' – whether he believes that marrying a girl as Machiavellian and promiscuous as Lulu would mean being ostracised by what is usually called 'polite society'. Soon, however, it becomes clear that he means plain suicide, and his prophecy is fulfilled when Lulu, having wrestled a particularly phallic-looking pistol from his hands, shoots him as the two of them are locked in an embrace, smoke billowing from between them like a joke about their loins being aflame. Brooks occasionally feels like an immediate danger to us because of her ability to stare out as if her eyes were meeting ours, as in a scene where yet another of her lovers is positioned directly behind the camera so that her seduction seems to break the fourth wall; she is a hair away from inviting us to join in on some or other form of mortally perilous mischief. Working as a critic in her later years, the actress will describe the ending of the movie thus: 'It is Christmas Eve, and [Lulu] is about to receive the gift that has been her dream since childhood: death by a sexual maniac.' This is an accurate description: Lulu, who has once again returned to sex work after six chaotic acts of sex and gunfire and adultery and marriage, is in London, and a Ripper – maybe Jack, though who's to say? – is killing women in the dark, until one fateful evening she receives him as a client. At first, he protests, wanting to resist his terrible impulses; he insists he has no money, and he throws away his knife. Lulu, ultraluminous with her proximity to nihility and destruction, tells him that she does not care if he can't pay her, since she likes him. In this instant, the immediate fellow-feeling and soul recognition of falling in love is replicated, as if in a funhouse mirror, as a moment of connection between murderer and victim, death and death-drive, knife and heart. While shooting, Brooks attempts to convince Pabst that when the final moment comes, the replacement blade the Ripper picks up from our desperate heroine's dresser ought to find its place not her breast, but in her cunt, and although technically this is impossible to attempt in the twenties, there is something of that spirit in the shot. Brooks' request proves her intimate understanding of her character – and it shows, too, how deeply she recognises the parity between this last violent act and sexual penetration. Perhaps audiences believe that she does nothing because they are not prepared to see the things she's really doing, many of which are psychosexually complex, emotionally rich, and gleefully contradictory. She does not yet know that one day, she will be described as both a genius and a sexual idol, although her unwillingness to compromise her intellect suggests that some small part of her might feel that day approaching with the same keen thrill that Lulu feels as she awaits the chill benediction of the knife.

VI. JUST LIKE HEAVEN

One year after the release of *Twilight* Kristen Stewart plays a love interest again, and this time she is not playing the hero, though she does not feel like an entirely conventional heroine, either. The film is *Adventureland*, a nostalgic romance set at a mid-eighties theme park. Her co-star is Jesse Eisenberg, who will flex the secret muscle of his cruelty in *The Social Network* in 2010 and, doing so, prove himself to be more than simply a sweet nebbish; for now, though, he is soft and new and wide-eyed, a boy-naif with visible puppy fat. Her first appearance in the movie is an archetypal Kristen Stewart moment, and its tone goes some way to establishing her enviably genderfucked appeal. She is the coolest, hottest and purportedly most unattainable chick working at the theme park Eisenberg's James has been hired at for the summer, and her coolness, hotness and purported unattainability all spring from an adult version of the self-same quality that let her radiate such evident charisma at the age of ten in *Panic Room*: her personality is as low-slung as her jeans, her lack of give-a-fuck undercut with a wry amusement at others' foolish excess of it. When she first looks at Eisenberg across the park, her posture – cross-legged, idly chewing on her lip, her green eyes shaded like the eyes of a cat looking at a curly-haired, virginal mouse – is lazily disdainful, but her smile is warm and hazy, as if she is looking at a treasured photograph rather than living in the present. As with her seeming ability to gaze into the future when we saw her playing Sarah, her performance here as a hip, jaded Pittsburghian teenager whose longing for excitement far exceeds her grasp is heightened by a sense that she is too wise far too young. It seems impossible that Eisenberg is seven years Stewart's senior, but then her sullen sophistication made it appear equally impossible that Pattinson's Edward Cullen was the older man in *Twilight*, and Cullen was quite literally a hundred-year-old vampire.

Em, Stewart's character in *Adventureland*, is a cinematic take on a very particular kind of teenage girl – the kind who appears wildly unapproachable and knowledgeable to boys simply because she owns a Lou Reed t-shirt, or because she has a Cure tape in the stereo of her car – and as such she is a humorous reminder of how little it requires for this very particular kind of teenage girl to seem impressive to a boy who has not ever, not once, actually had sex. She is the kind of sleepy-looking, long-limbed chick that often gets called 'cool' and 'smart' in the specific tone a person might use to address a dog they had seen walking on two legs, as if such qualities were hitherto unseen in girls and a startling evolutionary leap had taken place. 'No,' she tells James when he asks whether she has ever been in love, before clarifying with a forceful 'hell no'. She is unable to understand why, having realised he was not in love with his first girlfriend, he didn't just fuck her anyway, and when he rationalises the decision by invoking Shakespeare's sonnets, she reacts as if he's from another planet. *Adventureland* stills often appear in the memes circulating about Stewart's acting, and the point of their inclusion is that Em, in a static image, reveals very little of her emotional life – she does not suffer, she does nothing. In fact, Em's impassive looks are integral to her character as a girl who loathes emotion, and who believes vulnerability to be the most embarrassing quality on earth, and Stewart excels at playing guarded and cynical women: those who, perhaps once having been scorned themselves, cannot help but radiate their own scorn towards others like a sly, protective spell.

What could possibly be less cool than casually disclosing too much of oneself? Better to keep the mystery alive by staying fluid and inscrutable, especially if you are a babe with brains. If Em is not a full-throated, black-hearted deathly hedonist like Lulu, she retains a trace of that secretive darkness in her motivations and her actions: she is screwing a much older married man, she loathes her stepmother, she plays with James' heart, and so on. 'No, I never met a terribly introverted and damaged girl at a theme park in the eighties,' Stewart sighs to an interviewer who asks her if she's ever known someone like Em, before revealing a little more than she means to as she goes on. 'I could imagine what it would be like to not like yourself very much,' she admits, 'and [to] sort of be kicking it alone, and feel like you're sort of smarter than everyone, but no one gets it. I get all of that. Then the masochist[ic] aspects [of life] girls are good at, so I can relate on that level.' Far fewer people watch *Adventureland* than watched Stewart in *Twilight*, and as such news of the quality of her work does not circulate widely enough to dispel the public's notion of her as a terrible actress, a few instances of critical praise causing gentle ripples in the image but not breaking it entirely. One of the most curious things about the hatred Stewart faces is that it exists in opposition to the adoration Em receives from every adolescent nerd she meets, despite the fact that both reactions are provoked by the same thing – namely, her supposed difference from The Other Girls. One might expect her to have been embraced rather than pilloried for her sensual jadedness and her indifference, and the dissonance is possibly explained by either general fatigue around the archetype of 'manic pixie dream girl', or internalised misogyny on behalf of the predominantly female fanbase of the *Twilight* movies. Still, perhaps it's something else: a sense that Stewart is not quite what she appears to be, as though when she is in public she is always half there, half disappeared into some unknowable place. When she appears on *FHM*'s list of the sexiest actresses in Hollywood the following year, it seems jarring and bizarre, not because she is not sexy, but because there is so little sense that any part of her belongs to the specific demographic that reads *FHM*. Besides, she is so sui generis that she renders the idea of competition obsolete.

Stewart will go on to appear with Jesse Eisenberg in two more movies, a 2015 comedy about terrorism called *American Ultra*, and in 2016, a period romance set in the Golden Age of Hollywood called *Café Society*. (*American Ultra* is, controversially, written by Max Landis, who will be accused of sexual misconduct – falsely, he maintains – some years later; *Café Society* is, controversially, both written and directed by Woody Allen, who is Woody Allen.) They work admirably together, and what makes them fit is a shared tendency to feel as if each is muddling the other's gender binary, Eisenberg shy as an ingénue and Stewart tough as nails. In the latter film, the two are outside Joan Crawford's house, and Eisenberg's character Bobby says that, as a plain civilian, he can't even picture how it feels to be 'larger than life' like someone famous. Stewart's Vonnie, a tomboyish secretary, thinks a little, and delivers first a point, and then a counterpoint: 'It would be fun for a while. But I think I prefer being life size.'

VII. A HAPPY ANIMAL IN SATIN

It is surreal to see Louise Brooks looking like a bride, in a crown of pallid roses and an oddly babyish white dress, and even more surreal to realise that she is in fact not playing a bride, but playing a girl set to receive her first communion; stranger still that the man who at first appears as though he might be her much older and considerably less sprightly husband is her daddy. Daddy issues, in fact, run all the way through G. W. Pabst's 1929 film *The Diary of a Lost Girl*, be it in relation to, well, a relation, or in a more allegorical sense in which the 'daddy' is authority itself. Brooks plays Thymian, an innocent who is repeatedly exploited by both men and institutions. Her philandering father impregnates the family maid, and then when the pregnant maid takes her own life, he employs another woman who looks more or less the same, and whose name, in a detail that will one day prove especially amusing to audiences of the future, is 'Meta'. Meta rules the household with an iron fist, and when Thymian is raped by the frighteningly lupine man who mans the counter of her father's pharmacy, also becoming pregnant, Meta insists that the fallen daughter must be sent to a reform school that more closely resembles a women's prison.

Pabst cannily draws attention to Brooks' singularity by including a scene in which she's led into the institution's dining room in her civilian clothes, her oil-black bob and coruscating beauty deliberately contrasted by two neat rows of boiler-suited female inmates, drab and grey and spooning soup into their mouths in perfect unison. The message could not be more obvious: here is a woman who is not made to be hemmed in by convention, who could only ever be larger than life and never life-sized. When a girl called Erika plays footsie with her, making bedroom eyes in her direction, Pabst is not afraid to let us think that Thymian, and by implication Brooks, might be different from the other girls in other senses, too. (The school, because of course it is, is also run by a sadistic lesbian nun.) 'When I am dead, I believe that film writers will fasten on the story that I am a lesbian,' Brooks will later say. 'I have done lots to make it believable.' It is true that she fucks many women as well as many men, including Greta Garbo; it is also true that she believes herself to be essentially heterosexual, and that her pursuit of women is for the most part motivated by her self-avowed love of beauty. At several points in her personal history, she self-identifies as a homosexual man trapped in the body of a glamorous woman – 'not a lesbian,' she insists, quoting a queer friend, but 'a pansy.' Ultimately, her sexuality is mysterious, and Pabst – who also has her kiss a woman in *Pandora's Box* – appears to know this, the elusiveness around the sexual motivations of her characters in both his films feeling less like a result of zealous censorship, and more like a deliberate choice.

When Thymian and Erika escape from the reform school, they both quickly fall into one of the few careers that is then open to uneducated, unconnected women, and begin to operate out of a brothel. Logically, given the mores of the time, one might expect Pabst to suggest that they had leapt, as the old saying goes, out of the frying pan and into the fire – in fact, Thymian has never been more animated or exuberant than she is at a party where her sex is being auctioned off by lottery, and accordingly she has never looked more like Louise Brooks. ('A happy animal,' the critic Kenneth Tynan says of her appearance in the scene, 'in skintight satin.')

The event only turns sour when Thymian's father, by pure chance, is in attendance, narrowly missing out on buying a ticket for a night with his own daughter; until she is subject to the disapproval of her daddy, Thymian seems to feel no shame at all about her work. The suggestion seems to be that she has been exploited all her life, especially by men, without earning any money in the bargain, and that here she is at least granted the power of independence – it is money, and the need for it, which dictates how a woman's life is lived, and Thymian ends up giving her inheritance to her half-sister when her father dies because she recognises that this is the case. A series of contrivances lead to our heroine somehow being made a trustee of the reform school in the last scenes of the film, and as she is paying a visit Erika is brought in once again, condemned as an incurable and stubborn rebel. Thymian finally breaks, Brooks' fury radiating so intensely that it feels as though it ought to literally be possible for us to *feel* its heat, and she pours scorn on the institution and its cruel insistence that nominally bad girls should be punished for the things that genuinely bad men do to them. 'I know this house and its "blessings",' she snarls, holding Erika in an embrace that is more tender and more nakedly suggestive of the dynamic between a hero and a heroine in a romance than any Brooks has previously engaged in, at least onscreen. 'Your ignorance won't help her.' The invocation of 'ignorance' is unlikely to be a direct reference to sexual prejudice, but it certainly reads as one. Pabst's original plan was to show Thymian returning triumphantly to the brothel to operate it as a madam, and although

Brooks' liveliness makes the existing ending better than it might otherwise be, there is a sense that this would have been the most Brooksian finish – reminiscent, too, of Lulu, the happy animal-innocent slut – for another morality tale that is not really, has not ever been, a morality tale. During filming, Brooks spends all of her down-time partying and having sex with very wealthy men, in what is not quite a professional arrangement but which is also not *not* a professional arrangement, either, and Pabst chastises her once the movie is completed. *Carry on like this*, he says, *and you will end up like Lulu*. Brooks shrugs, fails to see the problem. It is strange that glimpsing her as what appears to be a blushing bride in the first scenes of *Diary of a Lost Girl* feels so wrong, as in the course of her life, Brooks gets married twice – being married feels somehow a little different, though, from being a bride or being a wife, and like Lulu, Louise Brooks is only ever married to the risk; the sex; the thrill; the pleasure of walking into a room full of other women and never once being confused with any of them. 'I have a gift for enraging people,' she is fond of saying, 'but if I ever bore you, it will be with a knife.'

VIII. TRAMPIRE

In 2012, Kristen Stewart is photographed kissing her director, who is middle-aged and married, and all hell breaks loose. The movie they are making is a Snow White adaptation in which Stewart's Snow White appears in a suit of armour brandishing a sword, a vision of retroactive female empowerment encased in steel. Most of the paparazzi images of the embrace themselves are unremarkable except for one that depicts Stewart in the front seat of his car playfully flexing one pale bicep, a mock-macho gesture that encourages the viewer to invent a more interesting narrative than the one probably behind it. Either way, whether or not Stewart's insistence that the affair never went beyond a kiss is true is hardly relevant, as media and fans alike behave as if the act might kick off a full-scale nuclear war. Teenage girls, already hostile to the Cool Girl lover of their boy-prince idol, make furious and tearful YouTube videos with titles like WHY DID YOU DO IT KRISTEN and HOW COULD KRISTEN CHEAT ON ROBERT PATTINSON?? The comedian Will Ferrell, in an interview with the late-night host Conan O'Brien, ostensibly satirises the hysteria by performing an amplified version of it, stage-sobbing about Stewart's infidelity and calling her a 'trampire', and the American public – not generally known for their good sense and sensitivity in separating irony from fact – seize on the neologism, wearing it on t-shirts and plastering it over social media. One social media user in particular, a moronic reality TV host and businessman, becomes frighteningly invested in the scandal, and at various intervals throughout 2012 he uses Twitter to extend his sympathy to Pattinson, the tweets occasionally tipping into something like harassment and exuding equal parts misogyny and lust. 'Everyone knows I am right that Robert Pattinson should dump Kristen Stewart. In a couple of years, he will thank me. Be smart, Robert,' the idiot businessman writes at 9.48 p.m. one day. 'After Friday's *Twilight* release, I hope Robert Pattinson will not be seen in public with Kristen – she will cheat on him again!' he fires off two or three weeks later around dinnertime. On and off, he spends a full month on the subject, giving the impression that it makes him just as frenzied as it makes the scores of teenage girls on YouTube weeping to their webcams. In spite of the fact that Kristen Stewart is not and has never been a public servant, she is required by the rules of fame, and female fame especially, to issue an apology, and she does so in the illustrious, glossy pages of the gossip publication *People*. 'I'm deeply sorry for the hurt and embarrassment I've caused to those close to me and everyone this has affected,' she writes. 'This momentary indiscretion has jeopardised the most important thing in my life, the person I love and respect the most, Rob. I love him, I love him, I'm so sorry.'

There is something sadly touching about the actress' repetition of 'I love him' in her statement, as though in spite of its having been prepared in advance and in writing, she is stumbling over her response because she feels too passionate about the subject to allow for concision. Nobody gets an answer in the moment as to why she chose to kiss the married man, although later she informs a journalist exactly what drove her to do it, and it is more or less exactly the motivation one would guess a girl might have for throwing herself at somebody's husband: she is trying to dramatically explode her life, which she believes intends to kill her via gradual suffocation. It is not only vampires who are capable of walking around dead, and perhaps feeling as if her path had already been set out with uncompromising certainty – the ethereally gorgeous co-star boyfriend; the five-film series of lightweight and high-grossing YA movies; an awareness of fame widening its mouth and drooling on her slender body like a beast, meaning to swallow her entirely – she confesses to going 'feral' to escape. Her apparent stillness, which is at once her most valuable asset and the thing she is most mocked for, is revealed to have been hiding a bottomless well of loneliness and desperation, and as little of a fuck as she appears to give about the public's opprobrium and derision, she cannot help but be hurt deep down inside by the continuing suggestion in the press that she is a talentless slut, a hanger-on to Pattinson, a scowling ingrate, *et cetera et cetera*. As it happens, the tweets by the insane businessman end up catalysing a change in Stewart's public image, to say nothing of her life, five years later when he goes on to become the President of the United States, and she goes on *SNL* and gives him hell. Delivering her opening monologue in a short dress with hanging leather straps, her hair close-cropped and dark, she addresses him directly in the sly tone of a child being made to apologise for something they are very proud of having done. 'If you didn't like me then, you're really not going to like me now,' she grins, 'because I'm hosting *SNL* and I'm like, *so gay, dude*.'

At the phrase *so gay, dude*, one hand flutters delicately to her mouth, a hammy burlesque of coyness that reveals she could not be less coy about being *so gay, dude* if she tried. It is hard to explain the precise vibe emanating from her, except to suggest that it is diametrically opposed to the one that once radiated miserably from her *People* magazine apology. This time, there is no 'I'm deeply sorry', and there is no room for a word like 'embarrassment', either – there is only her cockiness and her triumph, the metaphorical flexing of her bicep. Of course Stewart chose to crop her hair and wear an S&M-inflected dress to introduce the show; of course she threw the devil's horns, a universal gesture of alternateen defiance, as she walked onto the stage. She was always planning for this to be the very first moment of our meeting with the complete Kristen Stewart, an overtly queer star who channels the swaggering gaucho energy of her most assured screen performances into her offscreen self. Somehow, the revolting businessman and his obsession with her ex have allowed for a crack in the heavy armour of her public image, and as Stewart's fingers fly up to her grinning mouth during that monologue, it is hard not to think about another photograph of her from 2013 in which she has similar body language – namely, one in which she stands outside a Texas branch of Hooters in a backwards baseball cap, surrounded by a gaggle of buxom staff, trying to hide the fact that she looks like the cat that got the cream.

IX: WANTING TO BE ENSLAVED BY HER OR WANTING TO ENSLAVE HER

A great deal happens after Louise Brooks seems to be on the precipice of permanently becoming larger-than-life at the tail-end of the twenties, after her two films with Pabst move her definitively closer to the possibility of long-term global fame. One of those things is the pioneering and subsequent popularity of cinematic sound, heralding a different kind of picture that no longer requires actors to communicate in semaphore, making gesture suddenly far less important than good diction. It is not that Brooks does not have perfect diction – she has carefully trained the Kansas from her voice, the result pleasing and inordinately smooth, belonging to nowhere exactly except the America of the movies. Rather, the impediment to Brooks' continued fame is Hollywood's congenital inability to recognise the nature of her talent, coupled with her congenital inability to learn another language. In 1929, she goes to Paris and makes *Miss Europe*, a film in which she plays another character by the name of Lulu, albeit one with rather less of a destructive streak – a secretary who defies the uptight mores of her boyfriend by entering herself into Miss France. Because Brooks does not speak French, her lines are overdubbed by a French actress, and although the switch is purely practical its execution feels a little like a bad joke, the sight of another person's voice emerging from the mouth of this singular and uncompromising woman a little too apropos considering the industry's dislike of her outspokenness. That same year, an interview with Pabst is published in the US magazine *Motion Picture* in which Pabst, horrified at the idea of Brooks returning to the States, bemoans the idea that she ought to be expected to play 'silly little cuties'. 'The pettiness of [Hollywood],' he sighs ruefully to the reporter, 'the dullness, the monotony, the stupidity – no, no, that is no place for Louise Brooks.'

Proving him right, the head of the studio at Columbia offers her a contract, then insists on taking every meeting with her naked from the waist up; she decides instead to try her luck with individual pictures, and she appears in a few that are not especially notable, as well as a Western with an up-and-coming actor whose all-American masculinity makes for an interesting pairing with her haute-feminine sensuality. The movie, *Overland Stage Raiders*, is more or less forgotten; the all-American leading man, John Wayne, is in Brooks' words 'no actor, but the hero of all mythology miraculously brought to life', and he goes on to – well, everyone knows what he goes on to; suffice to say that he is remembered significantly better than the film.

Overland Stage Raiders is Louise Brooks' last appearance in the movies, and in 1940, she leaves Hollywood forever after a brief stint in copywriting; after this she is employed, variously, as a radio actor, a salesgirl at Saks, and – in all likelihood, although she remains evasive – as an extremely high-class escort with a small number of clients. Frequently, she ponders suicide, saying that she dreams of 'little bottles filled with yellow sleeping pills' but also joking, or perhaps not joking, that she cannot afford enough of the medication to successfully do the job; she becomes an alcoholic, living in a small New York apartment and intermittently working on a memoir that is titled, per a quote from Goethe's *Faust* about the dissolution of all youthful beauty, *Naked on my Goat*. In 1955, not long after she has thrown the manuscript into the fire after fearing that the text is not honest enough about her sexual life, a French film historian 'rediscovers' her and mounts a Louise Brooks film festival, rapturously explaining that 'There is no Garbo! There is no Dietrich! There is only Louise Brooks!' The newfound attention leads to contact from a film curator, James Card, who persuades her to relocate to Rochester, New York, and to take advantage of the George Eastman Museum film collection in order to learn more about cinema and theory and movie history. Proving Card's instincts about her gift for studying the medium entirely correct, Brooks surprises herself by successfully becoming something close to sober and beginning to produce, slowly at first and then with passionate speed, essays about film: works that seem to have emanated from another place, prefiguring a later school of criticism which – like Brooks' acting style – prizes detail over broad narrative gestures, subtlety over major sentiment. By 1979, she is spending almost all her time in bed – a state of affairs that would not be unusual enough to note if it were not for the fact that, now, she does so on her own, drunk again on gin and reading books, writing finespun arias of criticism about subjects that arrest her: W. C. Fields' shadowy loneliness; Margaret Sullavan's 'strange, fey, mysterious [voice] – like a voice singing in the snow'; the 'sympathy' of Joan Crawford's 'madness', and so on.

If this sounds like an unhappy life, Brooks does not seem to think it so, and she revels in the chance to spend her days expanding her intellectual horizons without being told, as she was several times when she worked as an actress, that the desire to read was unbecoming in a woman. One day, *The New Yorker* sends a theatre critic by the name of Kenneth

Tynan to her home in Rochester to profile her, and she opens the door to him in a pink nightgown, holding herself upright with a quad cane, and he falls immediately in love with her anyway – the two have been in conversation, first by letter and then by the telephone, but this is his first legitimate encounter with the staggering refulgency of her charisma. Her loveliness is still extraordinary, but it has changed, sexuality no longer being her most obvious currency; heat has turned to chill, sex to elegance, her movements and appearance suddenly more reminiscent of a dancer – and a ballet dancer in particular – than an actress. She is in her seventies, and the black helmet of her bob has given way to hair that runs down to her waist, silver as moonlight and pulled tightly at the crown. 'Her voice has the range of a dozen birdcalls,' Tynan rhapsodises, 'from the cry of a peacock to the fluting of a dove. Her articulation, at whatever speed, is impeccable, and her laughter soars like a kite.' Certainly, the two have what might be described as an intellectual affair, in the sense of two brilliant minds entwining and also in the less highfalutin sense that, in their heads, there is no doubt they fuck like bunnies; they are rumoured to have slept together in life, too, although Brooks' infirmity leaves some measure of doubt. The piece Tynan produces is a stellar piece of writing, but he plays second fiddle in it to his exalted lover-subject. Unlike other actresses whose performances try to dictate what the audience must feel, Tynan suggests, 'she does not care what we think of her. Indeed, she ignores us. We seem to be spying on unrehearsed reality,' and her personality in the context of an interview is more or less the same: she is fearlessly opinionated, casually brilliant, as loose as is befitting an entirely unrehearsed conversation and yet so stylistically consistent – bawdy, catty, naughty, sharp – that the whole exercise amounts to a towering performance by Louise Brooks as Louise Brooks. 'The great art of films does not consist in descriptive movements of face and body,' she herself claims, 'but in the movements of thought and soul transmitted in a kind of intense isolation.' No other writer, not even Tynan, has so perfectly and so succinctly put in words the nearly indescribable quality Brooks brings to her best roles, and her self-awareness makes it clear that if she has an animal's grace, she also has an analyst's mind. Her reasoning is that playing oneself is only difficult if one already *knows* it to be difficult, and because she always did it casually, as if by some inbuilt instinct, it came to her without trouble. Besides, wouldn't playing oneself be easier, anyway, if that self was hers – 'the only unrepentant hedonist,' as Tynan would go on to call her in a talk show interview, '[and] the only pure pleasure seeker I think I have ever met'?

Near the opening of his profile, Kenneth Tynan reproduces passages from his own diary regarding his youthful infatuation with Louise Brooks, and one comment in particular made immediately after his second viewing of *Pandora's Box* feels emblematic of her appeal as a sexual idol: '[She is] the only star actress,' he sighs, 'I can imagine either being enslaved by or wanting to enslave.' It is typical of Brooks to invite not only desire, but a simultaneous desire to be dominated by her and to own her, these being the kinds of feelings men tend to report experiencing when faced with a powerful phenomenon of nature. Why climb Everest? Because it is there. Why desire to possess, or to be possessed by, Louise Brooks? Because she is Louise Brooks. 'You're doing a terrible thing to me,' she tells Tynan as she ushers him into the house. 'I've been killing myself off for twenty years, and you're going to bring me back to life.' But Brooks has never been dead, really – even when she really, physically dies, the image of that black bob, the small white face underneath it luminous in the surrounding darkness, will endure; the ghost of her undulating across the screen and on the page. Until then, she has very good and very bad days; she receives bright tributes and endures interminably long and dark nights of the soul; she releases a hybrid memoir, entitled *Lulu in Hollywood*, which Roger Ebert describes as 'one of the few film books that can be called indispensable'. One thing she does not do, even when it would be easiest, is compromise, and it is this which makes her story – even with the poverty and the drink, the suicidal thoughts and the infuriating demands on her character by men who wish her to be stupid – one of triumph and not tragedy, her determination to play herself expanding from the screen and into every element of her life.

X. SHE'S NOT COMPLETELY ANTISEPTIC

Kristen Stewart is arguing with Juliette Binoche about a mainstream movie starlet, and the stories she is telling about the tabloid-frenzying sins the mainstream starlet has committed are at first generic – she drinks too much, she attends too many parties and drives drunk and is observed losing her head, she behaves horribly on set – and then suddenly entirely too specific. This wild girl, Stewart explains to Binoche, is hated by the media because she does not play the game, choosing to remain angular and aggressive rather than agreeably acquiescing to her objectification; there is, too, the problem of the starlet's recent breakup with her boyfriend, who is 'the biggest star' according to his 'preteen' audience. 'She took off and just started really fucking up,' Stewart observes. Later, we will see this actress, who is played by Chloë Grace Moretz, in a televised press conference which she treats with pure disdain: playing with her long and tangled brunette hair; rolling her heavily lidded eyes; having no idea of the full name of the director she is set to work with next. All of this is not because she does not care about the project, but because she does not care about the need to do publicity for it like a circus animal. 'I love her,' Stewart insists to Binoche, her defence becoming passionate enough that is not quite clear whether the root of it is fandom, lesbianism, or a kind of fellow feeling. 'She's not completely antiseptic like the rest of Hollywood.' Ultimately, Stewart and Binoche remain at odds: the older woman cannot understand why a girl who rose to stardom in the multiplex would want to trash her lucrative and stainless image for the sake of showing herself to be a punk and not a poppet, and she cannot understand why an actress of any integrity and intelligence would have made such terrible popcorn movies in the first place. It is possible that Binoche feels this way because she no longer remembers what being in the industry when you are very young is like. 'She's brave enough to be herself,' Stewart says, quietly. 'At [nineteen], I think that's pretty fucking cool.'

This is a scene from Olivier Assayas' 2014 *Clouds of Sils Maria*, in which Kristen Stewart plays the personal assistant of Binoche's respected middle-aged actress, the two women sharing an intense relationship that sometimes borders on eroticism, and sometimes nods nimbly to a genre the critic Miriam Bale once pegged as 'persona-swap movies'. In Assayas, Stewart has found her G. W. Pabst, a European visionary who is perceptive enough to look straight through her flimsy, faux Hollywood image and see her artistry; as with Brooks and Pabst, the two make a pair of nearly perfect films together in Europe, and those films act as a testament to the extreme modernity of each lead actress' onscreen style. Later in *Clouds of Sils Maria*, Stewart and Binoche attend a screening of a new Marvel-spoofing science-fiction film that stars Moretz's Jo-Ann Ellis, and Assayas takes the opportunity to mount his own defence of Stewart's performance in the *Twilight* films by putting his opinions in Stewart's own mouth: 'There's no less truth [in a blockbuster] than in a more supposedly serious film,' he has her say. 'She goes deep into the darker side of her character – it's daring, it's really daring, in such a big film.' Stewart's character says of theatre, thus of acting, that it is 'an interpretation of life that can be truer than life itself,' and this, too, demonstrates Assayas' understanding of what makes his actress' screen presence so special. Acting for her is not work, but a kind of rare and almost spiritual radiation, and her movements, interesting though they are, are never quite the focal point – what burns through the screen is her ability to telegraph with her eyes what might otherwise have been said with exposition or with narrative, leaving room for a director to be elusive or coy if he or she desires it. If this sounds like an obvious description of what acting *is*, it is worth noting that regardless, it is still not something the majority of actors do, helping to explain why sobbing scenes and weight gain and unusual accents still tend to win Oscars. Stewart is not melodramatic – she is truthful, and if truth is less arresting than a more exciting falsehood, it is also pure, pellucid, an ideal foundation for a genuine work of art.

Stewart and Assayas' follow-up, in 2016, is *Personal Shopper*, a film about a young woman named Maureen who is a fashion buyer for a catwalk model, and who spends her spare time talking to the dead: she is a medium, a funny little double-entendre playing on the fact that she works in an industry where *nobody* wears a medium that is also, thanks to the airtight synergy between the film's director and its lead, the catalyst for a breathtaking meditation on both grief and gender. Maureen's twin, a brother, has recently died, and the two siblings had a pact that whichever of them died first would send a message to the other from the afterlife; in between attempts at contacting him in the next world, Maureen hangs around in Paris, doing her job with such sangfroid and detached precision that she resembles a ghost herself. Maureen and her employer, Kyra, wear the same size, and the fact that they have mirrored bodies adds a faintly metaphysical element to Maureen's work: in spite of the encouragements of the staff at the boutiques she visits, she is totally forbidden from trying on Kyra's clothes, and as a result the items take on an electric, fetishistic quality for Maureen, who dresses simply, androgynously and hiply, i.e. just like Kristen Stewart. Maureen at once fears and desires the kind of high-femme trappings Kyra favours, and her fear is heavily implied to spring from her need to keep her brother alive in herself. The film's major set-piece, in what sounds as though it ought to be a contradiction in terms, is a thrilling text-message exchange conducted while Maureen is on the Eurostar, an anonymous number contacting her to ask questions that are so vague and so eerie that she at first wonders if she's speaking to her brother's ghost. The conversation begins with this mysterious figure sending her the most alarming of all possible text messages, a simple 'I know You' with the Y in 'you' deliberately capitalised, as if to imply something deeper, more essential, than mere physical familiarity. From there, things rapidly become baldly existential. 'R u a man or a woman?' Maureen asks. 'What difference does it make?' replies the texter. 'R u real?' Maureen counters. 'R u alive or dead?' Trembling, she begins to type the question she most wants to ask, and is most terrified to hear the answer to, and as she does Assayas cuts in close to Stewart's hand, so that we see her thumb begin to really shake as she taps out: L-E-W-I-S-?

When the film is released, Assayas tells a journalist that although some great movies might have theoretically worked just as well with different leads, there is no possible way he could have made *Personal Shopper* as effective as it was without collaborating with Stewart. 'Whatever this film is about is defined by the way Kristen appropriates it,' he suggests. 'It's about being in sync [with her], about being completely aware of her instincts, and being able to adapt to the way she is appropriating the material. She is the one person who is there within the shot.' The trust between the auteur and his actress is obvious: Stewart often behaving as if no one at all – no cast, no crew, no Assayas, no audience, no camera – is watching. The one sex scene is a sex scene with herself, when she finally slips on Kyra's evening dress and hypnotises herself in the mirror, masturbating and peacocking and adopting an entirely new set of mannerisms; her nakedness is the true and unselfconscious nakedness of someone performing a secret sexual ritual behind closed doors, and not the performative nakedness of an actress. Not one of her contemporaries could balance male and female, vulnerability and cockiness, or ease and unease, like she does, and thus nobody could make such a compelling and real figure out of Maureen, whose relationship with Lewis calls to mind what Katharine Hepburn often said about her own relationship with her late brother, Tom – that after his death, she had chosen to live for him and adopt some of his finest qualities, and that doing so had both helped to develop the masculine edge she was best known for, and driven her to succeed. Is Maureen a man or a woman? Is Maureen dead or alive? Stewart plays the character with the delicacy of a virtuoso musician playing a one-of-a-kind instrument – as though she is picking her up for the first time and, without practice, spontaneously performing in accordance with her instincts. 'It's extremely difficult to open a portal into the spirit world,' she croaks in one of the film's opening scenes, slipping a cigarette between her lips as if she'd just made the most obvious and natural observation. 'That's just how it is.'

It *is* extremely difficult to open up a portal to the spirit world, freeing something indefinable and then interpreting it with the appropriate note of grace, just as it is difficult to play oneself, or to transmit the essential movements of one's inner life. Stewart goes on to earn an Oscar nomination for her portrayal of the late Diana Spencer in 2020, in Pablo Larrain's *Spencer*, and although it is a good turn, faithful to its subject, it feels counterintuitive to ask an actress of such stunning naturalism to deliver an impersonation of a brittle woman with an accent, and the film's hysteric jewel-box style makes taxidermy of the woman at its centre. Many critics jokingly suggest that she is really being nominated for her work in *Personal Shopper*, an enduring career best and arguably one of the finest screen performances of the still young twenty-first century. With Stewart and Assayas, as with Brooks and Pabst, a kind of magic trick occurs in which both partners are colluding equally, the energy maintained as when participants are asked to hold hands in a séance. Like I said: contra to the myth, often perpetuated in cinema, of love happening at first sight, it is possible to see a person many times before one really *sees* them, and both European auteurs allow audiences to see their muses for exactly what they are, what might have seemed too quiet for the big screen is revealed to be exactly the right volume for the arthouse. Like sees like; work like this is made not with the body or the mind, but with the soul, and these are actresses who have more soul than most. An aptitude for minor and expressive gestures passes from the elder star to her millennial successor, and Stewart duly picks the thread up as if, like Maureen, she knew how to take dictation from the dead.

4

They Want a Woman, and I'm Good at That

On Joan Crawford and Jane Fonda

'The make-up job, of course, is the real star,' a critic for the *Boston Phoenix* said about Faye Dunaway's performance as Joan Crawford, camp and wild, in the 1981 biopic-cum-hit-job *Mommie Dearest*. '[Dunaway's Joan Crawford is] a Frankenstein's monster that hovers perilously between faces, between personas. There's something biologically askew here: a make-up man could create that face, but human genes and chromosomes couldn't.' When he says 'the make-up job', it seems likely that he means, in particular, the lips: the scarlet of Joan Crawford's, in life as in Dunaway's re-creation, was not that of a rose or a Valentine's heart, but that of a brand-new wound. Baboon-like in its signalling of sex and frightening in its scale, her mouth reinforced Goethe's claim that red, in colour theory, exerted a 'grave and magnificent effect'. Who could be graver, more magnificent, than her? If lips are supposedly an echo of the cunt, Joan Crawford's were a cunt as viewed through a funhouse mirror: less suggestive of fertility or sensuality than of a hostile, inhospitable take on the feminine ideal, as outrageous as a costume. On her face, both agony and ecstasy looked spooky-gorgeous, as precise in their doubled geometry as theatre masks of Thalia and Melpomene.

If the great Fontana slash of those lips did not do much to conjure a mother or a pretty, wifely woman, it was probably because she never wanted to be either: only a big, indelible star. To be a star, you also have to be a little like a monster, which is why they do recall, variously, the scowl of a clown, the scheming *moue* of a drag queen, and the bloodied mouth of a lioness in a wildlife photograph. 'Joan Crawford,' *The New Yorker* critic David Denby wrote in 2010, '[was] the prototype of the modern celebrity ... who places herself at the vanguard of current erotic taste and thereby becomes attractive and slightly threatening at the same time.' Insensitive to tenderness and hypersensitive to imperfection as she was, it was only logical that she would focus her attentions on being the best, the baddest, and the biggest bitch, a sex symbol too extreme and abstract in her self-presentation to be (hetero) sexually appealing. *If you want to see the girl next door*, she quipped over and over, *go next door*, as if the die-hard fans she had in later life were interested in seeing girls at all.

Rumour has it that the new and 'improved' shape of her mouth had its roots in disease. 'After altering the shape of her face by having her back teeth removed to give her cheekbones,' the Crawford biographer Shaun Considine wrote about a surgery she had in the late twenties, 'the painful procedure... infected her gums, which stretched her mouth. When the swelling subsided, it left her with a larger upper lip. Pleased with the extension, she decided to paint in her lower lip, giving the world "the Crawford mouth".' An alleged child abuse victim and a sexual conqueress so prolific that Bette Davis said she slept with 'every male star at MGM except Lassie', it was not unusual for Crawford to take pain and spin it into an exaggerated, eroticised source of pleasure. 'It has been said,' she is supposed to have claimed, 'that on screen, I personified the American woman.' To believe that she agreed with this interpretation of her affect is to fundamentally misunderstand her vision – the way that she meant her looks to be interpreted like semaphore, worshipped like scripture. Always, she was meant to personify something better, something larger, than the American woman, something never more evident than in the genesis and the evolution of the Crawford mouth. At twenty-four, as what F. Scott Fitzgerald called 'the best example of the flapper', her lips were two afterthoughts around a dazzling set of teeth; just four years later, they were wider, thicker, turned by a technique that the renowned make-up artist Max Factor called 'the smear' into something resembling the waxy, bright red-candy mouths they sell in joke shops.

Her most strongly held conviction – that she ought to be a star – took her from bit-parts as a dancer to an acting contract with MGM studios, which swiftly made her even better known than Garbo. She took elocution classes to get rid of her Southwestern accent, repeating any word whose pronunciation she was not familiar with a minimum of fifteen times; she read aloud from books and magazines, and from the dictionary, locked up in her bedroom, until she began to sound less and less like her actual self. 'Crawford,' her Wikipedia page says, brilliantly and succinctly, 'often played wealthy women in distress.' In 1945, she starred in *Mildred Pierce*, a noir-cum-melodrama that won her the Oscar for Best Actress, her greatest performance and the pinnacle of her achievements; for *Possessed* in 1947 and *Sudden Fear* in 1952, she received two more nominations. She herself became a very wealthy woman, and she also became talented at hiding her distress. Her flapper origins instilled in her a lasting sense of duty when it came to pleasing others with her face, her grace, the litheness of her body, and her willingness to be admired. 'I believe in the flapper as an artist in her particular field,' Zelda Fitzgerald once wrote, echoing her husband's sentiment: 'the art of being – being young, being lovely, being an object.' If youth is not possible as a permanent state, the last two can be worked on – tirelessly, borderline psychotically, like King Cnut apocryphally trying to tyrannise the waves. She would not return to being little lipless Lucille out of San Antonio, Texas, daughter to a housewife and a laundry labourer, stepdaughter to a pervert.

Fearing Lucille's return proved ultimately pointless, since three full decades of Joan had more or less succeeded in erasing her from Crawford's mind, the outcome being that in private she had no idea how to behave; no sense of her own opinions or desires. There were no lapses in character, no ill-advised moments of authenticity. By the mid-fifties, she was dressing as Joan Crawford to take out the trash; announcing 'hello, this is Joan Crawford' when calling up the operator; opening her fan mail in gowns that were specially designed for the occasion of answering Joan Crawford's fan mail. In an era when to do so seemed unthinkably gauche, she regularly called the paparazzi. 'No one decided to make Joan Crawford a star,' the MGM screenwriter Frederica Sagor Maas once said. 'Joan Crawford became a star because Joan Crawford decided to become a star.' 'In some ways,' she admitted, 'I'm a goddamn image, not a person ... even when I wasn't working, there was that image thing of looking like a star, conducting myself like a star.' Even her name was chosen by public consensus, voted on by readers of a magazine called *Movie Weekly*, after MGM's head of publicity decided that 'Lucille LeSueur' was, paradoxically, too starry, and accordingly too phoney.

Three weeks before her death, Joan Crawford put her back out polishing her parquet floor: seventy-three years old, dying of cancer and refusing treatment due to her newfound belief in Christian Science, she no longer kept a maid, and no longer believed that being in her inflexible Crawford costume all day every day was necessary. Evidently, she did still believe that cleanliness was next to godliness. 'I'm up early most mornings,' she had told a reporter in 1969, when she still lived in a nine-room apartment in Manhattan, 'doing the chores, driving everyone else crazy even though I have help.' At that time, she had downsized from living in a duplex on Fifth Avenue so large the master bedroom had a fountain – the apartment, white all over with white carpeting, could not have belonged to anyone except a movie star who was also a clean-freak, which is to say that it could not have belonged to anyone except Joan Crawford. Although this would seem to most civilians like a luxurious home, for a woman of Crawford's magnitude the change had been a minor but acute humiliation. She had moved to New York in part to lend a bohemian smokescreen to her drinking problem ('New York is a very wet town,' the biographer Fred Lawrence Guiles wrote in *Joan Crawford: The Last Word*, 'and the distinction between an alcoholic and a regular drinker is a fine one'), and had subsequently shaped that drinking problem to avoid staining her carpets or her furniture, so that her preferred drink was 100%-proof vodka, sipped, discreetly carried in a sterling silver flask. When nine rooms became too much for her to maintain along with this burgeoning hobby, even with a maid, she took on a five-room apartment elsewhere in the building, decorating it with flashes of jade green and mustard yellow, and leaving the walls as bright white and as sterile as a clinic. Doris Lilly, a newspaper columnist and writer, and a neighbour in her building, put it only slightly differently: 'A visit to Joan [Crawford's] apartment,' she told *People* magazine the year that Crawford died, 'was like a visit to a hospital operating room. A house-boy waxed the parquet floors every other day. "I gave up carpets years ago," [Crawford] explained, "when I realised I couldn't keep them clean all the time." Some live by the sword, but Joan Crawford lived by the mop ... Each and every piece of furniture – and the walls – had been treated with a vinylising process that could not be penetrated by dirt. There were no fresh flowers or plants ... [she] filled her apartment with yellow wax flowers and plastic plants – ones that could be swabbed with soap and water.'

Crawford spent four years in that apartment before dying, hidden from the public eye, in 1977, leaving behind a nursery of plants that could not die; five rooms that would not gather dust. 'With all this crap in the air,' she once told the interviewer Roy Newquist, 'nothing stays clean that isn't covered.' As a younger starlet, it was rumoured that Lucille LeSueur had not only danced nude in nightclubs, but that she had made three pornographic films – one of which was called, as if foreshadowing the evolution of her image, *Velvet Lips*. When she eventually arrived in Hollywood, the rumours followed, and when an aggressive blackmailer approached her studio claiming to have a reel that showed her in a compromising set-up, MGM denied the possibility of her involvement with such vehemence it was hard not to believe them. 'The picture could be anybody, anyone at all,' Louis B. Mayer blustered, adding: 'except our Lucille.' It might have been even easier to believe him if the house belonging to the blackmailer had not burned down, mysteriously and coincidentally, a few weeks after he made contact. Still: if Lucille had appeared on film *in flagrante delicto*, Joan had not, and if the body in the stag film was essentially the same one that inhabited her shoulder-padded gowns, the face was not at all her face.

As she aged, she became more neurotic. It had long been

rumoured that she would not smoke a cigarette unless she knew the pack was new; that she personally cleaned the floors of her hotel rooms, and constantly wore gloves for reasons that were not aesthetic; that she washed her hands obsessively like Lady Macbeth, favouring Jungle Gardenia and Estée Lauder over all the perfumes in Arabia. The root cause of her manic cleanliness was usually judged to be shame over her supposed dirtiness in sex, in drinking, and in the ignoble story of her origins: Lucille LeSueur the porno-flapper, Lucille LeSueur the unhappy dipsomaniac, Lucille LeSueur the hillbilly, all murdered nightly and staining indelibly her little movie star hands, her bright movie star attire, her white carpets and white couches and white walls. (Who would have thought the San Antonio whore to have had so much blood in her? *Out, out damned slut!*) The invention of Joan Crawford, in addition to allowing her to kill Lucille, prevented her from having to remember the indignities of Lucille's life – everything she did for money, the myriad ways in which she had debased herself in order to succeed. 'There's a lot I don't remember,' she admits in *Conversations with Joan Crawford*. 'A lot I don't want to remember.' Biographers are generally agreed on her having been sexually assaulted by at least one of her mother's husbands, with dissent as to which husband, when, and how severe the crime. 'It wasn't incest,' one records her saying, claiming that her first stepfather's penetrative sexual abuse began when she was just eleven. 'We weren't even related. He was gentle and kind, and I led him into it.' If this is quoted accurately – if even aged eleven, Crawford feels the need to see herself as the seducer, the perpetual sexual aggressor – it reveals something both sad and telling about her insistence on that falsified, sexualised, frighteningly unerotic image. This is one more way to read the Crawford mouth: as a manifestation of her trauma, worn the same way Jackie Kennedy wore her blood-spattered Chanel suit after the Kennedy assassination, saying in deed if not in word: *let them see what they have done.*

When Roland Barthes described the face of Greta Garbo as an idea, he was not only referring to its masklike qualities, but to the way it gestured to the mystical: 'At once fragile and compact ... perfect and ephemeral.' 'How many actresses,' he added, 'have consented to let the crowd see the ominous maturing of their beauty? Not she.' In 1957, when *Mythologies*, the book containing '*Le Visage de Garbo*', was first published, Greta Garbo had been living more or less as a recluse for nine years. She was one year younger than Joan Crawford, who would continue to allow audiences to see her maturing ominously until the mid-seventies, and who would never once be called 'fragile' or 'ephemeral'. Closer to the truth of Crawford's image is the way that Barthes describes, in the same collection of essays, the new Citroën DS: 'Almost the exact equivalent of the great Gothic cathedrals ... the supreme creation of the era ... a purely magical object.' If the face of Greta Garbo can be said to be an idea, Crawford's face can certainly be said to be – echoing, also, Zelda Fitzgerald's earlier definition of the flapper – an object. '[In *Johnny Guitar*], she is beyond considerations of beauty,' François Truffaut said. 'She has become unreal, a fantasy of herself ... She is a phenomenon. She is becoming more manly as she grows older. Her clipped, tense acting, pushed almost to paroxysm by [director Nicholas] Ray, is in itself a strange and fascinating spectacle.' By the time she appeared in that film at the age of fifty, the Crawford lips were more paint than biology, her face pre-emptively resembling that of a male Joan Crawford impersonator. 'Never seen a woman who was more a man,' a croupier says about her character, Vienna, a tough, butch bitch who owns a tavern. 'She thinks like one, she acts like one. It almost makes me feel I'm not.'

It's true that, like a man, Joan Crawford turned her fury and her suffering outwards as she hit impotent middle-age, projecting an eroticism that made sex seem like a war, and that like a man of her particular era she did not care to hear 'no' rather than 'yes'. Watch *Johnny Guitar* now, and what is striking about her performance is how well the character suits her – how effortlessly she slips into the attire and the postures of a man, in spite of a career otherwise spent in pursuit of the high-feminine. Crawford was commanding and uncompromising even when she tried to play soft, so that even the most romantic moments in her melodramas feel somehow hard and coercive, like a Dear John letter written entirely in capital letters, or a love poem delivered at the volume of a shout. As Vienna, she is given the opportunity to more literally wield the weapon she so often appeared to be hiding metaphorically in her gowns whenever she squared up to a love rival or a sexual opponent on the screen. She first appears on the mezzanine floor of her tavern, looming over her employees in a wide-legged, swaggering stance. 'I never believed I'd end my years workin' for a woman,' one of them observes with something close to awe, 'and likin' it.' Unusually, the film's antagonist is also female, a moralising and uptight townsperson named Emma who resents Vienna for her freedom, for her power, and for her refusal to repress her sexual desire. Vienna built her tavern, she admits, with the money she made lying on her back; if she'd also happened to enjoy the company of other men free and gratis at the same time, then so be it. When the film begins, she has a sometime-lover named the Dancin' Kid, an ostensibly good-for-nothing cowboy who seems to be good for *one* thing, at least, given that Emma and Vienna are both vying for his attention. Into the saloon walks Johnny Guitar, a tall, peaceful-seeming man with the film's titular instrument slung across his back. Heat, like a fire started by a casually upended oil lamp in a bar brawl, blooms immediately between Vienna and Johnny, and it is the kind of heat that is explicable only by a shared sexual and romantic history; it transpires that the two, once affianced, have not seen each other in five years, and that Johnny skipped town because he could not commit. (Judging from his name, we might assume he has since married his guitar.)

'How many men have you forgotten?' he enquires of Vienna – suddenly territorial, tediously macho. 'About as many women as you remember,' she replies. It is a verbal gunfight, and both shooters, aiming for the heart, hit their target. Truffaut's assessment of Joan Crawford in the movie would be pure misogyny if it were not also tinged with admiration, and if one did not truly believe that he meant it when he said that Crawford struck him as a genuine phenomenon. Nearly every line she delivers in *Johnny Guitar* has a combative ring to it, like the cocking of a pistol or the cracking of a whip. Her unbreakable façade and her immovable face make her more monument than woman – an indomitable force, etched in stone. Rarely does she smile, making the scene where Vienna describes Emma's ardour for the Dancin' Kid stand out: 'He makes her feel like a woman,' she says dreamily, her carmine lips curling almost imperceptibly into a sly grin of recognition, 'and that frightens her.' On this subject, Emma and Vienna are in stubborn, cool agreement: both believe that to self-identify as not just female but 'a woman' makes one vulnerable to risk, and vulnerable, too, to developing the specific strain of stupefying madness that is often referred to as 'love'. There is something interestingly masculine in and of itself about the way that Emma tries to disguise her lust as anger – an adoption of the historically patriarchal pastime of transmogrifying longing, with its possibility for failure and therefore for humiliation, into fury. The kicker is, of course, that for all of her resistance, Johnny makes Vienna feel quite like a woman too, so that even though the film ends with her shooting Emma dead and then embracing him while wearing a borrowed pair of men's blue jeans, the domesticating, sweetening effect of romance is still evident on her face. 'A man can lie, steal, and even kill,' Vienna snarls to Johnny, prior to their schmaltzy, somewhat disappointing reconciliation. 'But as long as he hangs on to his pride, he's still a man. All a woman has to do is slip once, and she's a tramp! Must be a great comfort to you to be a man.' Vienna, in other words, has adopted the costume and the poses of a man not only to absorb some of that sex's clichéd power, but to illustrate her own refusal to experience shame.

Few tools are as effective for quietening a too-loud voice or an opinionated individual as shame, and for all her borderline despotic control over her physical appearance and her public image, it is arguable that Joan Crawford never quite managed to resist her embarrassment and horror over her earlier life – her possible molestation, her alleged porn career, her poverty – to a degree that might have permitted her to play more characters like Vienna. Calcify a woman's image enough and her voice will cease to matter, the result being a curious sensation of disjointedness, as if we are looking at her face directly but hearing her speak from somewhere else – another room, another voice box, a script written by executives and managers and producers. This ventriloquism is echoed in the credit sequence of *Klute*, the magnificent and paranoid 1971 film by Alan J. Pakula, which begins with the sound of its lead Jane Fonda being played in isolation from a tape player as Bree Daniels, her character, talks to a john: 'As long as you don't hurt me more than I like to be hurt,' she purrs, 'I'll do anything you ask.' Bree, because she is a sex worker, is acting; Fonda, because she is both an actress and, by 1971, a woman with a history of being manipulated into self-presenting as a sex-kitten by men, does not seem as if she is. One senses Bree has adjusted to liking, or to tolerating, being hurt quite badly, both for money and for validation, and Fonda's delivery is delicately layered, a talented actress portraying another talented actress in such a way that it is obvious what she's saying is a lie, and also obvious why the men she's talking to tend to believe her. When we see Bree for the first time, she is silent, lined up in a casting cattle-call for models and being talked about as if she might be insentient, deaf, or mute. With the introduction of Bree Daniels as a voice without a face, and then a face without a voice, *Klute* announces its most interesting fixation, proving itself to be somewhat radical even five decades after it was first released – just as much as a New Hollywood thriller, it is a film about fractures in persona, the splitting of self and body as a matter of both sexuality and survival. It has this in common with *Johnny Guitar*, with both stories centring around a tough, intelligent and enterprising sex worker whose desire to be taken seriously is perceived by the men she meets as being somehow at odds with her willingness to sell her body.

Fonda's face, looking as it did almost exactly like that of her famous father Henry Fonda, carried nearly as much onscreen baggage as Joan Crawford's masklike features. To the public, she was a readymade icon, pre-cast in the image of a star from birth, and the recipient of both nepotistic kindness and cynical cruelty. To Henry himself, she was first a source of pride, and then a source of disappointment. As a small child, she was androgynous, tomboyish and bold, cutting an altogether more masculine figure than her sensitive and pretty brother Peter, and her father – evidently longing for a little self, a replica who might embody the same all-American macho qualities that he did – enjoyed seeing himself mirrored in her countenance. She was christened Lady Jane Seymour Fonda, and the idea of being a 'lady' in name or in practice made her shudder, so that she insisted on being Jane, plain Jane, instead. 'I used to think I really wanted to be a boy because that's where the action was,' she wrote in her 2006 memoir *My Life So Far*. 'Looking back, I think I just wanted to be exempt from what was required of girliness.' One afternoon, her father took her to a birthday party that was being thrown for one of Joan Crawford's daughters, and when she saw Crawford's children dressed up in their silly, frilly finery like unhappy dolls, she burst into tears and demanded to go home. 'I didn't know who [Joan Crawford] was,' she recalled in an interview with *The New York Times* in 2020, 'except that she had these dark eyebrows and she seemed to be very tall and imposing and she was responsible for this whole mishegoss.'

Like a lot of women who are simultaneously obsessed with and afraid of femininity, Fonda herself had Mommie Dearest issues, having watched her mother Frances Fonda's mental health deteriorate before her eyes for many years before finally, horribly, Frances slit her own throat with a straight razor in an asylum sometime around Jane's twelfth birthday. Because she knew that her father prized great beauty and exterior perfection, little Jane had blamed her parents' divorce on her mother's failure to maintain a flawless body, youthful tits, and a suitable level of joie de vivre, and if thinking of her mother in these terms was sick, a little evil, it was also eminently understandable given that Frances believed the very same thing of herself. A few days after the

Fondas first announced their separation, Frances insisted on showing her daughter the scar that wound its way across her abdomen after a recent kidney operation. Jane, clever but impressionable, internalised the idea that this surgical incision had, like the severing of a cord, somehow cut her father loose; when Frances also bared a mangled nipple, the result of a botched breast enlargement operation, the gesture's commingling of body-horror and sex and motherhood only further cemented Jane's conception of the ageing female body as a site of revulsion and distress. 'Well, all right, Hank,' Frances herself had said to Henry when he'd told her he was leaving her for a younger woman – adding 'good luck, Hank' as if she'd brought it on herself, or as if 'luck' could keep his new twenty-one-year-old wife from someday ageing just as she had.

The difference between Frances' body and the image Henry Fonda held in his mind of the perfect woman, unchanging and talismanic, proved to be irreconcilable, and the difference between Jane's body and that of the son he had imagined her to be became equally obvious as she reached her teens. As if overnight, the interactions between father and child changed; if Jane were to be Lady Jane, not Boy Jane, it was clear that she must be lady*like*, air-light, as slim and graceful as a second or third wife. 'Jane's got the body,' he remarked to her classmate's father when both families were holidaying together, 'but [your daughter's] got the face.' Previously, it had been Jane's face, his small mirror, which had interested him – now, she was nothing but a body, and accordingly he'd ceased to look at her and recognise himself.

'I was taught by my father that how I looked was all that mattered, frankly,' she said in 2011, adding that he often said of women: 'Unless you look perfect, you're not going to be loved.'

Like Crawford, Fonda was abused sexually at an early age, by a babysitter's boyfriend, and that formative experience helped solidify a feeling that would dog her for most of her adult life. When Christine Jorgensen, widely recognised as the first woman to publicly undergo gender reassignment surgery in America, began to appear in newspapers and magazines in 1952, the then-thirteen-year-old Jane began convincing herself that she might in fact be a trans man; she did not develop breasts or begin menstruating until she was seventeen, as if she had held her womanhood at bay by wishing to be boyish. 'For me,' she told the critic Michael Schulman in a 2018 profile in *The New Yorker*, 'being a woman meant being a victim, being the loser, being the one that'll be destroyed.' This statement, which recalls Vienna's observation about Emma in *Johnny Guitar*, is one that Fonda has made with extremely minor variations numerous times over the years. 'Being super-thin is a way to postpone womanliness, to put off victimhood,' she writes in *My Life So Far*. (Later in the book, when her thinness has failed to prevent her from conceiving her first child, she repeats herself more literally: 'Pregnancy was incontrovertible proof that I was actually a woman – which meant "victim", which meant that I would be destroyed, like my mother.') Already, in her teens, she had decided that the gender she had been assigned at birth was enough to consign her to a fate worse than death:

that of a girlfriend; then a wife; then a mother; then eventually a woman who was too old to be freshly 'pretty' in the sense her father might have meant it, and no longer smooth and malleable enough for a man to want to leave his fingerprints, as if in wet clay, on her body and her psyche.

When Fonda went to Warner Brothers in 1959 for her first film, an adaptation of the Broadway play *Tall Story*, she found herself drawn to a room on the lot that housed 'the muslin-covered body dummies of all the Warner Bros. stars: stout, thin, buxom, they had been created to the exact measurements of the stars' bodies, ready for the seamstresses to pin their patterns to the forms'. 'The dummies were headless,' she recalls in her autobiography, 'so if a particular shape intrigued you because of its dramatic curves (Marilyn's) or its petite size (Natalie Wood's), you'd have to ask one of the fifteen or so seamstresses whose it was.' The image of her faced with this room full of headless, silent facsimiles of famous women is a potent one – one pictures Bluebeard's wife in the folk tale, opening the door to a forbidden chamber in his palace and discovering the corpses of her predecessors hanging limply on the walls. The idea that the wardrobe department would expect the star to keep her body in line with that of her mannequin, rather than cutting a costume to an actress, proved to be one of the earliest indicators that the 'business of making movies', as she puts it, 'wasn't for people like me, who hated our bodies and faces'.

Shortly afterwards, she was funnelled into hair and make-up to be turned into a version of herself whose face audiences might like, at least: 'I lay back and presented my face to [make-up artist Gordon] Bau, confident that he would make me look like a movie star. When he'd finished I sat up and ... Oh, my God! Who is that in the mirror! Is that how he thinks I should look? I was horrified, dumbstruck. Who was I to tell him I didn't want to be that person in the mirror? But this wasn't me. My lips had a new shape and my eyebrows were dark and enormous, like eagle's wings.' The description of this face is familiar, to say the least, as is the mention of a surgery they offered her for 'a more chiselled look': 'Having [her] jaw broken and reset, and [her] back teeth pulled.' (Unlike Crawford, allegedly, she declined the alteration.) It is possible to find a studio photograph of Jane Fonda circa 1959 on the web, and it seems likely to be the very test shot from this heavily made-up reinvention: with her hair in a bouffant, her brows just as dark as she describes and her lips overdrawn into an artificial ripeness, her youth and the severity of her makeover combine to make her look like nothing so much as a toddler in a pageant. Evidently, she did not feel a particular kinship with the new and improved version of herself that the studio make-up artist had designed – as self-conscious as she felt about her looks, and as complicated as her feelings were about both men and sexuality, something inside her wanted to resist total subsumption into identikit sexiness for the sake of career success. The ideal actress in 1959 seemed to be a composite of one of those beheaded costume dummies – never fattening, never menstruating, incapable of being assaulted or abused – and a starkly painted, permanently smiling head.

'I have spent most of my life feeling and acting like an

Immaculate Conception in reverse,' Fonda once noted. 'Born of a man, without aid of a woman.' A more ideal comparison for her purposes than the virgin birth might be something more mythic, pre-Christian, like the birth of Athena from the head of Zeus – the junior Fonda springing fully formed from the forehead of her father; the trick being repeated every time a man she'd chosen as her lover remade her in his image, or a studio executive tried to remake her into someone else entirely. She would change herself for all three of her husbands: Roger Vadim, the French film director, who styled her as a skinnier, more Americanised version of his ex, Brigitte Bardot; Tom Hayden, the anti-war activist who at first used her fame and then disdained it; Ted Turner, the billionaire media mogul who wanted a clean-cut, glamorous trophy for a wife. It took Fonda until she was in her sixties to give up on changing herself for her men, but her first rebellion – even if it then ended up being curtailed by her second marriage – came around the time that she made *Klute*, hot on the heels of her divorce from Vadim, when she began to speak in an entirely different voice. After years of softening it to make it higher, sweeter and more feminine on film, she slyly dropped these modulations, so that *Klute* marked the first time audiences had been permitted to hear Jane Fonda speak exactly as she spoke in actual life, sounding deeper, tougher and less compromising than she had before. She had been a candy-coated space babe whose voice emanated from somewhere up in her wig; now, something in it rumbled, her intellect and pissed-off-ness bombinating underneath the things she said at a low register like electricity. There was a sense that after many years of sleeping with some version of her father, she had systematically, deliberately unsexed herself in order to become her own no-nonsense daddy – less a bimbo than a butch. 'I spent a whole lot of my life disembodied,' she told Schulman in that 2018 interview, 'trying to please men. Because if a man – especially a fascinating man, who knows what he's doing and where he's going – oh, my God, if *he* loves me, it means I'm worth something. Which means that I wasn't really in my body. I wasn't in my skin. It was all about pleasing. Starting with *Klute*, I began to re-inhabit myself, and my voice began to drop.'

'[*Klute*] was the first movie I made in which I identified myself as a feminist,' she remarked on *Oprah*. 'There was a resonance there because my voice was coming [from my diaphragm].' There is a resonance, too, in the scenes in *Klute* in which Bree sees her therapist, whom she has hired to 'cure' her of her desire to turn tricks. Asked about the difference between doing sex work and auditioning as an actress, Bree – whose answers have been improvised by Fonda, in a session lasting ninety minutes that was cut down to just six – immediately says that sex work is less taxing and humiliating 'because someone wants you'. 'They want a woman,' she says bluntly, able to remove herself enough from what she does to see exactly why she does it, 'and I know I'm good at that ... for an hour I'm the best actress in the world.' 'What I would really like to do,' she offers in a later session, 'is be faceless, and bodiless, and be left alone.' If it was bold and unexpected for both Pakula and Fonda to suggest that prostitution could feel better and be less psychically draining than being a woman in the movie industry in 1971, it was also extraordinarily vulnerable of Fonda to be willing to explore her own relationship with womanhood – with the wages and advantages of conventional beauty; the way sexiness can drown a woman's voice out like white noise – on camera, even if she happened to be doing so while in character as Bree.

Like Crawford (allegedly, at least), Fonda had her own brushes with X-rated material, with the difference being that, by the sixties, showing flesh had become more acceptable, even encouraged for a liberated woman. In her early twenties, she sat for a modelling shoot in which she had appeared coyly but definitively topless, with the final image only failing to be printed in a magazine because her father intervened. When she appeared in her then-husband Roger Vadim's film *Circle of Love* in 1964, one Broadway movie theatre in New York startled her by promoting the film with a billboard-sized image of her reclining naked in a bed – a tactic that was doubly surprising for the fact that no such shot appeared within the film. When she objected, threatening to sue, the movie theatre solved the problem by protecting her modesty with a haphazard sheet of canvas, and the whole debacle became a joke, with the absence left by the 'correction' – in true Derridean style – only drawing more attention to what lay beneath the censoring cloth. Making the cover of *Life* magazine just four years later, she was pictured dressed as Barbarella and brandishing an enormous space-age gun, looking every inch the warrior heroine; the fact that the interior spreads were mostly sultry photographs of her rolling around entirely naked on a beach, however, somewhat undercut that warlike stance, suggesting as the combination did that if desirable women were permitted to be powerful in other solar systems, other galaxies, they had not yet necessarily earned that right on planet earth. 'Fonda's little girl Jane,' per the issue's somewhat nauseating cover line, certainly looked out of this world without her clothes on, weapon or no weapon, activism or no activism, and that certainty was what her audience counted on. In a sense, she was being asked to embody the contradictions inherent in the sexual revolution of the sixties as many less famous female earthlings had experienced them: she could be strong if that strength expressed itself in being sexy, and she could be sexually open as long as it was the kind of openness that benefitted heterosexual men, i.e. an openness to casual bisexuality, and a breezy, no-muss disdain for commitment. In effect: girls should be seen – nude – and not heard.

Women everywhere, despite the undisputed joy of attaining the pill and finally being able to fuck on their own terms without getting pregnant, were being sold back their own objectification, repackaged to appear like something feminist and free. Barbarella, an animalistic innocent with no sexual hang-ups, was the ideal sixties sex object; she was also so unreal that her story, having first originated in a comic book, could only be realised as a work of science fiction. The actress who portrayed her – who had after all grown up occasionally longing to be 'John' rather than 'Jane' – was a different proposition, real enough beneath the construct of her image that this realness tended to express itself, onscreen and off, as what is described more favourably in male stars as 'intensity'. Even in her earliest roles, when she was more often than not confined to the status of a girlfriend or a wife, something seemed to sear her characters from the inside out, the way the cherry of a cigarette might burn through the fabric of a flimsy summer dress. In life, too, she dutifully played the role of wife or girlfriend, but seemed always to be wishing for a bigger, better part: on their wedding day, as he slipped the ring onto her finger, Roger Vadim would go on to say that he looked deep into her eyes and saw that she was thinking not *I love you* but *fuck you*. (She could at least, he must have thought, have added an *I want to*.)

With a string of exes that included Bardot and Catherine Deneuve, Vadim apparently favoured blondes – baby blondes and bottle blondes, nearly platinum in a way that toed the line between vulgar and angelic. Fonda's hair obsessed him similarly, and he could not help but see it as the source of his wife's femininity. Without it, he imagined she would lapse into unhappiness and ruin. In *The Game Is Over*, his 1966 adaptation of a novel by Émile Zola, he cast Jane as a woman flush with inherited money who has spent her whole life trading on her looks, and then had her character's jagged mental breakdown coincide with the chopping of her hair, as if the act had robbed her, Samson-like, of her purpose and her strength. The message was clear: beautiful women needed to stay beautiful according to a strict set of parameters in order to avoid being sunk by shame and loneliness and sin, never doing anything that might reasonably – or unreasonably – be construed as boyish. That year, *The New York Times* ran a profile of the couple with the headline *And Roger Vadim 'Created' Jane Fonda* – a riff on the title of a film he made in 1956 with Bardot, *And God Created Woman*, and a sly positioning of him as the slick, godlike manipulator of Jane Fonda's image. Vadim did not make his wife into a woman in the strictest sense, but he made her *more* of one, at least as he saw it. 'Women are a problem,' he once said. 'If they're intellectual they become aggressive; if not, they're boring.' How Jane was expected to express her intellect without this self-expression being mischaracterised as 'aggression' was not something that he found it necessary to explain, although perhaps requiring an explanation made a woman 'boring' or 'aggressive', too.

Eventually, Vadim's fixation on his wife's hairstyle passed onto Jane herself, and she began to loathe its imprisoning prettiness enough that when she won the lead in the 1968 film *They Shoot Horses, Don't They?*, she agreed to cut it off to better fit the role. 'Hair,' she would later observe ruefully, '[had] ruled me for many years.' This was a ritual rejection of that rule; an aesthetic coup. Her character in the movie, a Depression-era competition dancer by the name of Gloria, is no pin-up. If she wants to fuck anything at all, it is America itself, and preferably with a blade – she is a nihilist and not a sensualist, and where Barbarella's eyes were wide with pleasure, Gloria's have been forced open by a permanent proximity to pain. Fonda's presence in the movie makes it clear that the dance marathon is in some ways an entirely fitting metaphor for the spectacular abjection of large-scale female stardom: the hunger and exhaustion; the impossibility of stopping the performance and still staying in the spotlight; the unfortunate side-effect of sleepwalking through tasks while in a state of near, or occasionally full, psychosis. When Gloria begs to be shot in the final scene, broken and unwilling to continue, it is one of Fonda's finest onscreen moments, and the character's death – a mercy killing – feels a little like the execution of the old, complaisant Jane. Shortly afterwards, the actress took her transformation further, walking into the same barber shop frequented by Vadim and asking his barber, simply and unflinchingly, to 'do something' to make her someone else.

The resulting hairstyle, dark and choppy and above all else profoundly modern, brought her as close to being a Plain Jane as a woman with her assets could have ever hoped to be; the 'someone else' she became may not have been as marketable, but it could not be denied that she had also never been, in the parlance of the era, *groovier*, or more attuned to a world outside the movies. She had begun to display a sincere interest in political causes, campaigning against the war in Vietnam, and her apparent lack of patriotism quickly made her public enemy number one for many former soldiers, good American boys, and Republican voters, who called her 'Hanoi Jane'. 'This is what we wanted, and this is what we got,' a popular anti-Fonda poster read underneath, respectively, a photograph of her costumed as Barbarella, and an image of her in her more contemporary beatnik guise. Jane, slowly feeling her way into activism after a life of great and largely unexamined privilege, did sometimes speak before she thought, but for many, the idea that she was expressing herself politically at all was a terrible disappointment, as if they had gone to a burlesque show and been lectured by the half-nude dancer about economic inequality. She had dared to be a symbol of something other than pure, idiot sex, and that was seen as a betrayal; she had spiritually renounced her womanhood by passing comment on the world around her in a manner that was seen as more befitting of a man, and her quasi-androgynous clothes and cropped hairstyle made it easier still for some of her former male fans to redirect the energy they had once reserved for desiring her into loathing her, instead.

Fonda has one particularly funny line-reading in *Barbarella*, when the aptly named Dildano asks the space adventuress whether she is 'typical of earth women': 'I'm about average!' she chirps, the shot just wide enough to show her taut, bare stomach and her breasts packed into chainmail. What is perfect about her delivery is the fact that while her tone suggests that she believes what she is saying, her eyes do not. Vadim had originally wanted Bardot, Sophia Loren or Virna Lisi for the role, all women who were luscious in a way that Fonda, with her coltish figure and her father's face, had not been at all until her husband-director-Svengali-master had begun to shape her. If Bardot had claimed, standing there in a space-porno costume with her blonde hair teased halfway up to the Sputnik, to be 'average', the joke would have sprung entirely from the image – Fonda, though, draws the stupidity of the implication out with a few delicate movements of her face, suggesting that she knows just how atypical she is, and how much sacrifice it took for her to get there. At that point in her career, her self-maintenance was almost as much a matter of sexual science fiction as the film itself; she was not merely appearing in a work of fantasy, but embodying a fantasy in three dimensions. Bulimia, ballet, starvation, endless bleach, nights spent fucking socialites and sex workers with – *for*, more specifically – Vadim. Nobody tried harder to escape being average than Jane Fonda in the sixties, who believed for many years that the best way to be a superlative woman was to be a gorgeous and subservient one, in spite of the fact that her one truly exceptional, incomparable quality was her onscreen skill.

Eventually, once she had made and released *Klute*, her conception of herself began to shift, and with it, the perception of her as an actress in a wider sense. 'Jane Fonda's motor runs a little fast,' Pauline Kael wrote approvingly in her review of the film. 'As an actress, she has a special kind of smartness that takes the form of speed; she's always a little ahead of everybody, and this quicker beat – this quicker responsiveness – makes her more exciting to watch. She has somehow got to a plane of acting at which even the closest closeup never reveals a false thought.' At that time, Kael believed, there was no other American actress who could touch Fonda as far as verisimilitude and raw, unflinching power were concerned. Contrast this with the way she described Jane's airy performance in *Barbarella* in 1968, labelling her a 'fresh, bouncy American girl triumphing by her innocence over a lewd, sadistic world of the future', with 'the skittish naughtiness of a teenage voluptuary', and a change, in both Fonda's onscreen work and its reception, becomes clear. By

1971, she was no longer attempting to deny or triumph over the lewd and sadistic in contemporary film or contemporary life; she embraced it, using the resistance generated by pushing against it to electrify the engine of her talent.

By 1972, she had won her first Best Actress Oscar for her work as Bree, and Barbarella slipped into the rear-view mirror once and for all. Fonda was thirty-three when she made *Klute*, neither especially old nor especially young, and the feeling of some of her earlier *Barbarella* sexiness being replaced by something else must have both frightened her and thrilled her. It is difficult to watch that opening scene where Bree is sized up and found wanting and not wonder whether the experience made her think about her father's judgement of her face and body – his tendency to cruelly appraise her as if she were his wife and not his child, and to be just as exacting about Jane's already diminutive measurements as the studio had been when they kept that lean, unchanging mannequin on hand to make her costumes. (Jane, in response, slipping her delicate hand into a bottle of Dexedrine, or shoving her fingers down her throat.) Something had to give, and when it did it left a fault-line in the carapace of her patriarchally crafted self-perception that would, along with a number of successive periods of self-discovery between marriages and men, eventually allow Fonda to break free.

◆

Rather than that of the blue-jean adventuress Vienna, the defining Crawford role might be said to be that of Harriet

Craig, from the 1950 film of the same name. A domineering woman, married to a man with no discernible identity other than just how easily he's swayed by her inviting him to bed, Harriet is above all else in love with her perfect, bougie home, whose design is a triumph of good taste over unhappy, trashy breeding. Like Crawford herself, Harriet is low-born – the offspring of an unscrupulous and uncaring father, and accordingly a misandrist. She sees a heterosexual marriage as a business deal, and men as hustlers. 'The average woman [puts] her life in someone else's hands,' she purrs. 'Her husband's. That's why she usually comes to grief.' As a schemer with a mind that might be better suited to heading a corporation than selecting fabric swatches, her Machiavellian nature seems as much a product of her boredom as it is a product of her feminine desire for well-off domestic bliss, and her willingness to flirt shows as much of an awareness of her capital as it does an awareness of her duties as a wife. *Harriet Craig* alludes to, rather than explicitly reveals, the link between Harriet's marriage and her sexual aggressiveness; suffice to say, when one maid asks another why a man like Walter Craig would marry a woman like her, only to be met with the knowing answer *why'd you think?*, we do not have to think particularly hard to guess the reason. Crawford, whose preferred footwear in the very earliest years of her career is said to have inspired the idiom 'fuck-me shoes', was herself subjected to innumerable *why'd you think?*s in Hollywood, and this experience must have helped contribute to the way she so seamlessly embodies Harriet's contradictory qualities: the way her tolerance of loveless sex brushes up against her love of sterile, sexless order in the home. 'I've kept up my end of the bargain,' Harriet sneers at her husband when they fight. 'I've kept myself attractive and seen to it that you never got bored.' The line sounds a little like the ageing Joan – who was somewhere between forty-six and fifty when she made *Harriet Craig*, having been so vague about her 'real' age on record that her Wikipedia page still lists her birth year as '190?' – speaking directly to her public, with whom she maintained a similar contract. Had she not kept her promise to them by continuing to be Joan Crawford, even though doing so got harder every year? Wasn't their end of the bargain to continue buying tickets; ensuring her stardom; sending her fan mail; acting as if she still looked the way she had when she was twenty?

As a character, Harriet Craig shares with both Vienna and Bree a willingness to exchange sex for status and material goods, although ultimately some element of the equation appears to be missing in her case – the acquisition of real power on her part, perhaps, given that although she is an undeniably formidable presence, by the last scene of the film she has lost her maid, her personal assistant, her husband, and quite possibly her mind. Her spotless house, thank God, remains in her control. (If what Vienna says about men – that a man can lie, steal and even kill, and remain a man as long as he hangs on to his pride – is true, one wonders if a woman like Harriet Craig could remain a woman if she did not hang on to her home.) When Walter tells Harriet that she is 'at war with the whole world', he is right in the sense that the America of the fifties was a world built for men. Childless with no career, no love, and no apparent intellectual stimulation, it is not surprising that Harriet chooses to produce her own entertainment in the form of marital psychodrama, nor that she might choose to be brutal in the only sphere available to her, the heterosexually coupled homestead. It is bizarre in retrospect to watch *Harriet Craig*, and think of the film's source as a Pulitzer-winning play from 1925, when it so evidently seems to be in some way drawn from Crawford's life. Harriet hovers, spectre-like, over her actress. In the year before Joan died, the gap between them thinned to gossamer, each woman sadly echoing the other; the rigidly kept, unforgiving interiors of their houses mirroring the contours of their rigid, unforgiving minds. 'I'm a compulsive housekeeper,' Crawford told David Frost in 1970, dressed for the interview in a baby pink sequinned gown and matching turban. 'I played Harriet Craig once, and I was ready for the role.'

'It may be this picture was intended for sloppy housewives to make them feel superior to the tidy monster in it,' a reviewer at *The New York Times* sneered about *Harriet Craig* in 1950. Fearing herself to be a tidy monster, Crawford's terror in her final years proved prescient given her posthumous reputation as a mother-tyrant – as a germ-obsessed despot of the hearth whose compulsions made her violent, and whose violence made her frightening and ridiculous. When the young Jane Fonda visited her home and was spooked by the sight of Crawford's children trussed up in their clownish outfits, it seems likely that beyond her own burgeoning fear of femininity, what troubled her had been the sense that they were trapped – just as their mother was; just as Jane herself would later be for many years – in a prison of enforced, false perfection. Motherhood can make a set-designer of a woman; rarely does it make her the true star of her own life, so that what Sylvia Plath called 'viciousness in the kitchen!' can amount to something like a primal scream. ('The potatoes hiss,' the suicidal poet further spits. 'It is all Hollywood, windowless.') Joan accepted almost any film project suggested to her after she turned fifty or so, hoping to remain in the public eye – to avoid being only remembered as a mad housewife, a mad mother. The result was that that her early triumphs were balanced out by last-minute flops: her axe-murderesses and her blowsy sci-fi-scientists, her TV guest spots. 'Please don't ask me about any pictures that follow *Baby Jane*,' she sighed after retiring, thinking particularly of the idiotic caveman film she improbably made at the age of sixty-six, in 1970. 'I made them because I needed the money or because I was bored or both … If I weren't a Christian Scientist, and I saw *Trog* advertised on a marquee across the street, I think I'd contemplate suicide.' She must have felt a little like the last surviving caveperson herself: a living relic rattling the nerves of the townspeople, driven into hiding for the fact she'd dared to stay alive too long.

Referencing *A Woman's Face*, a Crawford noir from 1941 about a female criminal with a disfigurement who falls, coincidentally, in love with the world's premier plastic surgeon, the film critic Andrew Sarris argued that 'the scars of Joan Crawford's struggles can be seen in all her films'. 'No make-up man,' he added, 'could ever remove them.'

All her adult life, she had lived as a slave to men's desire, until what resulted near the end was a person who existed between dream and flesh: more than a woman, almost more than a star, and yet somehow so alienated from herself that she must sometimes have felt that she did not exist if nobody was watching. At home, she surrounded herself with reminders of her face as it had been in the past: a bust, in bronze, presented to her by the sculptor Yucca Salamunich in the forties, and two paintings of her by the artist Michael Vollbracht, one of which depicted only her eyes, her heavy brows, and her mile-wide lips. In 1974, at a book party in New York, she made her last public appearance while recovering from extensive dental surgery, just as she was rumoured to have been when she first fell in love with the haemorrhage bloom of her new mouth back in the twenties. Now, she felt differently about the version of Joan Crawford that she saw in photographs from the event, standing next to Rosalind Russell in a dowdy, silvery-brown wig. 'If that's the way I look,' she reportedly said, 'then they've seen the last of me.' 'My life as I had enjoyed living it was largely over,' she went on to add, 'because my life as Joan Crawford was over. I had to retire Joan Crawford from public view. What was left of me could only destroy that image.'

If the absurd mechanics of her maintenance had left her with almost no time for personal development, they also left her with a talent for designing every aspect of her life: she had made eighty-one legitimate films, and maybe a few more illegitimate ones, and what she did not know about perfection, the appearance of it in the face of pain and strife, was not worth knowing. In the last shoot she ever did, in 1976, she is again all eyes, mouth and eyebrows, like a version of Joan Crawford drawn from memory on a telephone pad. Lensed softly, she glows like the make-up mirror in a starlet's dressing room. Most conspicuous is the shade of her lips, which no longer look like a bloodied lioness', but like those of a grand dame: light, pearlescent, flattering to the pallor of her skin. What would usually be loud – *too loud* – is now pianissimo, eerily hushed. She mailed copies of these photographs out with her Christmas cards that year, five months before she died, attaching an excruciating postscript to her package for the director of *Harriet Craig*, Vince Sherman: 'If you do not like the picture, please throw it away. I'll understand.' She had begun, by then, to refer to herself as an 'ex movie star', making the concession after overhearing two gossiping women in her building talking about her as if she had died. 'I was waiting for an elevator,' she recalled, 'and I actually heard a woman beside me say to another: "See her? She used to be Joan Crawford."' By the time she died for real, she weighed roughly eighty-four pounds, a grey-haired shadow in a housecoat. Whether her retirement had been for her sake, or for ours, remained unclear. What was clear was that in those final photographs, mailed out with apologies, a message ran through each image like a melody: a requiem for a burned-out star who had orchestrated herself into inhuman oblivion. She wanted her audience to think always of Joan, and not Lucille, and she had accordingly finessed her appearance up until the end-most frame. The Crawford mouth, if less outré than before, was still mystical, masklike; as pristine as if it were shrink-wrapped in vinyl like a couch.

In 1977, the year Joan Crawford died, Jane Fonda turned forty, an age at which even un-famous women are too often made to feel obsolete. That November, she appeared on the cover of *US Weekly* in a feature with the cover-line *FONDA AT 40*, and the contrast between photographs of Crawford at roughly the same age and this barefaced, beaming shot of Fonda is (to say the very least) instructively stark. Reclining on a chaise in a studio portrait from 1944, Crawford is immaculate, vampiric, looking if she'd identified the beating of the heart – its marking time – as a catalyst for ageing, and then subsequently given up on having blood at all. Fonda, pictured with her laugh lines still intact, *does* look forty, but she also looks extraordinarily at ease. The following year, she won her second Oscar, a Best Actress trophy for *Coming Home*, a pioneering film in which she played a nurse who shared a tender, humanising sex scene with a disabled Vietnam veteran; the year after that, she won acclaim, and a Bafta, for her portrayal of a journalist reporting on a nuclear cover-up scandal in *The China Syndrome*. 'The three stars are splendid,' Vincent Canby wrote in his review of the latter in *The New York Times*, 'but maybe Miss Fonda is just a bit more than that. Her performance is not that of an actress in a star's role, but that of an actress creating a character that happens to be major within the film.' Canby's comment reflected, in a sense, the journey Fonda was making in her life at that time, albeit in fits and starts: from acting the part of the star – a Hollywood sure-thing born into the industry elite – to projecting a version of herself that, if not yet entirely authentic, certainly felt like a major and distinctive character rather than a celebrity trying to be real.

By 1979, in spite of her biggest films being fairly spaced out through the decade, the *Motion Picture Herald* named her cinema's most bankable actress. Further triumphs, personal and feminist, followed: in 1980, she appeared in *9 to 5*, a now iconic black comedy about workplace sexism that featured several deliciously misandrist fantasy sequences. Her best performances have always been those in which she evidently feels a kinship with the character at hand, her innate skill coupling with a psychic or experiential understanding of the woman she's portraying until what emerges seems not merely three-dimensional, but almost hyperreal. She has said that in each of these roles, it felt as if she were looking at the world out of someone else's eyes – as if the 'plane of acting' Pauline Kael suggested that she occupied in *Klute*, 'at which even the closest closeup never reveals a false thought', might be astral. In 1981, she appeared in *On Golden Pond*, starring opposite Henry Fonda as a daughter trying to win back her estranged father's love. She had purchased the rights to the original play with Henry in mind, as a gift or perhaps as a challenge: the central dynamic of the film so obviously replicates the offscreen struggle of the Fondas that the finished product feels almost unethical to watch. In one scene, her character Chelsea attempts a little tenderness, telling her father: 'I just want to be your friend.' 'I had stifled the urge to touch [Henry's] arm [in rehearsals], wanting to save it for when it would matter most: his close-up,' Fonda recalls in her autobiography. 'Dad very rarely had tears on camera, and I wanted him to have tears in this scene, which meant so much to me on a personal level.'

With the cameras rolling, Jane reached out and lightly grazed her father's elbow with her hand; just as she'd hoped, she surprised him. 'For a millisecond, he was caught off guard,' she continues. 'He seemed angry, even: *This isn't what we rehearsed*. Then the emotions hit him.' Henry Fonda's lifelong propensity for playing moral men must have felt deeply ironic to the daughter from whom he withheld his affections, and the contrast between the all-American, upright tenor of his work and the less virtuous nature of his private life makes his insistence on playing every scene as rehearsed explicable: he was a good actor, but he was not necessarily a good man, and sustaining such an illusion at this scale over decades takes considerable concentration. The shattering effect that occurs when Jane touches his arm – practice meeting spontaneity, a collapsing together of reality and fiction that produces a peculiar intensity of feeling – is the same one exerted on a moviegoing audience whenever she inhabits a character like Chelsea, or Bree: a sense of vital, energetic unpredictability that is usually only found offscreen. There is a loony artistry in Jane Fonda's decision to connect with her father, in addition to her viewers and the Oscar-voting Academy, by shepherding this heightened, Kaufmanesque simulacrum of a daddy-daughter vacation into being – a delicious touch of Hollywood eccentricity, too, in her being such consummate, from-birth showperson that making a fifteen-million-dollar movie felt like a more obvious route to a reconciliation than, say, family therapy. Going off-script might have made her father furious, but Fonda herself knew, with her wild, storied history in love and work and politics, that life had no rehearsals, and that sometimes it was necessary to throw away your lines if you wanted to express something true.

Taking in the full, doglegging scope of Fonda's life, to say nothing of her work, would be more daunting if she had not generously offered up, in 2006, her own suggested structure for analysis: in her autobiography, *My Life So Far*, the shape she imposes on her story – splitting it into three acts, as if it were a work of theatre or a screenplay – lets us know that we should not expect a tidy resolution to the problems posed in its first two-thirds until she is well into her sixties. 'Haven't you ever been to a play where the first two acts seemed confused,' she writes, 'then along came the third act and pulled it all together? ... to have a good third act, you need to understand what the first two have been about. To know where you're going, you must know where you've been.' In Fonda's telling, her third act began when she divorced her third husband, Ted Turner, a billionaire TV producer with whom she had been a preppier, peppier version of herself, all neat blowouts and pale-shaded couture outfits, and for whom she'd temporarily given up her career. If Joan Crawford complained that she was 'a goddamn image, not a person', from her final divorce onwards Fonda began working out a way to be both things. It seemed as though she had begun to recognise her childhood desire to be male for what it was: a need for the power that masculinity conveyed, and a longing to be able to display 'masculine' characteristics – outspokenness, political interest, sexual frankness and voraciousness, emotional strength – at the same time as perpetually renewing her attractiveness in such a way that one could never quite forget that she was *the* Jane Fonda, which was not quite the same thing as having to be *the* Joan Crawford every day in perpetuity.

Joan's mistake was trying to stretch her second act all the way to the curtain call – terrified of others finding out where she had been, she employed smoke and mirrors until, finally, she could no longer ignore where she was going: first into obscurity, and then into the grave. Her claim that she had 'personified the American woman', with its ironic suggestion that she was a relatable figure, is an observation that one might more easily make of Fonda, in spite of her having been born into a dynastic acting family, and in spite of her obvious genetic and artistic gifts. In 1977, she played Lillian Hellman in an adaptation of the author's 1973 book *Pentimento*, the title of which refers to the phenomenon via which the earliest versions of a painting remain visible beneath its final, finished version. 'Old paint on canvas, as it ages, sometimes becomes transparent,' she says in the film's opening scene. 'When that happens, it is possible in some pictures to see the original lines ... That is called a pentimento, because the painter repented: he changed his mind.' It would not be quite correct to say that Fonda wished to repent for any of her past incarnations; still, she is not scared to let them show beneath each new, burnished image she presents to the camera. This admission of the work inherent in navigating the world over numerous decades as a woman *and* a star is totally antithetical to the kind of fame that first found, then killed, Joan Crawford, and it is also the very quality that has permitted Jane Fonda to have a career that, at time of writing, has stretched from 1960 through to 2024, and counting. One might say that she personifies the American woman in the sense that at one time or another, she has embodied *every kind of woman in America*.

It is certainly no insult to say that over six decades as a very public figure, Jane Fonda has been a complex, fascinating mess of contradictions. Watch her development closely, and it is as if a diagram of the ascent of (wo)man had been made into a flick-book, albeit one where Homo sapiens is quite the looker: we can see her atomising and restructuring, fracturing into so many discrete selves that it occasionally seems as though she might have the kind of hysterical, invented personality disorder that Joan Crawford would once have pretended to be suffering from in a tasteless sixties hagsploitation movie. There is a touch in her, too, of those fish who change their genders midstream, with their dichoic glimmer between masculine and feminine: not for nothing did she once call herself, as Barbarella, 'a female impersonator'. She has been effortlessly hip and cool, and also totally neurotic; hyper-sensual and steely; an opinionated left-winger in public, and frequently submissive to men in her private life. ('I'm now five years older than my dad was when he died and I've realised that I am, in fact, stronger than he was. I'm stronger than all the men that I've been married to,' she said in 2020, maybe not realising how incestuous – how Freudian – the statement sounded, implying as it did that she might once have been married to her father.) She has had breast implants, and then removed them; self-identified as anti-feminist, and then become a fiery advocate for women's rights. Increasingly, she has approached her looks in accordance with the famous F. Scott Fitzgerald quote about first-rate intelligence, tweaking herself with the stringency of a restorer working on an artwork of great value, but admitting in the press that she knows caring so much about her appearance is in many ways beneath her – silly, and a little vain.

She has, in effect, changed with the times; the times have also changed with her, making it more and more acceptable for a woman to be sexy and still have an extraordinarily big mouth, in a very different sense than the one that we mean when we talk about Joan Crawford's lips. If the face of Greta Garbo is an idea, and the face of Joan Crawford is an object, how might we describe Jane Fonda's? As a lovely carbon copy of her father's, yes; as a site of careful surgical and cosmetic preservation, also. As the face of a woman in a mugshot, her fist raised aloft and her chin a little blotchy from sleeplessness – her lips set in a firm, serious line. It is certainly not, as Barthes also said of Garbo's, 'virtually sexless'. Perhaps we do not need to describe it at all, since doing so would only further detract from the sound of her voice, splitting her in two the way *Klute* splits Bree in its opening scenes. Or else, if we must divide her thus, then here is the picture to hold in your mind: at the 1972 Academy Awards, she appeared in a black, Mao-collared suit by Yves Saint Laurent, looking less like a star than a chic revolutionary. Her shag was newly cut, barely brushed; she wore no make-up. Her eyes glittered manically as if she was a prisoner who had recently escaped captivity – which, in a sense, she was. If the last shoot that Joan Crawford did in 1976 was a formal declaration of the death of her persona, all of the documentation of Fonda on this particular night feels like the inverse: an announcement of rebirth. 'There's a great deal to say,' she remarked on-stage when she collected her Oscar for *Klute*, 'and I'm not going to say it tonight.' In the footage, she appears to swallow something down. Make no mistake: she has said everything she wanted to in the ensuing years.

5

On One Side of the Magic, or the Other

On Pamela Anderson and Tula

This piece was adapted from the essay 'Blonde Ambition' first published by the Baffler *as part of issue 69 in July 2023*

There are two things that might be said to define her from the off, and they are absolutely not the two things that you might expect. The first thing is that she is not American, but Canadian, an accident of her birth that seems unthinkable when one considers how American she seems from the outside – how blonde, how plastic, how aspirational and saleable and generally designed to look just right rendered fourteen feet high on a billboard. The second is the fact that there was almost no 'her' to begin with: in 1967, her father totalled his green Ford Fairlane while trying to outrun the police, and her pregnant mother was thrown face-first through the glass of the car's windshield, in a smash that might have claimed three lives, but improbably ended with no casualties at all. In her memoir, she imagines how the scene played out, and the details she includes in her description (her mother's 'pretty head' going through the windshield; the 'soft cream interior' of the car being 'soaked in blood') are suggestive of a glamourpuss with an illicit taste for the macabre. This combination – sweet and bitter, with a happy ending invariably following an ordeal – characterises the entire book, which has the feel of a Grimm's fairy tale with extra sex.

'Life is a series of problems/we must navigate/with grace –/one problem solved/another arises,' she writes in verse in its opening pages. No problematic twist of fate, even a car accident, could prevent Pamela Denise Anderson, b. 1 July 1967, from becoming Pamela Anderson, model and actress and activist and eccentric, just as being born in Ladysmith, British Columbia could not prevent her from becoming an all-American icon. She is a self-made woman in every possible sense of the phrase 'self-made woman', and her whole career has been defined less by her talent than by her determination. To deny the wattage of Pamela Anderson's charisma at her peak would be absurd, like denying the existence of the sun. Her appearance on the jumbotron at a British Columbia Lions game in 1989 is an origin story on a par with the discovery of Lana Turner at a West Hollywood malt shop in the thirties, and one might imagine that on seeing herself at such awe-inspiring scale for the first time, larger-than-life in the manner of an actress on a cinema screen, Anderson might have immediately sensed her destiny – or that even if she hadn't, she might have been tempted to tweak history for the record and imply that this was *fate*, a cathecting incident in the trajectory of her life and her career that she would think of on her deathbed. Instead, whenever she refers to the incident in interviews, she merely says that she remembers thinking she looked old, as though what was being demonstrated to her in that moment by the universe was not the dazzling commencement of her stardom, but the end of her old life: her last innocent and unencumbered day of youth.

Her rum-soaked cherry of a memoir, *Love, Pamela*, paints femininity as a matter of both nature and nurture, something at once inherited as a kind of spiritual birthright from one's foremothers and worked at, tirelessly and sometimes expensively, for reasons that run the gamut from sex appeal to monetisation. One might also say that she makes the creation of femininity and desirability into a magic trick, making it entirely appropriate that in 2007, in between playing herself in the *Borat* movie and appearing at the Crazy Horse cabaret in Paris, she performed as an on-stage assistant to the square-jawed, lank-haired Teutonic illusionist Hans Klok in a show at the Planet Hollywood Resort & Casino in Las Vegas, entitled The Beauty of Magic. When the show first opened, Anderson was three weeks shy of turning forty, an age at which many sex symbols begin to think about how best to reinvent themselves so that they might transition into being a symbol of something else entirely. Instead, Pamela Anderson chose one of the vampiest, flashiest jobs of all, in one of the vampiest, flashiest cities in the world, and continued to be perfectly content being blonde, augmented, nearly naked, and an undeniable bombshell. In photographs from The Beauty of Magic's opening night, she looks utterly at home: as hard and golden as a trophy, traversing the stage with the sure stride of a prizewinning thoroughbred in her six-inch mirrored heels and her shimmering leotard. 'Being Canadian and a gymnast and an acrobat,' she wrote on her website after revealing she'd begun work with Klok, 'I always wanted to join Cirque du Soleil – I love it more than anything.' It figures that Anderson, of all people, would have dreams of running away to join the circus, not least because of her adventurous spirit and her taste for illustrated men.

Historically, the role of a magician's assistant has been controversial, owing to the fact it largely exists to allow a very pretty, often silent woman to serve as eye candy for the audience and – if she is lucky – to pretend to be sawn in half, or to have knives thrown at her while she is in bondage, or some other thrilling form of pseudo-torture. (One might say that the job amounts to 'a series of problems' that the distracting model in question 'must navigate with grace'.) 'The audience was not only complicit, but vital in making the magic happen through a connection that felt almost childlike at times,' the feminist academic and researcher Dr Naomi Paxton recalled in 2019, on the subject of her own time as a magician's assistant. 'They wanted to believe the impossible, but were also eager to know how it was done.' Read it carefully, and this sounds like it could also be the job description for an entirely different role – that of the contemporary pin-up, whose admirers accept her honed and modified physique as an impossible work of perfection, and whose detractors want her to admit exactly how she got so impossibly perfect in the first place. In both instances, the woman at the heart of the performance must be a gifted illusionist, and an excellent liar; she must make the work she does appear like nothing, while also insisting she is doing no work at all, or that if she *is*, it does not feel like graft to her. She is less a dove sequestered in the sleeve of a magician than a swan atop a lake: effortlessly lovely on the surface, furiously paddling the water underneath.

By the time she appeared on-stage in Las Vegas, Pamela Anderson had undergone a cruel, slow-motion media trial that would have made being pinned with throwing knives seem like a cinch. In 1995, a tape she had made on her honeymoon with her then-husband Tommy Lee was stolen from their home and then illegally circulated, both online and on VHS, and although the footage contained eight minutes of sex and forty-six minutes of them goofing off and being stupidly in love, comedians and talk-show hosts and talking heads alike united to declare Pamela Anderson a slut. Somehow, in spite of this, she remained successfully afloat, maybe floundering once or twice but ultimately still retaining the unflappable, parodic, throwback sexiness she had projected from the moment she became a public figure. That jumbotron appearance carried her from beer advertisements to *Playboy*, and from *Playboy* to a cameo role on the TV comedy *Home Improvement*, and from *Home Improvement* to the dumb, delightful swimsuit sleaze of *Baywatch*, which mostly required her to run slowly on the beach and look gorgeous while preventing various individuals from drowning. What made her ubiquitous during this period was not necessarily the quality of her work on serialised television, but the quality of her work as a model and a public figure: what else could Anderson, a woman with the figure of mud-flap girl and the bawdy sense of humour of an old-school broad, be *but* famous? Late-night hosts perpetually enquired about her breasts, her breasts, her breasts; when she was not actually on-set, they would make filthy jokes about her in their opening monologues, as if not having her most famous assets in their direct line of sight made it even easier to dehumanise her. A professional who knew it was a sin to break character in the middle of a show, she simply laughed, or played along, or rolled her eyes.

'My breasts have had a brilliant career,' she has often joked. 'I've just tagged along for the ride.' When that ride required her to climb on-stage in Las Vegas in a tiny glittering leotard just three weeks before she turned forty in order to perform tricks with flames and blades and all the other trappings of Vegas magic, she did so without complaint or hesitation. (That the show was originally meant to star Carmen Electra, and that Electra dropped out because several of the illusions made her 'queasy' per a piece in the *Las Vegas Review Journal*, speaks volumes about Anderson's athleticism, to say nothing of her inner strength – her gut may not always have led her in the right direction, as evidenced by her marriage to Kid Rock, but it did not fail her when it came to gastrointestinal fortitude.) 'My favorite parts of the [magic] act,' she recalls in *Love, Pamela*, 'were when I was levitated and when I had fire spikes driven through me. It was dangerous, but my double-jointed shoulders and flexibility came in handy.' Her flexibility has always come in handy in the tightest spots of her career, too, as if she were capable of folding herself into one half of the coffin-like confinement of her public image to escape the blade; time after time, she has been threatened with reputational dismemberment and still returned to the stage smiling and unscathed.

'In a traditional male-female double act where the man is considered to be the magician and the woman only a decorative mover of props,' Dr Paxton writes, 'there is enormous scope for misdirection and playing with presence and status.' The lovely assistant, in other words, takes the audience's underestimation of her as a comely woman and uses it for her own ends, turning a disadvantage into a professional boon. In another universe, Pamela Anderson might have gently inverted the generic title of the Vegas show and called her memoir *The Magic of Beauty*, and it might have documented her self-engineering and her rise to fame in a style that was less soft-hearted and more hardboiled than *Love, Pamela*'s – it might have been a how-to guide on surviving and exploiting the attention of an audience primed to see a blonde, large-breasted woman and assume the worst. For Anderson, the magic of beauty is that it has given her both a saleable asset and a mask to hide behind. A few terrible things have befallen her over the years; she has personally ensured that a greater number of good things have fallen into her bikini-clad lap since the early nineties, however, and to suggest that hers is simply a tragic tale of victimhood is to trip into the same trap a naive viewer falls into when they assume that the beautiful woman standing next to the magician has no purpose outside decoration. In fact, the trajectory of her life, both before and after the incident which at once traumatised her, and momentarily made her one of the most famous women in the world – namely, the theft of that sex tape – forms a fascinating case study about consent, the connection between sexuality and empowerment, and the relationship that the public has with female sexual icons. In effect, it is a perfect illustration of the difference between being a willing, active participant in a carefully orchestrated illusion, and simply being tricked.

The year 2023 was a major one for Pamela Anderson as a public figure – perhaps the most notable year since the release of that fateful tape, in fact. In addition to *Love, Pamela*, which she produced without the aid of a ghost-writer and with final approval on even the most minor of edits, she also provided access to decades of her personal VHS recordings to a documentary maker, Ryan White, and produced a film entitled *Pamela: A Love Story* for Netflix. Given that home videos are a loaded medium for Anderson, their use here as a ballast for the reclamation of her image feels especially fitting, and sometimes subtly funny. One clip, though, stands out especially, and it is not one from Anderson's private collection, but one from an unspecified magazine show. In the segment, it is 199-something, and Pamela Anderson is sitting on the pale sands of a beach that is presumably in California, dressed down in a pair of flip-flops, a white vest, and a flowery sarong. She looks impossibly radiant and very young, and she is being interviewed on television. 'Where'd I get my boobs done?' she asks her off-camera interlocutor, her forehead crinkling into a small, foxed frown. 'Geez, that's a personal question!'

It *is* a personal question; it is also one that she has probably already answered in a number of other interviews, and God knows how many untelevised and unrecorded conversations, and her irritation makes it obvious that she is not keen to answer it again. 'But,' she adds, in a voice that is both playful and sarcastic, 'let's talk about this.' On 'but', she lifts up her flip-flopped feet and swings her legs open in one aggressive movement, swift and pointed, until suddenly the camera is directly pointed at her sarong-covered crotch, the moment taking on the simultaneous air of a come-on and a tongue-in-cheek sexual threat. There is no ambiguity as to what the word 'this' refers to. It is impossible not to think of another nineties blonde using her genitalia to her tactical advantage, perhaps even in the same year this was filmed – the cool sexpot murderess Catherine Tramell in Paul Verhoeven's 1992 film *Basic Instinct*, portrayed by Sharon Stone. The scene in which Tramell is being interrogated is one of the most iconic in contemporary cinema, and part of this is obviously because it is a scene that encourages the audience to picture the vagina of a beautiful and famous woman, but part of it is also that Stone makes it paradoxically empowering, an exposure that challenges those observing her rather than leaving her defenceless. (The fact Stone later claimed she had been told that her genitals would not appear in the scene makes the legacy of this image obviously complicated, and those complications certainly have their own resonance vis-à-vis Pamela Anderson's history with stolen sexual imagery.) Unlike *Basic Instinct*, the short clip of Anderson does not take time to show us the reaction of the man she's speaking to – we don't see him sweat, or squirm, and in this edit we don't hear him reply, either – but it's clear she is not merely being cute.

Hidden in that gesture is the real reason that it was necessary for Pamela Anderson to offer up the one-two punch of a documentary and a memoir: because we seemed to have let it slip our minds that she was always knowing, funny and entirely in on the joke of herself, and accordingly we needed a reminder. In 2022, the fictionalised TV series *Pam & Tommy* presented a nominally feminist and moralising take on the events surrounding the theft and release of the sex tape, and its version of Pamela Anderson had not been accurate, exactly; the series' obsession with making Anderson stainless somehow resulted in its making her appear to be entirely brainless, instead, and as portrayed by the English actress Lily James under a thick layer of silicone and spray tan, this imagined Pam did little more than simper, lisp, pout, graphically fuck, and look befuddled. When an actor playing Hugh Hefner tells James' character that women like her 'come around once in a generation', it feels like a self-defeating joke, underscoring the creators' inability to actually find an actress who resembled Anderson without requiring paint and bleach, or accent coaching and a rubber breastplate, to complete the fantasy. The phrase 'they don't make 'em like that anymore' invariably crops up with regards to bona fide Golden Age movie stars, but in a sense they do not make them like Pamela Anderson now, either.

Absolute fidelity should be the goal of a celebrity impressionist; it need not necessarily be the goal of an actor who has been cast as a real person, which is why Cate Blanchett, with her hoarse, ethereal swagger, made the best Bob Dylan of the seven cast in Todd Haynes' *I'm Not There*, and why it did not matter too much when Ana de Armas played Marilyn Monroe with a Cuban accent in Andrew Dominik's hysterical horror movie *Blonde*, a film that blends *My Week With Marilyn* with *The Passion of the Christ*. More important than exactly resembling the celebrity at hand is the ability to effortlessly channel their particular glamour, in the oldest, most enchanted sense of the word. Nobody would be naive enough to believe that Pamela Anderson appeared to us in 1995 exactly as she had appeared to others as a younger and less famous person, and she made no move to hide the work she had put into her extraordinary face and body. Still, something evidently radiated from her on that jumbotron which caught the world's attention, and that something was not simply pulchritude. It was fortitude, an inner glow; an unexpectedly fierce intelligence under her regulation lipliner and Sun In. The gravest mistake the creators of *Pam & Tommy* made was to presume that in order to enhance her martyrdom and thus ensure their audience's sympathy, they should make their version of Pamela Anderson a dumb, surprised babe-in-the-woods who things happened *to*, and not a woman who more often made things happen – one who had spent much of her life making herself into exactly the person she desired to be. As it had with the real Pamela Anderson, a great deal of effort went into constructing an exterior for the character that screamed perfect femininity: a fem-bot shape, and eyebrows plucked to permanent suggestiveness, and lips so plush they seemed to kiss themselves. What was missing was a spark of life, of electricity, so that even this Pamela's horniness seemed somehow inauthentic, as if she were playing the sexual equivalent of a junkie in an anti-drug commercial.

When a source discussed Anderson's feelings about her portrayal in *Pam & Tommy* with a journalist at *Entertainment Weekly*, one line stuck out. 'Pamela,' the source said, 'has no regrets about her life.' It feels plausible that this phrase in particular did come directly from her, largely because it suggests her usual mix of optimism and pragmatism: a shrug; a proud upwards tilt of her delicate chin; an acknowledgement that her life was always going to be characterised by boom and bust. (The statement also makes perfect logical sense: why would Anderson regret making a consensual, often quite romantic sex tape with her husband, meant for private use? The sex crime – and it *was* a sex crime – was not any fault of hers, making the idea of regret irrelevant here, too.) In *Love, Pamela*, she expresses some sadness at the modification of her body – 'I agreed to amplify my chest like everyone else [in *Playboy*],' she writes, 'then endured years of sordid attention I wasn't ready for. Then came the complications, the unexpected injuries that led to more surgery, a vicious cycle. I was fine the way I was' – but also suggests that her 'un-thought-through' decisions are 'a part of [her] charm'. Does she occasionally contradict herself? Very well then, she contradicts herself; she contains multitudes as well as 400-odd-ccs of silicone, and in her memoir, she suggests she finds it heartening to be misinterpreted because it means that she is fluid vis-à-vis her identity and her image. In the subtitle of *Pamela: A Love Story*, the love story is between Pamela Anderson and her children, and arguably between Pamela Anderson and Tommy Lee, but above all else it is between Pamela Anderson *and Pamela Anderson.*

The word 'victim' appears only once in *Love, Pamela*, in the context of the phrase 'not a victim'. The word 'magic', or a variation on it, appears fifteen times, and the most notable use is in a passage where Anderson reveals that she was molested by a babysitter as a child. She leaves the details vague, and instead chooses to focus on the moment in which she finally snapped and chose to fight back: '"*I hope you die!*" I screamed through tears. Then I ran for my life,' Anderson writes. 'Soon after, she died in a car accident. I couldn't tell my parents that I'd killed her with my magical mind, or that she was touching me and making me touch her in ways I don't want to remember.' If this is an especially dark introduction to the idea that she might be possessed of some kind of thaumaturgic power, it is interesting for the way it links her so-called 'magic' – for good or for ill – with her sexuality, and that theme recurs even when the word is not literally being used. Anderson often suggests that the outline of her life has been shaped by the ability to manifest her dreams and her desires; when she speaks about doing her first nude shoot for *Playboy* in the documentary, she presents it as a mystic transformation, shucking off the trauma of her molestation and her rape at twelve by an older family friend, and thus reclaiming her body. 'That was the first time I'd broken free of something,' she explains. 'That's where a wild woman was born. I felt like it was kind of a gateway to another world. Now I was going to take the power of my sexuality back. And I did – in a really big way.'

'[I was] shy at first,' she wrote in her journal at the time. '[But] by the end of the week you had to stop me from running out the door naked.' This version of Pamela Anderson is entirely at odds with the one brought to life by Lily James in *Pam & Tommy*, and her ability to see her objectification as both a blessing and a curse, a source of disempowerment *and* empowerment depending on its context, makes it difficult to fit her into the tidy, orderly brand of feminist-revisionist history that is so popular at present, which too often insists that the famous woman being 'rehabilitated' behave like a sacrificial lamb. 'When I was little, I wanted to be a nun or a showgirl,' Anderson remarked to Ronan Farrow in *Interview* magazine in February 2023. 'Why can't [women] be both?' Certainly, she is no saint, but she has never claimed to be one, either, and there's nothing innocent about her near-supernatural command of her physicality and her charisma. To suggest that every element of her hypersexualised public persona is purely exploitative is to suggest that being a sex idol *in itself* is de facto humiliating or inhuman, and that she is not especially powerful or bright – a position that might be perceived as being just as antifeminist as simply calling her a slut, given its implication that no woman could possibly *choose* to live like Pam.

The truth of the matter, as it often is in cases that pertain to the commodification of sexuality, is more complicated than it might at first appear to be. Some feminists may baulk at Anderson's belief that her appearances in *Playboy*, posing nude for a predominantly male audience, gave her back her sexual agency, and some non-feminists may argue that because she had already presented her body to the public, the free distribution of her sex tape could not truly be considered a terrible violation in the same way that it might have been if it had happened to a tonier and less naked star. Both of these arguments misunderstand the nature of consent, and underestimate, too, how powerful it is possible to feel when one elects to do something of one's own free will that has previously been done under duress. Nude or not, the difference between posing for a photograph and having one snapped candidly in an extremely private moment is so great that it has spawned an entire genre of celebrity quotes distastefully describing the experience of being photographed by paparazzi as a 'rape', or 'like rape'. Anderson, who knows from experience the severity of rape as a term and an act, does not use the word in reference to the publication of the sex tape. Rather, in *Love, Pamela*, she reports having responded to the levelling of 'question after invasive question – about [her] body, sexual positions, sexual preferences, locations [she] had sex in' at the case's deposition with a single cool and rational question: 'What does any of this have to do with them stealing or selling our private property?'

It may be better, then, to think of Anderson as neither a saint nor a slut, but as both the skilled magician and the glamorous assistant in the conjuring act of her own life, taking full advantage of our gaze being focused on her outsized props in order to conduct her business. In Ann Patchett's 1997 novel *The Magician's Assistant*, another book like *Love, Pamela* in which magic and self-transformation are synonymous, a former assistant named Sabine learns that her late husband and stage partner, a magician who once performed under the name Parsifal, has a secret past. That past – an Andersonian hardscrabble childhood in an unglamorous place, with a violent father and a distinct lack of money – is at odds with her perception of him as a charismatic and sophisticated Californian. Parsifal was also gay, and Sabine acted as a beard as well as an assistant, both jobs requiring her beauty to act as a lure and a distraction. 'There was no such thing as being a magician's assistant without knowing the trick,' Sabine says, explaining why it can be advantageous to be underestimated when you're trying to sell a lie. 'People are misguided by the assistant's surprise, the way her mouth opens in childlike delight as her glove is turned into a dove. But if you didn't know how it would all turn out, you wouldn't know where to stand, how to turn yourself to shield the magician's hand or temporarily block the light.' Just as her former husband hid behind a new self he'd produced as casually as a rabbit from a hat, Sabine prides herself on being able to comport herself on-stage with grace even as she fights to keep from swaying in their levitation act, 'every muscle rip[ping] apart from its neighbour'. 'People long to be amazed, even as they fight it.' She shrugs. 'Once you amaze them, you own them.'

For those few months in 2007, Pamela Anderson amazed Las Vegas nightly, and as a result she came to briefly own Las Vegas, as if she were an interim monarch or a minor deity. She occupied the entire top floor of the Planet Hollywood Casino, and held court as she was visited by friends like Amy Winehouse, Thierry Mugler, and the drag queen Lady Bunny; she flew back to Malibu four times a week to drive her sons to school, occasionally catching sight of her reflection in the window of her car and realising her face 'was covered in glitter', her eyes 'blackened by last night's show's eyeliner'. As ever, she lived two lives: as the pneumatic, hedonistic Pamela Anderson, and as Pam, a kooky, frazzled single mother who never missed a kindergarten play, a PTA volunteering opportunity, or a karate tournament. 'The truth was,' she writes in *Love, Pamela*, 'I really did not like Vegas – but Vegas loved me ... They would even take the "L" out if I was in residence, so the sign up on high read PAMS.' It seems strange to think that Pamela Anderson would dislike Vegas, with its flash and 24/7 intoxication, although if Las Vegas loved Pamela Anderson, it was probably because it recognised something of itself in her outsized, unabashed style. It makes sense that a city built entirely on sleight of hand would find room in its heart for a woman who was capable of toggling between high glamour and the school run, public glitz and private grind, with such speed and ease that she appeared to be performing an illusion – something done with mirrors and timed carefully to the second, disappearing from one spot and then re-materialising in another to the sound of thunderous applause.

♦

On a Sunday morning in the summer of 1981, in the middle of a heatwave, the model Caroline Cossey – best known to the general public under the mononym 'Tula', which, depending who you asked, meant 'tree' or 'pure gold' or 'tranquillity' or 'mountain peak' – suddenly began to feel that she was being watched. That people, and especially men, enjoyed looking at her was not much of a surprise. That people, and especially men, were watching as she and her sister Pamela stripped down to their bikinis in a public park was not unusual, either. Cossey resembled a rangier Raquel Welch, and she was six feet tall, and if Mattel had cashed in on her newly blooming fame and made a Tula Barbie, they could probably have done so easily by simply scaling down her body to a twelve-inch height; she had the impossibly high cheekbones of a gorgeous jungle cat, and the kind of fluid and chatoyant beauty that allowed her to look like a dusky English rose one minute, and a golden Amazon the next. She had recently appeared in a James Bond film, where she wore a white bikini and got splashed with water from a pool and shrieked prettily with surprise, and although it was the kind of role about which people say 'blink and you'll miss her', missing somebody who looked like her – lest we forget, like Raquel Welch if Raquel Welch were a six-foot demigoddess carved from amber – was not easy. She had also recently done a print advertisement for Smirnoff vodka in which she water-skied with the Loch Ness Monster, somehow managing to draw the eye even more effectively than her cryptozoological co-star. ('Well,' the tagline read, 'they said anything could happen!' Looking back over her shoulder to look straight into the lens, her high-cut red swimsuit screaming *Baywatch* a full decade before *Baywatch* hit the air, her expression in the picture suggests several things at once, from alarm to apprehension to defiance.) A year previously, she had been the Painted Lady for a company that made motorcycle gear, following in the footsteps of the famous German supermodel Veruschka – a job that required her to stand entirely still for upwards of three hours while a team of artists painted clothing, 'right down to the individual teeth on a zipper', on her naked body for the campaign images.

So, yes, it is true that Caroline Cossey was by this point very used to being gawped at; it is also true that to survive being gawped at *as a job*, beautiful women must develop the ability to tell exactly what a look means in an instant, and whether it signals danger. That morning, she felt certain that the looks she was receiving were not lustful or admiring, but violent, as if the men watching did not want to fuck her, but to hurt her, or to mock her. The *News of the World* had just run a prurient article revealing that she had been assigned male at birth, under the headline JAMES BOND GIRL WAS A BOY, and although the piece was little more than a violatory excavation of her medical history, the newspaper had presented it as if it were the justified exposure of a double-cross. 'I was overwhelmed by feelings I hadn't experienced for years,' she would go on to write, 'an awareness that I was different, a freak, that when people knew they wanted to avoid me because I was an alien.' Public life is hard for any woman who refines her image with commercialism and consumption on her mind, making it so perfect that it provokes atavistic anger in her audience as well as drooling ardour. It is harder still, however, for a woman like Caroline Cossey, whose physical alterations were a matter of survival as well as one of aesthetic taste – a necessary evolution that allowed her to live as her most complete self, marrying the person in the mirror with the person she imagined herself to be in her dreams, or with her eyes closed, or when she took to the stage in feathers and a G-string as a wide-eyed and flat-chested teenage dancer, trying not to trip and fall.

That scene in the park appears in both of Cossey's memoirs, the first of which was released in 1981 in the immediate aftermath of her tabloid exposure; entitled *I Am A Woman*, it is by the author's own admission a frank, nakedly transparent account of her childhood, her career, and her transition, released swiftly in order to counter the bad-faith material that had begun to circulate within the British gutter press. The narrative structure of the book is at once terribly familiar, and brand-new – in a sense, *I Am A Woman* takes the classic rags-to-riches self-invention story of a female celebrity, from stifling rural life to showgirl squalor to the movies, and breathes new life into it by making its heroine's journey one that carries her not just to stardom, but to proudly inhabiting the role of a heroine in lieu of being forced to pretend she is a hero. Because it begins with the *News of the World* exposé and then rewinds to her childhood, the book begins with the words, 'I remember I felt very good that Sunday morning', a foreboding line that might as easily serve as the first sentence of a horror story as the opening of a memoir. In contrast to *Love, Pamela*'s alembic of sexual glamour and true grit, Cossey's memoir describes the various events of her life with a straightforward, unembellished plainness, perhaps because her previous attempts at being coy had done little but provide her enemies with further fuel for her pyre. The best way to appear reasonable – and to avoid the classically feminine charge of 'hysteria', which those eager to declaim her femininity would presumably still have been more than happy to apply – was to recount the facts clearly and coolly, as if she were giving evidence in court or showing us where she had been violated on the body of a doll. If this was a horror story, readers were left in no doubt as to her valorous, hard-won status as its Final Girl.

When she describes the surgeries that helped her attain the body she desired, the prose is at its sparsest, and her matter-of-fact delivery of the details helps to normalise them without fully stripping them of their horrific power. Likewise, when Cossey reports exposure to emotional violence, such as the scenes where her exposure in the press begins to unfold in terrible slow-motion, her unadorned and affectless style allows the cruelty, clear and stinging as ice water, to leave a perceptible, unhappy chill as it flows through the text. Born with a less fitting name in 1954, in the small village of Brooke in Norfolk, Cossey rechristened herself Caroline in her teens after meeting a trans woman for the first time at a Soho party. Like many rural girls who dream of something bigger, she had moved to London to become a different person, and the way she describes the immediate manifestation of the name 'Caroline' in her mind, like a thunderbolt from heaven, feels as fated as Pamela Anderson's discovery on the jumbotron. The professional name 'Tula' was assigned to her by a modelling agent, who already had a Caroline on her books and figured something more exotic might help Cossey capitalise on her elegant height and general dark-eyed magnificence. That simplification into a single-name brand turned out to suit her perfectly, allowing as it did for a personality split, letting Tula be the supermodel and Caroline Cossey be the woman who went home for Christmases in Norfolk, drank in hotel bars with her work girlfriends, and dreamed of eventually marrying a decent man (which she did, in 1992).

Already, she was used to altering herself in order to best fit the context she appeared in, amplifying or minimising certain characteristics for the sake of pleasing others; in becoming not just Caroline, but Tula, too, she finally had the chance to do so purely for herself. No part of her career better honed her aptitude for projecting the desired picture than the years she spent performing as a showgirl, a job which is not exactly the same as being a magician's assistant, but which certainly has crossover elements – a reliance on one's beauty to procure the audience's attention, for example, and an aptitude for making difficult things look extremely easy at the same time as traversing the stage, sometimes backwards, in a pair of four-inch heels. Cossey's unexpected aptitude for showgirl life mirrors, in a sense, her own transition, an inborn understanding of what might very broadly be termed *the feminine assignment* revealing itself as she auditions for a troupe in a scene in her memoir. Believing herself to be stricken with 'two left feet', she turns out to be a natural. Instinct, a bone-deep conviction that she's doing exactly what she is meant to, spurs her on. 'I gave that performance everything I had,' she writes. 'I smouldered with all the sex appeal I could muster. Even I was surprised by what I managed. With one deft move I loosened my hair and, as it tumbled down around my shoulders, I glowered at the audience. "Well, that should scorch them," I thought.' At the end of her audition, the room breaks into spontaneous applause, and it is easy to imagine how validated she felt, both as a dancer and a woman. There is nothing else quite like a crowd's roar, after all, to confirm that you are hitting all your marks.

When Cossey released her follow-up memoir ten years later, she gave it the simple and straightforward name *My Story*, as if having already declared her womanhood, she did not care to be asked to do it again. If *I Am A Woman* is plain-spoken, *My Story* has refined the tale to diamond sharpness, the way a familiar anecdote becomes streamlined in the telling. In *I Am A Woman*, she describes her journey home after being discharged from the hospital after her gender reassignment, and although she mocks herself for being frightened, her admission that she cannot stop imagining she will be sexually assaulted is both startling and raw. Her longed-for vagina suddenly feels to her like a biological booby trap, and her status as a woman, in her eyes, now also makes her easy prey. 'The train began to fill up with people and I realised, to my horror, that nearly all the passengers were men,' she recalls. 'I felt that every single one of them was looking at me, and they knew what I'd been through ... there was one man in particular who kept staring at me. I had a sudden fear that I was going to be raped. Obviously the drugs were still playing on my mind, but I couldn't get the fear of being raped out of my thoughts. Later, I realised how stupid I'd been and laughed at myself: the first time you travel [with a vagina] and all you can think about is being raped!' Contrast this with her later, less emotional record of that moment, and a shift becomes apparent, in delivery if not in perspective: '"They all know," I thought,' she writes. 'One man, dressed in a white shirt and a dark-blue suit, seemed to be paying me particular attention. I prayed for him to look the other way. For the first time in my life the attention of men was something I wished to avoid. "This is one aspect of feeling female that I hadn't expected," I thought to myself.' By this second account, she has maintained a certain level of ambiguity around her terror, and perhaps the most interesting thing about the change is that almost any woman, cis or trans, would read her description of the source of her unease – the sly 'one aspect of being female' – and intuit easily that she meant rape or harassment, with the passage still remaining broadly allusive enough that Cossey does not risk frightening (cis) male readers circa 1991 by coming across as, shock horror, a man-hating feminist or a scold.

This minor alteration functions in some ways as proof of her total immersion in her new life as what she defined as 'a complete woman', in the sense that she is performing a little sleight of hand, splitting the perception of her audience in two and allowing herself, figuratively speaking, to appear in two places at once. In 1991, she had plenty of new reasons to be frightened and suspicious when men stared at her in public, not least because by the time *My Story* was released, the *News of the World* had run another exposé, this time covering her marriage to the millionaire businessman Elias Fattal. Although Fattal knew his wife was trans, his Orthodox Jewish family did not, and the public revelation of her history was enough to make him ask for an immediate annulment and, in a volte face that is so cruel it results in some of the hardest-to-read lines in Cossey's book, to renounce her entirely by saying that he 'hate[d] queers', labelling her a 'freak'. 'The evidence of [his] eyes and my soul made precious little difference,' Cossey laments. Piggishly, the *News of the World* decided to conclude their article about her nuptials with the line 'she's really landed on her back this time'. They were not to know how little time Caroline Cossey had spent on her back – minus the time spent on the operating table – for most of her adult life because of her sexually paralysing fear of being 'found out' as a 'boy', nor how badly she had wanted to be loved sincerely for herself. In a sense, the fact that what they saw was a perfect trophy wife, a supermodel who had set out to position herself as a prize for a rich man, felt like a sick confirmation of her gender, since in painting her as nothing but a bauble they had had to admit exactly what Cossey described as 'the evidence of [their] eyes'. It should not be a requirement for any woman, trans or cis, to be beautiful or flawless, but it also could not be denied that Cossey remained breathtakingly so. She had self-actualised into a shape that many men who desired women might be pleased by, and that in itself seemed to be what inflamed the ire of the press.

'The prejudice, cruelty and ignorance that [trans women] had to face could easily break a personality and leave it fractured beyond repair,' she notes in *My Story*. 'I had hoped for a different life, a life of domestic peace and tranquillity with a man I could love. I had never wanted to take up the banner that I was now holding. But fate had given me no choice. Time and time again I had been forced into the public arena and treated with disrespect.' '[The media] seemed to feel,' she adds, sadly, 'that my [trans status] was some vast joke made at the expense of an unsuspecting public.' The mistake the papers made was imagining that if any trick had been pulled off, it was one at their expense, and not one that was entirely for Cossey's benefit. The *News of the World* tried to imply that, by transitioning, she had somehow succeeded in hypnotising or otherwise fooling her male audience, making them believe that they saw one thing when really, they were looking at another. In fact, if Cossey had performed any illusion, it was one that must have felt for her like the trick where a magician places the two halves of the assistant he has sawn in half together again: a making whole, a flash of savage cruelty being undone with a unifying gesture. (In literature, a relevant analogy for

Cossey's surgeries might be the scene in Peter S. Beagle's 1982 novel *The Last Unicorn* in which a witch who runs a carnival captures the titular beast and then, because unicorns appear as mere white mares to lumpen mortals, casts a spell on her to create the illusion of the magic that she already possesses, and was born with – a transformation that, as the witch puts it, allows onlookers to 'know [her] for [her]self'.) It is interesting that so much opprobrium has been directed at trans women for the supposed transgression of 'deceiving' their male audience, when so many cis stars have also had extensive surgery in order to achieve the 'right' exterior. Ultimately, whether a female celebrity is cis or trans, there will be speculation on the authenticity of her body, and to suggest that one kind of surgical transformation is more acceptable, or more 'moral', than another is at best naive, and at worst disingenuous. The global beauty industry is currently on track to become a 580-billion-dollar market by 2027, and although the internet is full of memes made by men about how women 'can't be trusted' because of their tendency to draw on different, prettier faces, it remains the case that we are told almost constantly by media and advertising that the faces we were born with are not adequate – too thin-lipped, too full-cheeked, too creased, too un-Caucasian, and so on. It is a double-bind: do you want to be a liar, or do you want to be desirable; be loved; be *enough*?

No cis woman can ever entirely understand how it feels to occupy the world as a trans woman, especially a trans woman in the public eye. Still, both Pamela Anderson and Tula went to great lengths to offer us a smooth, idealised vision of traditionally feminine beauty, and in both instances, they were cruelly punished, not because they put a foot wrong, but because we could not keep ourselves from trying to see behind the velvet curtain of each woman's image. As with Anderson, too, the media made the error of believing that Caroline Cossey, because she was attractive, would also be compliant and silent. Their error was to her advantage, allowing her to take them by surprise by claiming her own narrative, both in her memoirs and in various interviews in other publications. 'I've been very honest, and I've put right some of the inaccuracies that have appeared in the press... I've always refused to be put down. Whatever this book does to me, I'll struggle on,' she writes at the end of *I Am A Woman*; by the end of *My Story*, she is no less blazing with determination, vowing to act as 'a voice ... for those who had been silenced by their fear of exposure', and a 'champion [of] the rights of men and women who ... had been born into a sex to which they did not belong'. In the same year that *My Story* was released, she made history for being the first openly trans woman to appear in *Playboy*, in a shoot that saw her posing in a jungle waterfall in leopard-print, both to accentuate her tan and Amazonian height, and to subtly imply that there was something about her that was exotic. On the cover, she wore an androgynous suit and pretended she was pulling down the zipper, and the strapline asked: 'Would YOU sleep with THIS woman? See inside – then decide.' As far as promotional gimmicks go, it was offensive, but it was also entirely nonsensical, since if Cossey had continued to pull down her fly she would have revealed a vulva. Evidently, for a certain kind of reader, the idea of being 'tricked' was the erotic point, ensuring that the model ended up saddled with yet another – for her – inconvenient and unwanted phallus: a phantom one, yes, but still a phallus all the same.

In spite of the attendant indignities in the packaging of *Playboy*'s shoot, Tula is still rightly proud of having been the magazine's first trans model. Asked then, she might have said – just as Pamela Anderson did when she described using her own *Playboy* shoot as a corrective for the traumatising past that made her unjustly resentful of her body – that with the publication of that shoot she had broken free of something to become a wild woman, wild not because she happened to be wearing leopard-print and situated in a jungle but because she had done something brave, and free. Bravery, a glib concept in media and advertising with regards to women's bodies in the present day, is usually mentioned in the context of a model or an actress having the temerity to pose in a bikini with cellulite, or post-partum, or at a size twelve; in this particular circumstance, however, it is difficult to know how else to describe Cossey's actions. By appearing in the world's most popular softcore magazine as a trans woman, she presented her body as a body worth desiring, making the resulting objectification, complicatedly and sort of paradoxically, a form of social progress. As Anderson would also say, she took the power of her sexuality back; by signifying to a wider audience that she *had* a sexuality in the first place, and that furthermore it was the kind of sexuality they might like to see displayed, she helped to change the conversation, taking a small but significant step in the still-ongoing journey for sexual, legal and political parity for cis and trans women. '*Playboy*'s readership is mostly male and heterosexual, so it allowed me to get out there and prove that people like myself can be sexy and attractive,' she said in a later interview with the magazine in 2015. 'That's what I aimed to do at that point. I wanted to fight for the right of recognition. And *Playboy* gave me the opportunity to ask for a whole hour on most of the talk shows ... It gave people the chance to get to know me ... and hopefully gain empathy and understanding.'

In January of 2023, Pamela Anderson made yet another of her own talk-show appearances on Jimmy Kimmel to promote the dual release of *Love, Pamela* and *Pamela: A Love Story*, and the resulting footage certainly showcases her ability to use her carefully crafted image as a good-time bimbo for her own personal gain. 'I'm so impressed that you wrote all your experiences down in a journal so diligently,' Kimmel says regarding the material used for the documentary voiceover, his tone suggesting for a moment that the sentence might end after 'wrote'. Seeing an opportunity for mirth, he mentions her residency in Las Vegas. 'You worked as a magician's assistant in Las Vegas,' he points out. 'And at that time, you also learned how to make balloon animals.' 'Well, I didn't want to waste any time, so while I was getting my make-up done I hired a clown to teach me how to make balloon animals,' Anderson deadpans, before adding with crackerjack comic timing: 'You know, something to fall back on.' Kimmel pulls out a long red balloon and Anderson tries to demurely deflect, before taking the balloon and shaping it with some degree of confidence. 'The funny thing about balloon animals is that they can pop at any second,' she says, an arched eyebrow evident in her voice even if it is not technically evident on her face, before producing a 'poodle' that is definitely, no bones about it, actually a dick, and brandishing it at Jimmy Kimmel. In that instant, it appears to hit her that the object she has made is accidentally lewd, and Pamela Anderson – who would turn fifty-six that year, and whose laugh combines the kittenish mannerisms of a schoolgirl with the throaty cackle of a woman who has seen a lot and lived to tell the tale – throws the balloon onto the desk and puts her palms up to her cheeks, mock-horrified.

When Kimmel expresses some astonishment at the idea of Pamela Anderson, 'a huge star', having wanted to act as the assistant to a magician, she reacts as though it had been the most self-explanatory career move of her life. 'It was one of my favourite things I've ever done,' she says, proudly. 'Because I feel like you're on one side of the magic or the other, and I always wanted to be on that side of the magic.' Obviously, she is being self-deprecating – she has never really been on our side of the magic. For more than three decades we have collectively allowed ourselves to be amazed by her, even though we've sometimes fought it, and whether or not we realise it, she owns us; and she owns all of her own sexed-up and controversial and sometimes embarrassing shit, too. Even after replaying the Jimmy Kimmel interview numerous times, it is not entirely clear whether this bit of business with the balloon has been scripted and rehearsed, or whether it works out just as perfectly as if it had been, because Anderson takes one look at that red balloon, and knows exactly how the play is going to go. If you are Pamela Anderson and the host of a talk show offers you a long, bright red balloon, pressing it into the French-manicured hands that most of America remembers being wrapped around a famous drummer's penis, of course what he wants is for you to produce a phallic symbol – to appear as if whatever you are doing, you can't help but bring the subject back to sex. Give the nice man what he wants, and the audience will cheer and holler, and your memoir will end up on the best-seller list, so who here is really the illusionist, and who's the mark? 'Pamela', lest we forget, 'has no regrets about her life'.

'Why become a model if you've had a [gender reassignment] operation?' is the cry of so many ignorant people who believe that [being trans] carries with it the penalty of humble obscurity,' Caroline Cossey writes in *My Story*, an eye-roll detectable even in writing. 'They seem to feel that [trans women] who become successful are courting publicity and deserve the treatment they get.' In this passage, Cossey puts her finger on a timeless and infuriating fact of womanhood: that it is important for a female-bodied person to be desirable, but it is also the case that being *too* desirable, or desirable in the 'wrong' way, makes you a hate object, a pariah, or the subject of some arcane social punishment like, say, public humiliation in the gutter press. This particular contradiction is so central to contemporary feminine life that even putting it in writing yet again feels tiring and banal – and yet living it is tiring and banal, too, and somehow there is no end to it at present, however much corrective feminism we apply to the extremely recent past. Shortly after the *News of the World* ran their exposé of Caroline Cossey, they printed a pin-up photograph of her in swimwear in a round-up of bikini beauties, as if to admit that although they felt she deserved to be pilloried for her body, they were also not yet ready to stop looking at it.

The year after the release of Pamela Anderson's stolen sex tape, *Playboy* ran her image on the cover once again, and this time they used a close-up of her face, which was by this point so iconic and instantly recognisable that the reader could imagine all too easily what was inside the magazine. In the picture, her powder-blue eyes are half-closed like a cat's, and although the look is meant to be seductive, there is steel in it, as if she might be issuing a challenge.

A 2023 interview in *The New York Times* entitled 'Pamela Anderson Doesn't Need Redemption, She's Just Fine' opened with the journalist showing Anderson a new app that allowed users to transform themselves into a version of her circa the sex tape, 'hair in a tousled top bun, pencil-thin eyebrows, mouth in a lip-lined pout', and Anderson, laughing, firmly refusing to try the filter on herself. She had been that woman once – she had originated her, *designed* her. Why revisit her again? 'If, in some impossible, unimaginable circumstance, the trick was not explained to the assistant,' Sabine suggests in *The Magician's Assistant*, 'she would get it sooner or later out of sheer repetition: The egg comes out of your ear, the rabbit is between your breasts, your head is sawed off, it happens over and over and over again.' Both Cossey and Anderson made a career, at least for a certain period of time, out of pulling proverbial rabbits from between their breasts for an interested audience, knowing – like a good assistant; like a good magician – that nobody can actually saw your head off if the one you're offering them is a decoy in the first place. Tula was, for a brief shining moment, a Bond Girl and a supermodel; Caroline Cossey now lives a life of relative obscurity, aside from giving the occasional interview about trans rights, looking in more recent photographs like your wealthiest schoolmate's gorgeous, bohemian mother. Pamela Anderson reappeared on the promotional circuit, in a tour that included her balloon trick on Jimmy Kimmel, for just long enough to sell her documentary and her memoir, and then largely returned to being Pam, happily wandering the dunes of a Canadian beach in Uggs and a white kaftan, her face bare, her famous chest left unsupported and unheralded. To survive as a professional babe in a world that both wants you and wants to destroy you, it is necessary to learn a few tricks, and it is also necessary to know how and when to – as if by simply saying abracadabra – make yourself disappear.

6

Less an Actress Than a Great Natural Wonder

On Lindsay Lohan and Elizabeth Taylor

Is it possible to be the reincarnation of a person who is not actually dead? Certainly, in 2012 at least, Lindsay Lohan seemed to think so. That Elizabeth Taylor had also found fame at twelve; that she had also been forced to make a smooth transition between being a feted baby-actress and being a sexual icon; that she too had shuttled in and out of rehab; that her stupidest mistakes with men, some of which were very dumb indeed, had also been intensely documented, and that they had also sometimes taken precedence over her talent as far as the public's interest was concerned – these were not small coincidences, and in promotional interviews that year for *Liz & Dick*, the Lifetime movie in which she played Taylor, Lohan wore them like expensive jewellery: proudly, flashily, and not always in good taste. (In fact, when she had first met with the TV movie producer Larry Thompson at the Polo Lounge to discuss being cast in *Liz & Dick*, Lohan had been on supervised probation for the uncontested theft of a two-thousand-dollar necklace, and although the felony itself had not been very Tayloresque, one had to concede that the mad, obliterating need for glamour it suggested was appropriate in spirit.) It could not have escaped anyone's notice that there was one crucial difference between Lindsay Lohan and Elizabeth Taylor – two, in fact, given that Taylor had won the Academy Award for Best Actress twice, once for *BUtterfield 8* in 1960 and again for *Who's Afraid of Virginia Woolf?* in 1966. Still, Lohan was ambitious, and in 2012 she was still telling everyone who'd listen that she'd have her own Oscar by thirty. She was sure that fate, so often a supporting player in most tales of stardom, would still show up in her second act.

'You can never be a clone of a person, so you do have to bring something of yourself to it,' she told a producer at *Good Morning America* that year, her young face plush with fillers. 'I was lucky because I do relate to Elizabeth Taylor in a lot of ways.' What Lohan brought of herself to the movie was a touch of angst, an unmistakable weariness, so that some of her most accurate scenes occur later in the runtime when she plays a late-middle-aged woman – the preternatural maturity that marked both the young Taylor and the preteen Lohan out as being preordained for stardom had continued, somehow, to accelerate in Lindsay, the result being that at twenty-six she was already giving the impression that no one had ever been so old, so tired of living. The deadness in her eyes did not seem to be the emptiness of inactivity or inability, but that of a kind of existential fuckedness; her best line-reading is that of the phrase 'I guess I never had anybody say no to me before', a throaty near-sob that pitches in and out, half cracked, like a broken radio signal. Who had said no to Lindsay Lohan by 2012? A great many people, owing to her criminal convictions and her lofty claims that she was owed an Oscar, that the world would come to see her genius even though she did not care to come to set on time or give up going to bed at dawn.

The sting so evident in her delivery of that line, in other words, might have sprung from Lohan's realisation of that moment being, for her, ancient history – not merely in the sense that she was playing a woman from the past, but in the sense that being rejected was now so much a part of her Hollywood experience that this, a Lifetime movie, was her best chance of a comeback. 'Yes', with all its Faustian sweetness and seductiveness, lay in the rear-view mirror, and it was no longer clear to audiences or to directors whether Lindsay Lohan was still in the driver's seat of her own life at any rate. She may not have burned through four marriages by twenty-nine, as Taylor had by the time she met Richard Burton, but at twenty-six it often seemed as if she'd been through several ugly deaths and rebirths, several cycles of unmaking and remaking. She had already been a Disney tween; a once-in-a-generation actress; an ungrateful, snotty bitch; a party girl; a convicted criminal who'd been to jail; a redheaded sexual terrorist; a bone-thin blonde; a dark-haired femme fatale. This explains why it had seemed so feasible to Lindsay Lohan that she could be a reincarnation of the still-living Taylor – both women had had nine lives, endless lovers, endless stamina, endless talent, and many things that by rights ought to have killed them hadn't done so, as if death itself was loathe to snuff them out.

One night, deep into her affair with Richard Burton, Elizabeth Taylor had awoken to find her then-husband Eddie Fisher standing by the bed, holding a gun. 'I would never kill you, Elizabeth,' he supposedly said. 'You're too beautiful.' Beauty, in this instance, proved to be her saving grace, in both the colloquial and the God-given sense. It was also the same thing that drove her husband to the gun safe in the first place – the same thing that had made Burton, when he'd picked up the phone once to Fisher himself at the Fisher-Taylor residence, simply remark, 'I've just been fucking your wife,' as if the act were so inevitable that it could not be immoral, only natural. Beauty itself might be seen to be a little like a gun, a source of power and also a source of danger, and as with a firearm there is a change in risk depending who is handling it. Viewed from one angle, a woman like Taylor might be seen to have the ability to dominate a room, to say nothing of a man, because of her possession of a face that Burton once described as 'unquestioningly gorgeous' and 'too bloody much', and a body that he frequently said far less elegant things about. (It is interesting, incidentally, that Burton said that Taylor's face was 'unquestioningly gorgeous', when it seems as though he might have meant 'unquestionably', instead – a woman who does not ask too many questions, even with her perfect face, has her own appeal for men, and although by all accounts Burton adored Taylor for her mind as well as for her looks, here he landed on a deeper truth merely by muddling his words.) That said, while sometimes women get to point weapons at men, statistically it is more often the other way around. Taylor's overt sexiness may have earned her roles; it also continually acted against her being taken seriously, and it helped to make her fascinating to a group of people she unwittingly helped usher into existence by being so gorgeous that the public felt every bit as entitled to her image as they might if she had been a tourist landmark, or a piece of sculpture.

Something else that is a little like a gun is a camera, with which one is also 'shot', especially if one happens to be beautiful. In 1960, the same year that Elizabeth Taylor won her first Best Actress Oscar for playing a sex worker who self-identified as 'the slut of all time' in *BUtterfield 8*, two other films helped to explain a new relationship between desirable women and the camera: Michael Powell's *Peeping Tom*, the ur-text for the phallus as a combination camera-weapon, and Federico Fellini's *La Dolce Vita*, whose photographer character Paparazzo would go on to lend his name to a new, rather dishonourable profession. Starring Carl Boehm as Mark Lewis – a man whose dream is to become a bigtime filmmaker, and whose fixation is the serial, sexual murder of young women with his rolling blade-tipped camera – *Peeping Tom* is notable for its modern sexual style, for its aestheticised heterosexual violence, and for its acknowledgement that the containment of the latter in the former would eventually come to be almost ubiquitous. *La Dolce Vita*, meanwhile, began production in Rome at the same time that Taylor and Burton began their affair, and Fellini drew some direct inspiration from his observation of the flurry of activity and noise that invariably followed them each time they were together. 'Every night, the same story,' a socialite sighs to the film's journalist protagonist Marcello in its opening scenes, having once more run a gamut of scrambling, shouting, flashing hangers-on outside a club. 'You should be used to it now,' says Marcello. 'You're a public figure.' It's a subtly ironic joke, as is Marcello's claim that Rome is 'sort of a moderate, tranquil jungle where one can hide' – this kind of photographic coverage was so new, and so novel, that nobody was especially used to it in 1960, and the Italian capital was less a jungle than a fishbowl, with Burton and Taylor being its biggest, most resplendent fish.

Liz & Dick, in its own characteristically clumsy way, attempts to deal with the advent of what we now know as paparazzi coverage, showing the producer Darryl Zanuck reacting with horror to an Italian paper printing photographs of Taylor and Burton holding hands. 'It's just kids on motor scooters, Rome is infested with them,' a character we might as well call 'Jimmy Exposition' tells him. 'They call them "Paparazzi" – it means "little buzzing insects". I think Fellini actually coined the word.' Because the image on the front page is of Lohan standing in for Taylor, what might otherwise have been a throwaway moment in a subpar biopic requires closer observation, acting as it does as an accidental piece of meta-commentary on the history of celebrity journalism. When Taylor and Burton began openly consorting with each other on and off the set of *Cleopatra* in 1961, there was not yet an expectation that everything famous people did in public would be filmed and photographed and shouted from the rooftops, and the newness of this way of life – the seeming obscenity of suddenly existing in a panopticon of salacious gossip, an idea that must at first have been so strange as to feel dreamlike or unreal – meant that many stars were not appropriately cautious. The peak of Taylor's fame arrived concurrently with this mania for candid images, and the Vatican would probably not have felt quite as pressed to issue a condemnatory statement about her 'erotic vagrancy' if there had not been quite so many pictures of the lovers in the press, always looking as if they were breaking at least three of the commandments at the same time. Taylor's racy public image 'was a kind of reverse method acting, in which she drew on her theatrical roles', such as her turn in *Cleopatra*, 'to provide direction and add lustre to her life', the journalist Sam Kashner wrote, in his 2009 Burton-Taylor biography *Furious Love: Elizabeth Taylor, Richard Burton, and the Marriage of the Century*. 'On the face of it,' the famous gossip columnist Liz Smith once bitched, 'Elizabeth Taylor was just totally arrogant ... That's part of what excited the public: her vulgarity and her arrogance and the money.'

And then there in *Liz & Dick*, in the photograph adorning that mocked-up Italian newspaper, is Lindsay Lohan, whose own face graced so many blogs and tabloids in her twenties that it began to seem as if *TMZ* and the *National*

Enquirer, and not the screen, were her primary medium for self-expression. Lohan did not always have the money Taylor had, but her arrogance and her vulgarity were not in question, and although both qualities were eminently understandable in a stunning, famous woman who had proven herself to be effortlessly skilled in her early screen performances, they were not exactly tolerated by the general public. There are many paparazzi photographs of Lindsay Lohan which might reasonably be described as iconic: the 2007 shot of her sitting in a car with Paris Hilton and Britney Spears that the *National Enquirer* ran with the headline BIMBO SUMMIT, for example, or the images of her wearing an ankle bracelet at the pool party she threw to celebrate her twenty-first from the next year – pictures which are funny and a little knowing on Lohan's part precisely because the device is there to monitor her alcohol consumption, and the soirée marked the first event at which she could legally have a drink. Perhaps the most indelible tabloid moment in her career, though, was indelible for all of the wrong reasons, and its cruelty stuns even now: in 2010, the *Enquirer* ran another cover on which Lindsay Lohan appeared centre stage, pictured crying in court, and next to a subheading referring to her 'jail hell', 'suicide fears', and 'addictions', the feature's headline screamed WHO'LL DIE FIRST! [sic].

When another character in *Peeping Tom* asks Lewis what kind of magazines sell the largest number of copies, he replies, 'those with girls on the front covers and no front covers on the girls'. *Plus ça change*; sex sells, and so does death, and a hot woman who appears to be hurtling headlong towards death will sell most of all. If you choose to hasten her along with your camera, is it murder, or good business sense? Lewis' primary fixation is the possibility of capturing the expression on a woman's face at the very moment of her terrible demise, and his preoccupation with this image – as well as prefiguring the kind of tabloid coverage the *National Enquirer* specialises in – is in some ways a pre-empting of another work of art that was produced a little later in the decade: Andy Warhol's *Marilyn Diptych* (1962), which uses a familiar promotional shot of Monroe from 1953's *Niagara* to suggest the actress' deterioration unto death. When Warhol painted Elizabeth Taylor that same year, he depicted her in a similarly smudged and etiolated style, using a publicity shot from her role as Cleopatra; in 1963, he repeated the same technique with an image of her from the 1944 film *National Velvet*, in which she played a twelve-year-old who disguises herself as a jockey. The artist's decision to invoke the same deathly qualities in his portraits of the living actress might be explained by several factors: firstly, that in 1961, Taylor was gravely ill with pneumonia, and it was believed that she might die, with one news agency erroneously reporting that she had; secondly, that the expiry of her third husband Mike Todd in a plane crash in 1958 had cast a pall over her life and image, making her proximate to death even as she lived; thirdly, that most of the paintings Andy Warhol made of actresses contained within them a suggestion that violence and death were intrinsic factors in the manufacture of a famous woman, and that the very machinery which makes stars has the power to destroy them.

Six years prior to *Liz & Dick*, Lohan appeared on the cover of *Interview* magazine at twenty years old, portraying Taylor in *Cat on a Hot Tin Roof*. It is difficult to believe just how young she is when looking at the shot. Taylor herself was twenty-six when she played Maggie in 1958, and she had seemed older besides – less because of her appearance than because of the sheer, knowing force of her erotic power, which animated her even at rest. Puberty can be a killer for a famous child who was best known for being cute, or for playing up their innocence; for stars like Lohan and Taylor, both of whom impressed not with their sweetness but with their evident ability and sophistication, adolescence brings the challenge of being seen as too mature in an entirely new way. One of the most memorable posed images of Lohan's career is one where she is sitting on a bed in what appears to be a hotel, wearing a purple and pink bikini in a Pucci pattern – something about the picture, which appeared in *Vanity Fair* in 2004, feels as though it has been art-directed by a man who'd kept a countdown to her eighteenth birthday. Her green eyes and marzipan-smooth cheeks are puppyish in contrast to her body, which is stupidly voluptuous, and the piercing in her navel adds a note of teen rebellion. 'I want people to know me for the work that I'm doing, not for this party girl image,' she had said in the accompanying profile, 'which is just vile and disgusting, and not fair, because I work so hard.' It could not be ignored that Lohan played hard, too, and though her earliest performances suggested a singular promise, her preferred extracurricular activities gestured towards a fatalistic nature – a desire to self-immolate in the most spectacular fashion.

The Mark Lewis of the noughties, the moustachioed photographer and professional sleaze Terry Richardson, photographed her while she was making *Liz & Dick*, and decided to literalise the parities between the camera and the gun. In one shot, she has the weapon in her mouth; in another, it is pressed against her temple, and if her brilliance as an actress had ever been in doubt, her face in this image re-cements it. It ought to be a contradiction to describe someone as terrified *and* weary, but somehow Lohan manages it, and it makes her look like someone who is equally afraid of life and death. It is the expression of a person who has undergone some slow, lingering torture, and now knows that it will end, even if the end itself is frightening or painful. The photograph is not a fashion photograph, or even a candid image, but a documentation of a performance, and perhaps even – per certain age-old superstitions – a snapshot of her soul. Ten days before it was taken, the *Hollywood Reporter* notes, 'paramedics were called to Lindsay Lohan's Ritz Carlton hotel room in Marina del Rey because she was in such a deep sleep that she couldn't be roused'. Maybe Lohan was just very, very tired – of being looked at, of being overlooked, of being made to look foolish and incompetent. Richardson has since been accused of being a sexual predator, and appears to have been more or less ousted from the fashion industry. Nevertheless, his images of Lindsay Lohan are her best, exposing as they do the dangerous, acuminated edge that makes her interesting as an actress and a public figure. For the cover of *Purple* magazine, he shot her dressed as Jesus Christ in a designer crown of thorns, her arms thrown out in a pose redolent of the crucifixion; in another image for *GQ*, he showed her setting fire to a gossip rag with her own picture in it, her eyes as wide as a startled deer's. Perhaps sickness recognised sickness, with Richardson seeing the extent of Lohan's injury and capitalising on it to produce (if half accidentally) several documents of her celebrity that are so truthful and provocative it's tempting to categorise them as art. Where the *National Enquirer* saw fit to speculate on the possible date of the actress' death, Richardson understood her enough to depict her as a figure capable of a kinky, perverse form of resurrection, and to let her play with fire without getting burned.

'The story of child stars who go haywire,' the journalist Caryn James wrote in 2009, in a profile of Lindsay Lohan, 'is as old as Elizabeth Taylor.' While there were inarguably child stars before Taylor, and some of those child stars certainly went psychologically off-piste in later years, the fact that Taylor was often described as being the most famous woman in the world at the height of her career does make her a particularly memorable example of the trope. ('She is less an actress than a great natural wonder, like Niagara or the Alps,' *The New Yorker* critic Brendan Gill wrote in 1963, reviewing *Cleopatra*, 'and it was right of the director to deal with her as the thing she has become – the most famous woman of her time, and probably of all time.') 'I've been pronounced dead, and I've read my own obituaries,' she once said. 'And they were the best reviews I ever read.' Technically, she was talking about the erroneous announcements of her death that followed her bout of pneumonia in the early sixties; figuratively, she was also offering up a pithy statement about her continuing survival as an icon in the face of the many inconvenient, unpleasant developments in both her life, and her coverage in the press. Born to a mild-mannered antique-dealer father and a pushy actress mother – whose micromanaging of Elizabeth's career predates the neologism 'momager', but suits it nonetheless – she appeared in *Lassie Come Home* at the age of ten, and quickly found herself being subsumed into the studio system, chaperoned to the degree that she was not allowed to use the bathroom by herself. Roughly a year later, she was in *National Velvet*, swiftly gathering an entourage of hangers-on and yes-men; staff at Metro Goldwyn Mayer were on hand to teach her how to walk, and talk, and move, and how to answer questions like a canny actress instead of a preteen girl. The power she held in her babywoman's face, with its violet eyes and imperious, feline bones, soon become evident to her, and this realisation seemed to thrill her and infuriate her at the same time, proving as it did both that she had been born for stardom, and that nobody cared much about anything other than her looks. She developed a foul mouth, and a tendency to start – and to win – belching competitions, signalling that she was not the china doll her fans expected her to be.

At eighteen, she married Conrad 'Nicky' Hilton Jr, a hotel heir with a gambling addiction and cruel fists, as a promotional stunt for the film *Father of the Bride*, in which she starred as Spencer Tracy's daughter. After six months, and after Hilton allegedly kicked Taylor in the abdomen and brought on a miscarriage, the marriage ended on the grounds of 'mental cruelty', with the husband claiming that he'd only become violent because he had been unable to deal with the pressure of being married to a star, and the wife claiming that she had only capitulated to the PR merger because of what she described as 'feelings that could not be indulged outside of marriage'. Taylor's glorious sex drive, and her joy at inhabiting her increasingly Rubenesque adult body, would contribute to some of the most difficult moments in her public life – not because she ever behaved badly, necessarily, but because she behaved in accordance with her instincts. The pursuit of reckless pleasure was, for her, as much of an art form as her acting. The passion that inspired her greatest sexual and romantic affairs was the same passion that animated her in her best and most moving performances, a feeling that she contained too much life for it to be fully contained inside her soft and queenly body. She took the same approach to eating and to drinking, her weight fluctuating as she habitually overindulged in champagne and fried chicken, beer and cream cake. Warhol, her court painter, claimed that women who wore diamonds tended to live longer lives because of the spiritually rejuvenating power of crystals, and as Kashner notes, Taylor's love of jewels and her endurance in the face of great pain – including a tracheotomy during that terrible bout of pneumonia – seemed to bear this out. In a film like *Suddenly Last Summer*, one feels in spite of her marmoreal pallor that she might be molten to the touch – her skin appearing white in the feverish, ardent sense of 'white-hot', rather than white like a frigid snowdrift.

All in all, Taylor married seven times, and although her third husband Mike Todd had been a great love for her, no other man mattered quite as much as Burton, whom she married twice. In 1950, there was Michael Wilding, a man mostly notable for being another husband chosen by the studio, and for being closer to her father's age; they divorced after five years, possibly because if Taylor had been left with any issues by her parents they were not the Daddy kind, and she married Todd one year later. When he died in 1958 in that plane crash after just three years of marriage, she sought solace in his close friend Eddie Fisher, somewhat inconveniently for Fisher's then-wife, Debbie Reynolds. What Taylor had loved in Todd was his unvarnished masculinity, and his status as a self-made man. He could drink and fuck and fight exactly as she liked, and as was befitting an incontrovertible diva of her stature, she preferred to live a life that was dramatic; souped-up; full of sex and emotional warfare. Fisher, an acolyte of Todd's as well as his best friend, did his best to live up to his predecessor, and yet he was not quite as much of a champion at what might be euphemistically referred to as the natural arts. Taylor, as if by contrast, often inhabited both sets of traditional gender roles in her marriages: acting as the breadwinner but doting on her husbands; dressing like a perfect mannequin in public but demanding to be screwed more or less constantly behind closed doors. 'She was a "man's woman",' the film critic Molly Haskell once suggested, the phrase doing double duty in its implication that men lusted after her, and that she could stand toe-to-toe with them in conversation and in work, '[and] she had the ego to survive and become a power.' The ego, certainly – and the money, and the fortitude, and the fame, and the libido. If she was going to be the most famous woman in Hollywood, she may as well act like it, and while she was at it why not behave as if she were the most famous man there, too?

When a tabloid headline screamed *Blood Thirsty Widow Liz Vampires Eddie* on the eve of her marriage to Fisher, Taylor hit back by exclaiming: 'Mike is dead, and I'm alive!' A reference to her famous role as Maggie in *Cat on a Hot Tin Roof*, she did not mean for the statement to be callous – only for it to remind her fans and enemies alike that she refused to give up her pursuit of pleasure. For all of the studio's attempts to mould her in her childhood, she refused to alter her more adult impulses in order to be liked, perhaps sensing the approach of a revolution in both sex and stardom, or perhaps simply being too much of a hedonist to care. The first time Richard Burton met her on the set of *Cleopatra*, filming opposite her as Marc Anthony, he asked her facetiously: 'Has anyone ever told you you're a very pretty girl?' Taylor, mistaking the understatement for a clumsy attempt at what would currently be called 'negging', merely scoffed. In fact, Burton was being drily ironic, and his irony perfectly demonstrated how immediately he understood her. Taylor had not been a 'girl' even when she was a girl – she had been a prodigy, a marvel, a preternaturally wise child-sage, and now she was absolutely not a girl, but a goddess. Together, they were instantly explosive, and their hot-bloodedness was bound to attract, as that minor character in *Liz & Dick* described them, little buzzing insects. When the two rented a private villa in which to conduct their extramarital affair, paparazzi gathered in the trees around their pool, sometimes hanging from the branches to achieve the perfect shot. Through it all they fucked and bickered, fucked and bickered, marrying in 1964, divorcing in 1974, remarrying in 1975 and re-divorcing one year later, as if they were so committed to their favoured routine of falling out and then having make-up sex that they'd decided to take it to another and more binding level.

Taylor's long string of marriages, as far as tabloid fodder is concerned, might be said to outstrip all of Lindsay Lohan's crimes and misdemeanours in their irrationality and eccentricity – legal, yes, but suggestive of a devotion to wifehood, or more accurately to men, that bordered on insanity. Had the internet existed in the period during which Burton and Taylor were on-again-or-was-it-off-again in their interminable cycle, it would no doubt have combusted just as fiercely as the couple did themselves behind closed doors. For all of their similarities, this may be the fundamental difference between Lohan and her heroine, Taylor: the former's bad behaviour, even when it was not technically all that bad in the first place, flooded not only the tabloids but the web and social media, sometimes within moments of the actual infraction, and the reach of each misstep expanded exponentially like ripples in a pond, until it appeared so distractingly large that nobody looked too closely at the struggling young woman – who was not waving, but drowning – at its centre. Eddie Fisher may have humiliated Elizabeth Taylor by performing a cabaret act called *Cleo, Nympho of the Nile* in the wake of their divorce, but when oil heir Brandon Davis saw fit to bestow the name 'firecrotch' on Lindsay Lohan in front of a videographer from TMZ, half the world saw it immediately and began calling her that, too; when Taylor turned eighteen, a culture did not yet exist in which it would be deemed permissible to publish, as *Rolling Stone* did when Lohan turned that age in 2004, a cover image of her licking her teeth and flicking her hair next to a headline that said *HOT, READY, AND LEGAL!* Just as Taylor had been forced to grapple with a new form of media coverage when the paparazzi began swarming, Lohan and her peers had been caught, quite often literally, with their knickers down by the sudden advent of 24/7 press. The period of adjustment in which many of them had to learn to permanently, perpetually modify their conduct any time they left the house (and occasionally, when camera-phone images or videos leaked that had been taken by friends and hangers-on in private, *in* their homes, as well) was cruel and exposing, producing 'exclusive' content that was simultaneously hard to countenance and hard to look away from. No wonder Lohan drank, and sometimes drugged, and drove her car as if she hoped she'd die. No wonder being 'in such a deep sleep that she couldn't be roused' felt entirely necessary, and no wonder her career ended up entering into an equally deep, deathlike slumber as the scrutiny increased. Is it possible that she might eventually end up being resurrected, not as a reincarnation of Elizabeth Taylor, but as a new version of herself? Yes – but to understand how, and why this is necessary in the first place, we ought to rewind to the beginning. We must throw away the telescopic, leering paparazzi lens, and zoom out so we can see the bigger picture.

Lindsay Lohan – whose middle name is either 'Dee' or 'Morgan', depending on who's asking – was born in 1986, to Dinah, an ex-understudy for the Rockettes, and Michael, who is introduced in a 2005 *W* magazine profile of his daughter as: 'a man who is prohibited by fourteen court orders from approaching his wife and daughter; who has had numerous arrests for assault, disorderly conduct, jumping bail and issuing bad checks; who has a long history of alcohol and drug abuse; and who was incarcerated in 1990 after defrauding people in connection with commodities futures trading'. ('Let's not forget,' Lohan tweeted in 2010, 'that my father kidnapped me from a court room when i [sic] was 4 years old and is crazy.') She grew up in Long Island, a location that feels like a perfect breeding ground for her throaty all-American charm, seeming as she does – or did, at least, at the height of her adult fame – like the human equivalent of a Long Island iced tea: appealingly and unashamedly trashy, far stronger than you'd think, and laced with an intoxicating kick. At three years old, she became the first redheaded child model ever to be signed by Ford – her red hair, like Elizabeth Taylor's purple-blue eyes, would go on to serve as her calling card, and it gave her a similar air of singularity and specialness. (Only 1 to 2 per cent of people globally have red hair; fewer than 1 per cent have violet irises like

Taylor.) Lohan grew up idolising actresses from the fifties and the sixties, in particular Ann-Margret, Marilyn Monroe and, of course, Elizabeth Taylor; at ten, she began working on a long-defunct soap opera called *Another World*, whose eccentric Wikipedia entry describes it, somewhat grandiosely, as a show about 'exotic melodrama[s] between families of different classes and philosophies'. Her breakthrough performance in Disney's 1998 remake of *The Parent Trap* technically required her to fill two roles, as the identical twins Hallie and Annie, but because both girls had different accents, and in several scenes she had to play them *playing each other*, it ended up seeming more like four. In the credits, she is introduced by name over a shot of fireworks exploding, as if foreshadowing some later sound and fury. No one could have known just how explosive, how *like* fireworks, her adult life in the public eye would eventually turn out to be.

In a 2016 essay, Zadie Smith compares two ballet dancers, the cool perfectionist Mikhail Baryshnikov and the pantherish satyr Rudolf Nureyev, and describes them as 'trying to please' and 'so fierce and neurotic, so vulnerable, so beautiful' respectively. She suggests that her love of Baryshnikov springs from his efforts to be entertaining, and that Nureyev pleases her because he is a 'miracle'. Both are obviously extraordinary dancers, but it is certainly Nureyev who feels the most *impossible* – there is a snippet online of his American TV debut in 1963, and in that clip it seems as if a scientific error has occurred when he takes flight. He is in the air a beat too long; he is almost too possessed of the animal energy Smith so admires in him. Even Lindsay

Lohan's earliest performances have a touch of that Nureyev quality, and her public appearances as Lindsay Lohan in her late teens and her twenties tended to, as well. (Lest we forget, Nureyev was something of a gorgeous sybarite himself.) Many child stars, growing up not just as tits-and-teeth show-people but as inveterate show-offs, cannot keep themselves from straining to win audiences' hearts; when Lindsay Lohan appeared in *The Parent Trap*, it was clear that whatever permitted her to convincingly play identical twins with divergent accents, it had less to do with hard work than it did with something mysterious and intuitive, and she seemed less interested in providing entertainment than she did in thoroughly inhabiting her roles. She shared with the young Macaulay Culkin an air of sophisticated naturalism, as if she were simultaneously twelve and fifty-five. 'Miss Lohan ... plays the dual role with apparent effortlessness and with so much forcefulness that she seems to have been taking shy violet lessons from Sharon Stone,' Manohla Dargis offered in *The New York Times* – a curious observation, given that Lohan was not yet in her teens, and Sharon Stone was then best known for *Basic Instinct*, in which she played a bisexual nymphomaniac murderess, and for her Best-Actress-winning turn in *Casino* as a fatally desirable ex-sex worker. What Dargis was seeing, though, was that Nureyev-ness, that fierceness and neuroticism, in its infancy; it was not Stone's famous sexuality she saw reflected in this small redheaded child, but her determination.

When the adult Lindsay Lohan tries to seem sincere or sweet, it reads as phoney, but when she plays furious and hard-nosed – like Bette Davis in a Rita Hayworth body, or Barbara Stanwyck if Barbara Stanwyck had multiple DUIs and a cracked iPhone – some power still remains, even in her later work. 'Her weakness is her inability to fake it,' Paul Schrader once said, after working with her on 2013's *The Canyons*. 'She feels she must be experiencing an emotion in order to play it. This leads to all sorts of emotional turmoil, not to mention on-set delays and melodrama. It also leads, when the gods smile, to movie magic.' It did not often feel as though the gods had smiled on Lindsay Lohan in the noughties, but that magic burned through sometimes nonetheless, albeit with less and less frequency as she grew older and more jaded, and as the intervention of the fates in her affairs seemed increasingly unkind. As her jadedness developed, so did her affinity for darker scenes, the bright screwball comedienne of 2004's *Mean Girls* transmogrifying into the tabloid fodder bitch who, in 2012, reportedly punched a psychic in the face. 'I grew up really fast,' a twenty-four-year-old Lohan informed Nancy Jo Sales in a 2010 interview for *Vanity Fair*, 'just because of the situations I was subjected to because of my father.' Those of us who had been closely following her exploits did not need to be told twice.

'The things that girls must do,' Lohan tweeted the same year that *Vanity Fair* profile was released. 'If you only knew.' She did not have to tell us this twice, either. Fans had been familiar with many of the things Lohan had done, or had chosen not to do, since she was in her late teens, largely because she had done them all in public, and because voracious tabloid coverage had recorded them for whatever the obverse of posterity is. A car crash – now a common metaphor for a woman with a self-destructive streak – compels rubberneckers precisely because the sight of it provokes a feeling of alarming nearness to its heat, and people do not hesitate to warm their hands on Lindsay Lohan's blazing reputation, nor to fan its flames by pointing to her worst mistakes. (Number of times that Lindsay Lohan has attended rehab, according to Google: more than six. Number of times that Lindsay Lohan has done cocaine, according to Lindsay Lohan: not more than ten or fifteen.) For almost as long as I've been writing about women and celebrity, Lindsay Lohan has been a personal touchstone for me, a fact that I once explained by citing her precocious skill, and which I am now more likely to elucidate by pointing out that she is representative of a millennial obsession with early-life promise and adult disaster. The enduring and memetic popularity of famous women whose once-dazzling careers have clattered downhill at tremendous speed at one time or another suggests a vicarious thrill at the explosive, public way they waste themselves. In a child, a gift like Lohan's can seem gloriously preordained, almost holy; in an adult star who has more DUIs than Oscar nominations, it begins to look more like a wasted opportunity. In the case of 'a great talent with a really sexy voice' per Robert Altman, not to mention 'a terrific actress' in the eyes of Meryl Streep, this egregious squandering of talent felt like the equivalent of flicking a lit cigarette at the gas tank of a Porsche.

Jane Fonda, who played opposite Lindsay Lohan in the 2006 film *Georgia Rule*, once said that she wished that she could take her in her arms and simply 'hold her until she becomes [a] grown-up'. 'She's so young and she's so alone out there in the world in terms of structure and, you know, people to nurture her,' Fonda sighed to the *Los Angeles Daily News* that year. 'And she's so talented.' *Georgia Rule*, a film by Garry Marshall in which Lohan plays a cynical and clever teenage girl with a knack for promiscuity and a sexually abusive stepfather, may be one of the most tonally confusing family comedies ever made – it balances incestuous rape with slapstick, alcoholism and generational trauma with erection gags, and perhaps most bizarrely, a clutch of broad, small-town Mormon kooks with raw, serious central performances by Lindsay Lohan and Jane Fonda. It was arguably the first film in which Lohan played a character whose outward qualities closely aligned with those of her then-troubled public image; even her appearance carries the suggestion of a person still caught on the brink of growing up, her abdominals as taut as those of a Victoria's Secret model and her facial features cushioned by a touching layer of baby fat. Her thousand-a-day rumble, once wholly incongruous with her person, comes into its own, suggesting the kind of hoarseness that arises from whispering so as not to be discovered, or from screaming out in anger or in ecstasy. She proves herself to be an innately physical onscreen presence, a master at commanding her own lazy, sexy, bratty body language – at her best, it is as if her voice and form share a synesthetic sameness, one art translated into two mediums, until she begins to sound like a cigarette clamped between fake-tanned fingers, or a pair of bronzed legs propped up on a convertible dashboard.

If Lindsay Lohan is not and has never been two women in the strictest sense, audiences might be forgiven for believing something different: twice now, she has multiplied herself onscreen, repeating the neat, bifurcating trick of her performance in *The Parent Trap* for a brassy, brainless adult thriller called *I Know Who Killed Me* in 2007. This time, playing twins splits her like an atom going nuclear, or a middle and an index finger signing out 'fuck you': she is both Aubrey Fleming, a piano-playing ingénue in glasses who writes bad, short fiction about bad, lost women, and Dakota Moss, a stripper with an attitude as filthy as her mouth, and it is obvious from the jump which of the two estranged sisters Lohan finds it easiest to bring to life. Her work as Dakota seems expressly designed to serve as an announcement that – in this decade, at least – she no longer wanted to belong to any Mickey Mouse Club that would have her as a member. A fan of the films of David Lynch, the film's writer-director Chris Sivertson conjures red rooms and blue roses, and the guidance of a group of owls; a man who masturbates a log; a killer who makes weapons out of glass. What he has forgotten is to put the 'psych' in 'psychosexual mystery', so that what's mysterious isn't necessarily that deep. The owls, here, are exactly what they seem. The girls are, too – a 50/50 representative of sex and scholarship, virtue and vice, like illustrations from a child's picture book about opposites that for some reason features copious use of the word 'slut'.

'She knew a trick,' Aubrey writes in one of her interminable, auto-fictional short stories. 'She knew how to turn her life into a movie, and watch things happen. Not to her, but to a girl who looked just like her ... She always felt like half a person. Half a person with half a soul. Sometimes, if she dreamed hard enough, she could bring the two halves together. But she always awoke with the same feeling of loneliness and loss.' Because Aubrey at this point has no idea she has a twin, she believes the girl 'who look[s] just like her' she imagines sometimes – in what turn out to be psychic visions – is another version of herself, an alternate personality with dyed black hair and a dark lifestyle. Where Aubrey is polite and virginal and sweet, Dakota is a nihilistic nymphomaniac; where Aubrey longs to make her money with her mind, Dakota makes it with her body. Aubrey grew up in the suburbs in a loving, all-American family; Dakota's crackhead biological mother 'ODed, *duh*'.

Lohan's casting in this dual role is, in other words, extravagantly meta, not only because she first achieved fame playing identical sisters, but because she herself has performed some version of these archetypes in public, and because throughout the noughties and the 2010s, it occasionally felt as though she was being dogged by a shadow-Lohan who was hellbent on destroying her career – as if, having ritually killed off her child-actress self, she was struggling to prevent her adult incarnation from cleaving, sometimes messily, in half. 'Unfortunately,' as a writer put it at the *Daily Beast* in 2017, 'the life that Lohan would like to live is frequently undermined by Lindsay Lohan herself.' This second Lindsay is the one who, allegedly drunk and apparently desperate for the contact high of true A-List celebrity, once drove recklessly down Mulholland Drive at 2 a.m. to see Jack

Nicholson; who buzzed the intercom for half an hour; who endlessly requested, 'Jack, open the gate, Jack, open the gate,' until he did; who left three hours later, wrecked like a starlet's Maserati in the canyon. She is certainly the Lindsay who was accused of shoplifting that two-thousand-dollar necklace even though she was, at that time, a legitimately famous person; the one who ensured that the other Lindsay never got to work on time – who made her uninsurable, and mean with nausea, and incapable of saying sorry without making an excuse.

One imagines that the Lindsay Lohan who believed she'd have an Oscar by the age of thirty must have sometimes watched this other Lindsay with the kind of dissociative distance reserved for seeing things occur not to yourself, but to a girl who looks just like you, feeling loss and loneliness as well as horror. Perhaps all former child stars are forced to develop split personalities, duelling selves – more so, even, than those who enter Hollywood as adults. One of the industry's very first child stars was Baby Peggy, née Diana Serra Cary, who became a star of silent cinema in her infancy, and who was nicknamed 'Million Dollar Baby' after her $1.5 million annual salary (roughly $25.6 million now). By the age of five, Cary was so popular that she had a sprawling range of merchandise, from Baby Peggy dolls to Baby Peggy-endorsed milk; her film career ended abruptly shortly after she turned seven, in 1925, after her stuntman father had a falling-out with a producer and her contract with the studio was cancelled. When the actor and filmmaker Alex Winter met Cary for a 2020 documentary, *Showbiz*

Kids – with Cary now a full century old – he told *The New Yorker* that although at first she had insisted that her early life had not been traumatising, she eventually admitted to suffering a full-blown nervous breakdown at the tail-end of her teens. 'The identity that I constructed for myself [as a child star],' she told Winter, 'was a false identity. And when it shattered, I didn't have an underlying identity to replace it with.' 'It was almost as if you had ceased to be alive [in your teens],' she says in the resulting documentary, quietly. 'You were adorable, you were wanted, you were loved, and then one day, just when [you] were becoming [a] full adult human being, [you] were told: you're finished.'

In general, stars are loved for impermanent attributes – little in life is as reliably fleeting as youth, and beauty, too, is ephemeral as hell, as hard to guarantee as it is to rationalise or explain. Elizabeth Taylor, that 'great natural wonder', struggled with her weight across the course of her career, the impossible task of being perfect butting up against the universal fact of getting older, and of having a natural tendency towards soft, fertile-looking lushness. Indulging like a civilian made her look, in the eyes of the gossip press, more like a civilian, and the result was that she spent many years apparently at war with herself, fighting her own proclivity for cream and sugar just as Lindsay Lohan fought her desire for self-destruction. In truth, both women have done their fair share of time in rehab; both have looked at times like someone other than themselves, either because of surgery or weight gain or weight loss or some other more inexplicable change in their usual image. No woman remains one continuous version of herself, year by year or day by day, however talented her surgeon, however well-paid her stylist, however devoted her personal trainer and dietician.

'Like [Bette] Davis,' the film critic David Thompson wrote in Elizabeth Taylor's 2011 obituary for the *Guardian*, on the subject of her contradictory selves, 'Taylor was monster and empress, sweetheart and scold, idiot and wise woman. We went in awe of her, but with one word or a knowing smile she assured us she was one of us. So beautiful, she could go crazy, too – and then move on.' Taylor's Monster-Empress status is in some ways typified by the two roles she won Best Actress Oscars for, the second of which – after her sixties turn as a gorgeously movie-fied sex worker in *BUtterfield 8* – was that of Martha, the bitter and alcoholic spouse of a professor in Mike Nichols' 1966 *Who's Afraid of Virginia Woolf?* Adapted from a play by Edward Albee, *Woolf* already had a reputation as a vicious, modern text full of vicious, modern language, laced with profanity and sexual innuendo, making it an ostensibly unusual project for Taylor and Burton, who ended up playing Martha's henpecked, impotent husband George alongside his real-life wife. Her performance is magnificent: ripe, furious, not so much a rebuttal of her former image as the world's loveliest woman as the casual detonation of it. Martha is not ugly in any conceivable sense of the word, at least as far as her exterior is concerned, but her ruthlessness and unpredictability make her compellingly loathsome. When she proclaims herself to be 'the Earth Mother', it feels right because the natural world itself is, despite often being beautiful, undeniably savage: red, which nature is 'in tooth and claw' per Tennyson, is a maternal, menstrual colour as well as a supposedly fiery one, and although *Woolf* is in black and white, we know instantly that the lipstick Martha wears when she comes back downstairs in her flashiest, trashiest outfit must be crimson, jezebel-bright and excessive. As in *Cat on a Hot Tin Roof*, in which she played a woman incapable of seducing her closeted husband, there was a deliberate, heavily implied perversion in the casting of a world-conquering sexual goddess like Elizabeth Taylor as a desperate and desperately un-fucked woman, just as there was a deliberate, heavily implied perversion in the very idea of Richard Burton playing a cowed, bespectacled eunuch. Burton and Taylor loved to verbally spar in private, and there must have been a thrill inherent in seeing Taylor sound out ugly words with those famous rosebud lips – in watching her iconic violet eyes fill up with fury until they were hot and lambent with it, glittering like gemstones set into her perfect face. In *Virginia Woolf*, though, the couple engaged in a different kind of conflict, neutered and unpleasant. There would be no make-up sex, one sensed, unless it took the abstract form of screaming. 'Martha completely took me over. When I left the set, I couldn't take off my Martha suit,' Taylor recalled in her book *An Informal Memoir*. 'Richard and I would be out with friends and I'd hear myself saying to him, "For Chrissakes, shut up. I'm not finished talking." And then the next morning, I would think, "That wasn't me, it was Martha." I had to fight to regain myself.'

'Elizabeth Taylor is the prettiest girl in the world,' *The New York Times* review of *An Informal Memoir* began, nodding to the fact that this was a truth universally acknowledged, 'and no gentleman would quibble about where a girl leaves off and a woman begins. A pretty girl is allowed reticences.' In contrast to the tone of her book, the whole point of Taylor playing Martha was that it was a real opportunity for her to show no reticence at all, and although she had left off as a girl and begun as a woman practically at birth, this felt like a new shift altogether. It was less that Taylor had gone Method than that she had somehow used the opportunity to exorcise her inner Martha, to face head-on the imagined future conjured up by judgemental gossip columnists – the beauty gone to seed, the shrill harridan who drove off men, the has-been with the too-big tits – and had turned it into greatness, into art. Here was another case of furious psychic splitting – but this time, rather than damaging her reputation or her mental health or both, it paid critical and artistic dividends. If she never again equalled that performance, it is arguable that she never needed to in order to secure her place in the pantheon of cinematic brilliance. Burton often said he learned how to behave in front of a camera from his wife; that because he had been used to acting on the stage when he first began making films, he had looked at her on set and found her frustratingly quiet and still, only to realise when he watched the footage back that she had simply learned to radiate emotion without physically emoting all the way up to the gods. Watch her playing Martha, and at first it is difficult to imagine this being true as she bulldozes and rails her way across the screen. Listen, though, for the subtler, more plangent notes beneath the din, minor and breviloquent but inarguably present. She is hiding fear beneath her anger, and the anger cannot fully drown it out.

To bear the strain of tapping into this deep horror, one imagines it is necessary to be good at compartmentalising for self-preservation. Fail to do so in the right way, and you run the risk of being lost forever. The terrible bind of examining Lindsay Lohan's best adult performances – many of which are limited to discrete moments in dud movies, owing to the dearth of good material she's been provided with since she turned roughly twenty – is that all of them tend to feed on her inner well of suffering, and to be further electrified by her defiance in the face of bad luck and bad treatment and, yes, her own bad behaviour. It is undoubtedly true that she should not have had to suffer through the slings and arrows of outrageously unfortunate and fucked-up tabloid coverage in order to develop this ability to channel pain; to present herself as if her body had been stripped of all its freckled skin to expose her bare nerves. Still, all great actors are not just celebrities, but artists, and at one time Lohan certainly had the potential to become one of the greatest artists in her field, and of her era. Referring to 'the gaps that Lohan's travails have torn in her career and the holes they have likely torn in her psyche' in 2012, *The New Yorker* critic Richard Brody argued that 'her very presence comes packed with an intensity and an anguish that perhaps no other actor of her generation can offer, regardless of technical skill'. 'Other young actresses with other talents have come to the fore,' he writes elsewhere, 'but none has her distinctive blend of voracity and innocence, of will and vulnerability; her performances haven't been missing from movies we've seen, but, rather, movies meant for her haven't been made.' By 2012, perhaps the best example of this quality being permitted to fully express itself had been a single scene in *Georgia Rule*, in which a nobly widowed veterinarian played by Dermot Mulroney informs Lohan's character, as the two sit at a picnic table at a country fete, that she doesn't 'have a clue about surviving'. Mistaken for *just a girl*, an innocent and thus a fool, she is incensed; her eyes flash with icy malice. 'And you invented it, didn't you?' she snaps. 'We can all tell. The survivor. You wear it so well in your walk, in your face, in your eyes. You've got a dead wife and a dead baby. And we're all so proud you're still even here. Do you know I was twelve years old when my stepfather first started having sex with me? I *loved* him. He was *nice* to me. We can all survive, *Simon*. You just don't have to be so damn sad doing it.'

By turns cruel and wounded, childlike and profane, Lohan's portrayal of a teen sharpening her hurt into a sleek, defensive weapon feels almost too charged to watch. If the actress did not have any idea of what it might feel like to have been sexually abused, she certainly knew how it felt to be surveilled from the tender age of twelve, and to be reduced to her sexuality before that sexuality had even fully taken shape. When Disney were rumoured to have shrunk her breasts onscreen for the 2005 kiddie comedy *Herbie: Reloaded*, this probably apocryphal suggestion carried within it a sly implication that the barely legal Lohan's chest might otherwise draw too much focus from a certain segment of the population – dads, perhaps, attending with their children, more interested in the va-va-voom of the teen redhead in the driver's seat than in the talking car. In 2009, the former owner of the famous New York strip joint Scores, Elliot Osher, told the *New York Daily News* that Lohan's father was a regular, and that he had very specific tastes. '[He] sat down and described the kind of dancer he was looking for,' Osher claims. 'We sent some girls over. Funny, they all seemed to look like Lindsay.' True or not, the anecdote is certainly *funny*, if not necessarily funny ha-ha, and its publication must have stung her either way. All told, choosing to be a party girl in lieu of being a straightforward victim of the media was Lohan's own way of wearing her survival 'in [her] walk, in [her] face [and] in [her] eyes' without being 'so damn sad doing it'. If she wanted to put in appearances at so-called Bimbo Summits, or to fall down drinking at Les Deux, or to appear in court with 'FUK U' written on her middle fingernail in small, delicate letters, well, at least nobody had won by betting on her in the *National Enquirer*'s death pool yet.

'I'm impatient to see [the then-forthcoming] *The Canyons*,' Brody also wrote in 2012, 'in which she will have the vast benefit of Paul Schrader's direction – and in which the director has the great chance to work, with Lohan, a big-screen reconfiguration on the exemplary paradigm of what Quentin Tarantino achieved with John Travolta in *Pulp Fiction*.' Those of us who had hoped for brilliance from 2013's *The Canyons*, on Lohan's part and on Schrader's, were ultimately left wanting – sometimes amusingly camp, sometimes interestingly chilly, the film nevertheless remains curiously un-transgressive when it comes to sex and violence, and its satire is as flaccid as its onscreen cocks. The screenplay, written by Bret Easton Ellis in his own inimitable half-clinical, half-lobotomised style, presents a challenge for almost all of the actors who appear in it, from the now-disgraced adult star James Deen to the featherlight performers who make up all of the rest of the film's parts. Lohan, though, makes something admirably truthful out of Easton Ellis' unnatural dialogue – she does not so much spit acid as allow it to drool slowly from her mouth, and her luscious blend of jadedness and savagery elevates what might be soap opera material into a millennial take on a classic Tennessee Williams lush. In *The Canyons*, she's an ageing diva who is barely twenty-six, a mini-Martha – hissing, flexing, pouting, vogueing horribly with her smokes. 'Lindsay,' as Schrader put it delicately at a Q&A in New York, 'is out of her ingénue period.' Because of her insistence on doing her hair and make-up by herself, she appears to belong in an entirely different movie from the people she is acting alongside, and that movie is quite possibly a blue one. Her foundation, thick and orange, is a mask; her cat eyes, inspired by Elizabeth Taylor's *Cleopatra* look, are outrageous, looking as if it might take paint-stripper to remove them. (We might call the adult picture Lohan is made up for *Cleo, Nympho of the Nile*.) Her character, Tara, is an actress who is bored with cinema, and furthermore with life itself – she has a voice like tyres on gravel headed for a steep escarpment, and an affect that radiates both power and terror, like a predator and also like an animal predated.

'Okay, tell me something,' Tara asks a friend she's out at brunch with, Lohan barely holding back a smirk at the obviousness of the screenplay. 'Do you really like movies? Really, *really* like movies? When's the last time you went to see a movie in the theatre? ... Not premieres. Premieres don't count. I don't know, I guess maybe it's just not my thing anymore.' It does not take a leap of imagination to interpret Schrader's use of static shots of derelict movie theatres in *The Canyons*' credits not only as a metonym for cinema itself, but as a mirror for Lindsay Lohan, who was also underused by 2013, but who nevertheless remained iconic and profoundly cinematic, touched with the perma-dignity of something once held to be indisputably majestic. There is something of *Virginia Woolf* in the dynamic of the movie's central quartet, with two all-American innocents set to be corrupted by the two furious, warlike leads, and *The Canyons* seems to be about the corruption of 'real' values by hollower, meaner ones in general. It posits that true art is helpless in the face of self-absorption and self-interest and, perhaps most importantly, the internet. 'I guess I'd like to keep some parts of my life private,' Lohan's Tara hisses, in a lovers' quarrel. 'Nobody has a private life anymore, Tara,' her sadistic boyfriend shoots back, talking to her as if she's an idiotic child. Already, by the time Elizabeth Taylor had ascended to the peak of her international fame, the idea of celebrities getting to have truly private 'private lives' had begun to seem antiquated, even if ordinary people were not yet under the microscope in the same way; by 2013, the phones in our hands and pockets, just like the ones that facilitate the stalking and the hook-ups and the double-crosses in *The Canyons*, ensured that very few of us had complete privacy in any traditional sense, and that stars were treated more than ever like commodities.

In an exposé of Lohan's rampant naughtiness disguised as on-set coverage of *The Canyons*, *The New York Times*' Stephen Rodrick describes witnessing a scene of such bathetic and discomfiting intensity that it is, frankly, quite surprising that it did not generate more discussion online at the time. 'Deen came to life,' he writes about a rough assault scene in the film, 'throwing the negligée-wearing Lohan hard to the ground and pounding his fist into a wall with such fury I wondered if he had broken his hand. Lohan lay slumped on the floor, her hands guarding her face, shoulders shaking, tears pouring down her cheeks . . . [After shooting] someone complimented her work. "Well," [she said], "I've got a lot of experience with that from my dad." She didn't elaborate, and no one asked.' The gulf between the things that Lohan was frequently asked about, or at least the thing that generated interest from the public and the press – her sex life, her addictions, her jail time, her failures and her fallings-out – and the aspects of her life that arguably should have been interrogated for the sake of her own happiness and safety suddenly felt ultra-apparent. If we are not asking famous women how they really feel, how are they supposed to tell us? As privacy vanishes for them, so that every pose, every trip out of the house and every drink is documented, and as all these things are judged with unreasonable harshness, it must feel increasingly hard to freely express oneself while being *oneself*. Better to be somebody else who looks just like you, but is not you. Give in to your sickest impulses while in a nightclub, and the world will call you 'whore' or 'junkie'; give in to them under the legitimising cover of a role, and you may yet win an Oscar. If an actress feels she cannot speak to us directly, she may still be able to be truthful with us through her work.

After *The Canyons*, Lindsay Lohan stood at the convergence of two roads that led into the future. Ultimately, she did not select the one that might have let her exorcise her demons through her craft. Between 2013 and 2021, her CV contained nothing but bit-parts in TV comedies, roles in shorts that almost nobody had heard of, and a lead performance in a low-rent horror film as a detective who was also a werewolf; briefly, she opened a holiday resort in Mykonos, and appeared in a little-seen reality show about the venture. Partly, she lacked work because her behaviour on-set and off-set made her uninsurable. Partly, it was that she wanted something nobody was going to offer: although she might once have revived her career by taking her rebellious streak and her seen-it-all, ex-Mouseketeer mien to the arthouse to appear in something like *Spring Breakers*, she did not seem willing to give up on the opportunity of having one more shot at a new *Mean Girls*. In the winter of 2022, she re-emerged from her hiatus to appear in a festive romcom made for Netflix called *Falling for Christmas*. In it, she plays Sierra Belmont, a hotel heiress whose name is a spoof of Paris Hilton's. Sierra is as fawned over and cosseted as a beloved lapdog; her job, if she can be said to have any job at all, is to be attended to by a small coterie of terrified assistants, who spend every morning spooning caviar into her open mouth and, one senses, nervously anticipating any temper tantrums. Early in the film, she tumbles down a mountain, hits her head, and then awakes with no memory of her name, no memory of her former status, and too little sense to resist the romantic overtures of an uninteresting, stolid man. Workshy and impetuous, exacting in the manner of a person on the edge, pre-injury Sierra is a very PG take on the former image of the woman who portrays her, and accordingly when we eventually see her transform from an out-of-touch rich chick into a compassionate would-be wife-and-mother, we are meant to see the alteration as reflective of a shift in Lohan's image, too. 'She's never been arrested,' the sheriff notes when explaining why Sierra has no fingerprints on file, before issuing another meta-judgement: 'And possibly never been employed.'

Here, it feels a little as if the film is suggesting that we undergo our own bout of amnesia with regards to the old Lindsay Lohan, seeing her anew as a fresh-faced Hallmark heroine: plucky, squeaky clean, and so outwardly asexual that even the children she eventually produces might as well have been conceived immaculately. Offscreen, Lohan married, and she and her husband had a baby. In November 2023, she appeared in an ad for Walmart that spoofed *Mean Girls*, and in doing so offered audiences a glimpse of a Lohan whose life had run on a parallel track, as if she were the real Lohan's good, piano-practising, short-story-writing twin – glowing like a woman with a genius aesthetician, her hair back to its usual red, she looked more or less exactly as we might have pictured the middle-aged Lindsay Lohan to look when we'd seen her onscreen as a teenager, and her fleeting onscreen moments had a comic snap. A second romcom for Netflix, *Irish Wish*, was released; then a third, also set at Christmas, *Our Little Secret*. By late 2024, a *Freaky Friday* sequel had been announced, suggesting that Lohan might finally be getting the Disneyfied comeback she had yearned for ever since *The Canyons*, in spite of her vérité performance, did not win her an Oscar nomination. It is only humane to want this particular Lindsay Lohan to endure, given that she appears to be healthier than ever, and that, as far as anyone knows, she is content, and sober, and at peace. As a cinephile, though, it is difficult not to miss the full-throttle Lindsay of her past: the girl who'd evidently seen too much but also seemed perpetually in need of seeing – of consuming, ever-famished – even more. Paul Schrader, who admits himself that *The Canyons* did not end up being his best work, produced perhaps the finest film of his career in 2017, with *First Reformed*, and one wonders what he might have been able to do with Lohan if rather than hiring Bret Easton Ellis, he had written her a movie of his own. 'She is so fucking charismatic,' he sighed in an interview with the *Independent* in 2014, even as he admitted that she was a liability. 'You can't take your eyes off her. She has that thing that we watch in movies.'

If Lohan had to be the reincarnation of either Marilyn Monroe or Elizabeth Taylor, Taylor, who lived into old age and remained beloved, was undoubtedly the wisest choice. Still, after *Who's Afraid Of Virginia Woolf?*, even Taylor's screen career did not reach the same heights again, and as with Lohan, part of this came down to the immovable, iconic image of her that had firmly lodged itself in the imagination of the public. By the mid to late sixties, 'Elizabeth Taylor was just too famous to disappear into another character, and her lush, glossy appearance and increasingly voluptuous figure made her unsuited to play the newly emerging American woman who came into being in the "swinging 1960s",' Kashner writes in *Furious Love*. 'By the age of thirty-two, with five marriages, four children, thirty-one films, and world infamy behind her, she simply had too much history to play a "new woman". She was a queen, and there would be few queenly roles for women in the next three decades.' *Woolf*, for which she'd tapped into her raging id, had been a lucky exception to the rule, at least in Kashner's estimation. In fact, the suggestion that her quasi-retirement from the screen had been due to a lack of 'queenly roles' may not have pleased Taylor all that much, as evidenced by a 2011 interview she granted Kim Kardashian in *Harper's Bazaar*. When Kardashian asks her for advice on 'how to be a queen', riffing on her role in *Cleopatra*, Taylor demurs, exclaiming that she 'never wanted to be' one in the first place. 'The real Cleopatra had an incredibly complicated life,' she adds, 'and she had to be very, very canny to survive as long as she did.' The canniest thing that Taylor did was to spend the length of her career building her image into that of something other than a queen – more specifically, a diva, who by definition is still worshipped by her public even when her mainstream popularity has passed its apex. This kind of divadom tends to spring from a certain commitment to remote glamour, so that even if the star in question chooses to disclose certain facts about her personal or sexual life, she somehow manages to do so without ever seeming genuinely messy.

Perhaps it is more challenging to be a diva in this classic sense, as opposed to in the pejorative sense that is effectively a synonym for 'total bitch', in the age of the internet, when mysteriousness is harder still to cultivate: a Google search for 'Lindsay Lohan diva' returns 2.25 million results, but most of them refer to her 'setting the record straight' about whether or not she has ever displayed 'diva-like' attributes on-set, or to Oprah Winfrey saying 'fuck' on-air when lecturing her about 'diva behaviour'. As each of them matured in the eye of a newly blazing storm of paradigm-shifting and invasive coverage, Taylor and Lohan fixed their personas in stone in different ways. Taylor did it by becoming so aware of the gaze of the paparazzi that she began to perform for them as diligently, if defiantly, as she did for her directors; Lohan did it by behaving as if she were utterly impervious or indifferent to them, so that she had no qualms about coming across like a demented millennial hellion. 'When confronted with the gale force winds of Lindsay Lohan,' Paul Schrader told *Deadline* in 2014, 'people just can't resist.' His awestruck, primal language is indicative of both Lohan's greatest asset as an artist, and her biggest handicap as a commercial prospect. Her storied, public damage and wild, irresistible screen presence are inextricably linked, and it remains to be seen whether her recent push to rebrand as a wholesome romcom heroine will improve her reputation, and if so, whether that alteration also snuffs out the most vital quality in her work.

Choose the 'good' self, and be happy; choose the 'bad' self, and be brilliant. This is a simplification of the matter, and yet in the case of stars who wear their histories like second-skin couture, it feels uncomfortably accurate. If she is to be reborn, reincarnated as a nicer and more palatable star, it can only be hoped that she retains, or rekindles, at least a touch of her earlier dangerous heat. 'I think back like, "Oh my God, did I act like that? Ten years ago?"' Lohan said in an interview in 2018. I knew when she said 'act', she was talking about bad behaviour. Still, it did not keep me from thinking about how she used to act onscreen, the way that even barely flexing, in repose, she could be moving – so beautiful even though, or perhaps because, she could go crazy, too.

7

Some Damnbody Is Always Trying to Embalm Me

On Amy Winehouse and Billie Holiday

I. A ROMANTIC IN THE GRAVEST, SADDEST, BEST AND MOST RIDICULOUS SENSE

Three things make it the afterimage of Amy Winehouse that I still hold in my mind, more than a decade after hearing of her death. The first is her stance, a lean that suggests a woman propped up in a dive bar at three in the afternoon, nowhere to be and in no hurry to be served. The second is the one-two punch of those first lyrics – rhyming 'regret' with 'kept his dick wet' – which are sad and then all of a sudden very funny, very filthy, and thus quintessentially her. The third is of course that voice, and in particular the ease with which it leaves her tiny body, the smoothness of the action only further emphasised by the absolute audacity of that insouciant lean. Winehouse is recording 'Back to Black', a single from her 2006 album of the same name, in a clip that is perhaps best known from the 2015 documentary *Amy*, and we are watching her draw art from the very deepest part of herself with such little effort that we know the trick cannot last; that repeating it in perpetuity will leech something from her that can never be replenished. When the song is over, she is silent for no more than a few seconds, but her face in those few seconds is that of a person who is exiting a trance. She is twenty-three years old, and in four years she will be dead, killed by a return to alcohol after a period of sobriety, and by the weakening of her body from bulimia. For now, she just grins and turns to Mark Ronson, her producer, and says, lightly: 'It's a bit upsetting at the end, isn't it?'

Winehouse's story was more than a bit upsetting long before the end, but there was glory in it, too, and she was good at making something gorgeous out of hurt at any rate. Some of the pain in her voice was borrowed from the Black American jazz and soul singers whom she so admired, and the borrowing of that pain by a woman like Amy Winehouse was correctly seen by music journalists as problematic – as the trying-on of a costume that a white girl had no business wearing in the first place. Some of it, though, was real, as bone-deep and undeniable as her voice, and that true pain kept her from ever sounding actually phoney. The writer Nick Tosches once said of the late music critic Lester Bangs that he was 'a romantic in the gravest, saddest, best and most ridiculous sense of that worn-out word'. I believe she was that, too, and I believe it was why she could sing like a person who had suffered something. She seemed to belong to another time, which might help to explain why she could not bring herself to stay in ours for very long. One of the great running themes of *Amy* is her need, the great aching pit of it in her gut, and the way that it keeps encouraging her lovers to describe her as unfeminine. 'You're like a powerful man,' one ex-boyfriend tells her, and when her ex-husband Blake Fielder-Civil talks about her storied sex life, he says that her promiscuity made her 'like a man', too. When Bobby Womack introduces her for a performance of the song 'Stronger Than Me', he refers to it as 'Stronger Than Men', a bit of accidental editorialising that feels somehow far more complimentary than either of her exes' observations. Having a guitar slung across her body, she said in a promotional interview for Fender in 2004, felt 'akin to having a dick'. 'When I go on-stage and I've got a guitar, I feel like no one can touch me,' she continued, grinning. 'It's all my strength *here*. It represents the music that's inside me, but external. I guess that's why it's like having a dick: it's like myself but out.' Later in her career, as she became more successful and began to find herself being marketed more like a pop idol than a rock musician, she rarely appeared with a guitar, allegedly at the instruction of her label. One wonders whether for her, this might have felt like a symbolic castration: all her strength no longer *here* where she could feel it, but in someone else's hands – a loss of power that was reflected in the self-conscious, compensatory way she made her hair bigger and bigger, and her personal style ever more feminine and outré.

The double-bind of Winehouse's voice was that it was not only good enough to give her what she wanted most – a reputation as a jazz singer for the ages – but also good enough to ensure that she almost instantly surpassed the level of public recognition she was built to withstand. If she did not stop or shy away, it was because she had no idea how to stop wanting, even as the things she got proved terrible for her. More love, more romance, more yearning, more passion, more sex, more drink, more drugs; not more fame, necessarily, but *better* fame, better songs played in better venues for an audience who could understand her references, her genius. Amy Winehouse ached for all these things with such focus and intensity that the heat of her desire was too much for her to bear. She is one of only two celebrities whose death has made me cry, with the other being David Bowie. Part of this, I think, was for youthful, embarrassingly solipsistic reasons: Amy and I knew, however tenuously, some of the same people; we made what I might euphemistically describe as some of the same mistakes; we were just five years apart in age. I did not know what it was like to be able to produce something casually ecstatic with my body the way Winehouse did when she sang, and I did not know what it would be like for the very thing that you loved most in the world, your gift and purpose, to eventually become the thing that hung you out to dry. I did know, though, what it was like to be a woman in her twenties with the constitution and the appetites of, for want of a better phrase, an old-school male artist. It was like this: alongside the urge to chase art and pleasure, you felt an equal and commensurate urge to chase it harder than anyone else around, and in doing so to prove that you could be, as Bobby Womack put it with his fitting little slip of the tongue, stronger than men. (Drinking alcohol, as well as taking certain other substances, might also be said to help facilitate the act of being 'like [your]self but out'.)

Mostly though, I was so bereft on learning that she'd died because, quite simply, it was always evident that she was special. Who among us heard that voice and did not feel the same? It helped that she did not look like a classic starlet, or really like anyone else you might see on television or in mainstream music videos, and that this difference only served to enhance her offbeat eroticism. I don't know that I would ever say that Amy Winehouse had been 'pretty', largely because it seems to me to be impossible for someone to be 'pretty' and also be swaggeringly sexy. I might say that she was handsome, a word that does not mean the same thing for a woman as it does for a man – consider that Mick Jagger mouth, that lioness nose, those brown eyes that widened with sardonic disapproval every time an interviewer underestimated her, all of it conspiring to produce a face that seemed to move in every direction at once, rubbery and fantastic. When she smiled, the smile itself seemed to take up roughly one-third of her head, and on seeing it you understood how badly you would like to make her laugh. Her mordant, gobby wit made her, when she remained sober enough to function properly, panel-show gold. 'When she showed up for our first [recording] session she was wearing a pair of jeans that had completely fallen apart with "I Love Sinatra" embroidered on the arse. That's so Amy. I just fell in love with her,' the producer Felix Howard told the *Guardian* in 2004. 'Also, she has the power to scare the shit out of very seasoned, salty jazz people. I was doing her session with some very serious players. And when she started singing, they were like, "Jesus Christ!"' *Jesus Christ* is more or less what I thought when I saw that clip of her in the booth with Mark Ronson, unleashing her magnificence with the unbothered nonchalance of a yawn. It was not that she was made to be a star, exactly. It was that the firmament of stardom was in sore need of an Amy Winehouse, as if she had done celebrity itself the favour and not the other way around.

One of the Black American jazz singers whose pain Winehouse occasionally adopted in a bit of vocal burlesque, slipping it on like a pair of bloodstained ballet pumps, was Billie Holiday – also a titanic vocalist; also a titanic heroin addict; also a voracious fan of men; also dead far too young for her own good and, more importantly, far too young for ours. Bowie, that other much-missed star, used the phrase 'plastic soul' to describe his own forays into such music, reasoning that his efforts were a step removed from authentic soul music as a result of having been written and performed 'by a white limey'. Winehouse was a white limey, too: a working-class North Londoner with Jewish roots. 'I'm like an old Jewish man,' she once told an interviewer, and although she was talking about her music taste at the time, the observation did not feel entirely inaccurate in a more general sense. She certainly took after one particular old

Jewish woman: her beloved paternal grandmother Cynthia, a former nightclub singer whose romantic history included a dalliance with the saxophonist and nightclub owner Ronnie Scott. As for the 'man' part, aside from all of her previously mentioned credentials in relation to the culturally accepted definition of machismo, she often felt that she'd inherited her father's wandering eye – his tendency towards philandering and faithlessness, family be damned. Of course, her struggle with the fallout of her parents' acrimonious divorce paled in comparison to the many trials of a figure like Billie Holiday: another working-class woman, yes, but one whose formative experiences also included government-mandated racial segregation, physical and sexual violence, and adolescent sex work. Still, like Bowie, Winehouse approached traditionally Black music with genuine reverence, and she studied her musical heroes with a dedication that bordered on the academic. Some of the biggest influences on her vocal style were not even vocalists at all – she often said that she listened to Thelonious Monk in order to figure out the way her voice should move, and this makes sense when you listen to her live performances, in which she treats the melody as something mutable, feeling her way through the song rather than following its on-record structure.

Billie Holiday, as it happens, once said something very similar about her own inspirations. 'I don't think I'm singing,' she wrote (or had ghost-written for her, at least) in her 1956 memoir *Lady Sings the Blues*. 'I feel like I'm playing a horn. I try to improvise like Les Young, like Louis Armstrong, or someone else I admire.' Learning from another artist you are moved by is a rite of passage for a person who performs for a living, although the line between mimicry and homage can be dangerously thin. 'Her deliberate affectation of Holiday's unmistakable vocal tics can't help but suggest the narrative we're supposed to buy into,' an especially mean-spirited review of the American reissue of Amy Winehouse's debut album, *Frank*, suggested in 2007. If Winehouse's borrowing of certain familiar vocal techniques was more obvious on this first record, it is probably because she was extremely young when she both wrote and recorded it, and it is not surprising that a teenager would wear her influences proudly, maybe even gauchely. On that album, she sings the jazz standard '(There Is) No Greater Love', which Holiday also recorded in 1947, and listening to the two tracks side-by-side, it is certainly the case that there are very similar inflections. 'I've been told that nobody sings the word "hunger" like I do,' Holiday also wrote. 'Or the word "love".' In this track we get to hear her sing the latter, and we get to hear Winehouse sing it, too. (The word 'hunger' does not, I don't think, appear in any Amy Winehouse song, although the *suggestion* of her hunger is ever-present, as per the impatient and exasperated way she addresses a needy, too-sweet lover she wants solely for his body in 'Stronger Than Me'.) Billie Holiday's 'love' is a trill as crisp as birdsong, lifted by what sounds like an audible smile; for all of Holiday's real-life hardness, this 'love' is sentimental, tender, a romantic's 'love' that contains no hint of irony. Winehouse's is almost exactly the same: a faithful reproduction of a voice that, as Holiday herself says, ought to be irreproducible. What Amy

Winehouse doesn't sound like on her version of '(There Is) No Greater Love' is Amy Winehouse, and so although it is a beautiful performance of the song, it lacks un-plastic soul, or perhaps some other quality that is just as esoteric and impossible to define.

That quality might be 'authenticity', a concept that in music is as fraught as it is worshipped. In 1964, the Supreme Court Justice Potter Stewart defined obscenity by saying, vaguely but truthfully, 'I know it when I see it.' Authenticity reverses the formula, turning it on its head so that we are the ones being seen by the art we are consuming. When a songwriter or performer is authentic, their work seems to reach into us in some significant and profound way, and to reflect something that we recognise as being identifiably 'real'. Our pain does not need to be the same as the singer's pain for us to believe that hers is credible; our love affairs do not need to have been as passionate or doomed for us to feel her heat, her broken heart. At her best, Winehouse has what The Kinks once called 'a dark-brown voice', with a sound like richly dyed, expensive velvet and a raw, feral power – not, in fact, like Holiday's at all, which famously emanated from her sinuses, and which was less about sheer volume than it was about delicate expressiveness: a light melodic touch, and a stretched-elastic cadence. Both women's voices are equally miraculous, but their miraculousness is both separate and distinct. Listen to Winehouse on 'In My Bed', the track that immediately follows '(There Is) No Greater Love' on *Frank*, and it is clear that when she sings her own material, her vocal idiosyncrasies are already in place even before she's left her teens. The song is another irritable lament about male sexual inadequacy; in the music video, which features Winehouse prowling a hotel, her body language and her singing match each other, plush and lewd and lazy. If it feels crass to notice the music implicit in the Marilyn-like sway of her ass, it also cannot be denied that sex, like the blast of a brass band, makes itself heard above all her best performances. Her voice may have been at times transcendent, but her physical form remained earthly, even earthy – an instrument to be played, or played with, rather than a distant object to be worshipped.

Questions about authenticity with regards to Amy Winehouse have become even more relevant of late, since she has been given – or, more accurately, been subjected to – the biopic treatment, in a film by the Brit-Artist-turned-filmmaker Sam Taylor-Johnson entitled *Back to Black*. Released in 2024, over a decade after Winehouse's death, *Back to Black* received largely negative reviews, some of which were genuinely furious at the movie's willingness to launder the reputations of the men in the late singer's life. Ill-advisedly, it elects to recreate the studio scene I described earlier where Amy is recording with Mark Ronson, and that re-creation becomes, in a sense, synecdochic vis-à-vis the movie's failures: its precision, suffocating any chance of movement, illustrates in miniature the problem with the wider text, which is that any copy of a true original is condemned to feel uncanny. Marisa Abela, *Black to Black*'s lead actress, has doubtlessly studied Winehouse with great care, and she replicates the singer's chewy accent and maximal physical tics slavishly, almost eerily, as if the goal were not merely to conjure up her essence, but to commit identity theft. The film is, in a sense, hamstrung by Abela's skill – when she appears in a simulacrum of Winehouse's Grammy performance of 'Rehab' circa 2008, every snarl and every scatting spit is on point, and yet the very thing which made the original version so extraordinary and memorable was its unpredictability. Drugs and drink robbed Winehouse of her spontaneity, and this, more than the loss of control, was what made her late performances so heart-breaking to watch. In better times, her voice would waver and careen, skipping the beats that were familiar from her records to hit new ones. The reason she could play, could perhaps surprise even herself, was that she also knew that, being Amy Winehouse, she could stick the landing.

What is a faithful re-creation of a truly unforced, unpremeditated work of art? It is at best a contradiction, and at worst a failure. Abela's vocals have also been autotuned in certain scenes in *Back to Black*, sounding flat – not in terms of pitch, but in terms of complexity and resonance – and almost coldly metallic. The plot of the film has been subjected to the narrative equivalent of autotune, too, resulting in an arc that is equally lacking in depth, warmth, and realness. The story is essentially the same as in life: Winehouse arrives already writing odd, funny songs that showcase her singular voice; she is co-opted by the industry; she meets, and falls in love with, a dangerous wideboy with a drug habit; she becomes a global phenomenon; her romantic grief as she and this toxic man tear chunks out of each other fuels her music, and it also drives her towards heroin and crack; she dies tragically at twenty-seven. What is missing is any emotional or artistic intensity, so that what we end up seeing feels like a Lifetime movie about junkie love: *Mother, May I Sleep with Wasters?* One way the film does deviate from being merely a bare-bones repetition of the facts is in its bizarre apportioning of blame. 'I'm not a feminist,' Amy grins in its central meet-cute, tongue-in-cheek, 'because I like boys too much.' At times, *Back to Black* seems to admit to the same bias itself, letting both Winehouse's father, Mitch, and her onetime husband, Blake Fielder-Civil, off the hook. In real life, Mitch Winehouse famously suggested that his daughter did not need to go to rehab, and turned up with reality-TV cameras while she was attempting to kick drugs in St Lucia; Fielder-Civil has admitted to being the one to introduce her to both crack and heroin in the first place. 'It's more like [Amy and Blake] are a loved-up Disney princess and her prince,' one of Winehouse's best friends complained to the *Daily Mail* after seeing *Back to Black* – a fitting observation, as much like a Disney princess, this fictional Winehouse cannot seem to get away from little woodland creatures, whether it is the canary in a cage that reoccurs as an obvious and patronising visual motif, or the fox she makes dramatic eye contact with on a damp Camden street.

As far as metaphors go, likening a dead female singer to a songbird in a cage is not especially smart or novel, but then *Back to Black* is not an especially smart or novel film. Just as Taylor-Johnson's adaptation of the bestselling spanked-by-a-billionaire fantasy *Fifty Shades of Grey* continued its fairly vanilla source material's crusade to strip the dangerous heat out of S&M, *Back to Black* robs Winehouse of all interest or complicity in her drug-taking or her self-destructive love affairs, thus denying the thrill implicit in even the scariest forms of masochism. To suggest that Winehouse was in any way empowered by her addiction would be stupid, but to say that taking drugs is never fun or pleasurable would be naive. Heroin, a totally illegal product with no marketing that nevertheless continues to enjoy widespread popularity, sells itself by virtue of the promise that its benefits must logically outweigh the risks – of sickness, death, infirmity, infection, the breakdown of relationships and the loss of employment – that are known to be attendant to it. Like love, it can destroy you from the inside out, but it can also make you feel as if you exist beyond pain, and beyond considerations of 'real life'. The addict's dislocation from the Real in favour of creating a new world of pure sensation is perfectly illustrated by an incident in which, on seeing her husband accidentally cut himself on broken glass, Winehouse slashed a matching wound into her own arm. It was a bid, as she put it at the time, to 'feel everything he felt'. This insane and blinding love, and her belief in the importance of it, made her want to live her life as if the two of them were not just man and wife, but twin souls occupying a single strung-out body. Her interest in hard drugs was just as romantic, then, as it was reckless – one more attempt at crawling inside her beloved, like a needle stealing fluidly into a vein. Contrast this with the version of her that appears in *Back to Black*, babbling about babies and apparently never having heard 'Leader of the Pack' by the Shangri-Las before, in spite of the actual Winehouse's reputation as a woman with a near-encyclopaedic knowledge of the music of the sixties. The scene that depicts Blake Fielder-Civil playing her the song on a jukebox fails to demonstrate that while Amy may have been the sad girl in the song mourning her dead bad-news boyfriend, she was the bad-news boyfriend, too.

Biopics are identikit by nature, which would be less strange if we did not routinely make them about the most unusual people on the planet. The most interesting thing about Taylor-Johnson's movie is this hollow space between the real thing and its reproduction, which only serves to enhance the singularity and specialness of the person being mimicked. It becomes a demonstration of a thing that is almost impossible to demonstrate, and even more difficult to quantify or qualify; there is an absence at its core that serves only to remind us of a former presence, and thus make us feel nostalgic for it. Billie Holiday herself first got the biopic treatment in 1972, and to do her justice it was only logical that they would cast another Black musical icon: not merely *a* singer but one of *the* singers of her era, the luminous Diana Ross. Rather than offering up an impersonation, it is notable that Ross performs in what is more or less her own voice for the film's musical interludes, largely eschewing the idiosyncratic sinus-forward quality of Holiday's in favour of something crisper, brighter – less eccentric, perhaps, but no less immediately recognisable. 'Diana Ross,' boasts the movie's tagline, 'IS Billie Holiday.' In fact, the vocal scenes in *Lady Sings the Blues* only work because if Diana Ross 'IS' anyone when she sings Holiday's music, it is Diana Ross, sparing us the eerie feeling that we are watching an impression – a representation of real life that, by dint of only being a few degrees removed from the real thing, becomes unsettling – in favour of an accurate depiction of watching a Black icon on the stage, even if it happens to be one who is contemporary rather than historical. Ross and Holiday do not look or sound that similar, but each had her own particular charisma, and each proved important in her own distinctive way. Ross joined the Supremes (then called the Primettes) in 1959, the year that Billie Holiday died, and if seeing them sing 'You Can't Hurry Love' on *The Ed Sullivan Show* in 1966 was not quite the same thing as seeing Billie Holiday perform in a New York nightclub in 1939, its impact on the viewer's brain and body would, I think, have been at least a little similar – a rewiring, a sense that something fundamentally new and significant had happened.

There was a before Billie Holiday, and an after Billie Holiday; there was a before Diana Ross, and there is now. All great artists fuck with time by remaking our present and, in doing so, propelling us at breakneck speed into the future. No wonder trying to represent such figures fictionally feels like an unnerving, borderline-catastrophic collapse of several decades into one amorphous blur, transforming what had once appeared to be a vision of tomorrow into something more like synthesised kitsch. If these individuals had been easy to reproduce or to replicate, they would not have enjoyed such era-defining success in the first place, and their respective talents would not have been so frequently mentioned in the same breath as the phrase 'once in a generation'. 'Talent', in fact, feels like a faintly minimising word to describe what marks out a star like Amy Winehouse – or like Billie Holiday, or like Diana Ross. Originally it stemmed from the Ancient Greek word for a form of currency, and thinking of a voice like Winehouse's in such terms is rather sad, even if many of those around her were, in life, more than happy to reduce her to a conduit for cash. Consider instead another Ancient Greek word, 'daimon', translated as 'genius', and its closeness to the English word 'demonic'. There is something devilish and otherworldly about this kind of brilliance, and there is something wicked about the temptations that arise from the possession of such power when it results in renown. 'How big do you think you're going to be?' an interviewer asked Amy Winehouse in 2003. 'I don't [think I'm going to be famous] at all,' she replied, 'because my music's not on that scale . . . I don't think I could handle it. I'd probably go mad.'

Fame, of course, makes everybody mad to some degree – it is designed to work that way. Seeing yourself recorded in the public eye must be a little like being forced to watch your own biopic 24/7, observing yourself being depicted by a you who is not you; your voice being distorted by the deadening chill of autotune, reduced to an impersonation; your movements and your mannerisms being writ larger, somehow stranger, than they feel from the inside. Celebrity reflects you back at yourself from strange angles, like the familiar, stomach-dropping moment when seeing an un-posed photograph makes you wonder what you actually look like, only magnified, the subject being refracted into image after image until nothing else is visible. For Winehouse, many of these photographs were of her in a state of deep intoxication, sometimes bleeding from a fight or crying from a marital disagreement, making their extensive reproduction all the more disturbing, as if we were witnessing her deterioration frame by frame. Her bulimia – a disorder I recognise from experience as one that appeals to the sufferer for its seductive, then destructive, ability to facilitate great personal excess and swift physical diminishment at once – seemed like an entirely understandable response to all of this documentation: the behaviour of a woman who believed that her voice was far readier for the stage than her face and body were for the cameras. For the papers, this willingness to be messy, even frightening to look at, was a worse betrayal for the fact she was a woman, and that women who sold albums and won Grammys were supposed to look attractive rather than like starving, raving junkies, using their addictions to stay skinny or awake but never actually being driven crazy by them. 'The problem for Amy Winehouse was that she was female,' the musician Nick Cave – himself a onetime heroin addict – suggested in 2014, three years after her death. 'The English press couldn't handle her. If she'd been a guy, nothing would have happened. But a woman [who does heroin] gets hunted through the village.'

Amy Winehouse was, I think, angry in the later years of her career, partly because of the fact that she was kept under such close surveillance, and partly because she felt that she was being miscategorised as a mainstream pop star and a messy good-time girl. It was possible to see her harden over time, becoming cynical and self-destructive. She was no longer the life and soul of the party, and because her livelihood had hitherto relied on the grandeur of her soul, her work began to sicken and to suffer. In a 2008 video that has since seemingly been scrubbed from the internet, an intoxicated Winehouse snarls 'fuck *her*' when she is asked about Billie Holiday on the red carpet – a reaction that seems inexplicable until one considers the unpleasant, sneering subtext of that earlier *Pitchfork* piece, to say nothing of what she might have perceived as an unpleasant, sneering subtext to the comparisons being made between herself and Holiday in general. Both women were remarkable vocalists, yes, but both women were also junkies, and the fact that Holiday died at forty-four made the line that journalists were drawing between them feel every bit as morbid as it did laudatory. 'The worms of every kind of excess,' *The New York Times* journalist Gilbert Millstein wrote two years after Holiday's death, in 1961, 'had eaten her.' It was obviously at the forefront of the media's collective mind in 2008 that the worms of excess might devour Winehouse, and however blasé she was being, she might have imagined herself being devoured in this way, too. Distancing herself from Holiday was a way of distancing herself from what increasingly seemed inescapable, even if this move was only temporary, only superficial. It was a dismissal that was born of recognition, and seeing Holiday snuffed out by her addictions must have made it obvious to Winehouse that even talent in great quantities was not enough to counteract the mean black magic of the dope. The one thing that keeps you from wanting to die is so often the same thing that knocks you dead; the medicine that stops the hurt finally stops the heart, instead. 'All dope can do is kill you,' as Holiday wrote. 'Kill you the long, slow way.'

First, though, the dope takes liberties. In June of 2011, a month before she died, Winehouse played a concert in Belgrade that quickly became the last word in the story of her deterioration, as an artist and a woman. She had been unconscious in London when her team had bundled her onto the plane, waking up abroad and discovering that, in spite of her earlier protestations to the contrary, she was expected to perform. In a sense, this was what had happened to her generally when she'd first signed a contract, then released an album – her ascent to global fame, unexpected because who could have expected a working-class London jazz singer to end up being one of the most famous artists in the world, seemed to happen so swiftly and inexorably that it was as if she had in some way slept through that bewildering ascent into the heavens, too. Was it any wonder that heroin – a ravishing downer of a drug, as lush and dark brown as her voice – was so appealing, given its ability to lull the user back into a dream world that was soft at the edges, half like death and just as mercifully quiet? Down came the jet of Amy's consciousness, and down came her once-soaring voice, and it did not seem to matter much to her in that particular moment whether it all burned. As the crowd jeered, you could see a kind of reckless and unhappy wickedness begin to spread across her face, as if she'd realised that refusal was the one thing she had left. *No, no, no. I said no, no, no.* Without her gift, what was there left to lose? When she did sing in Belgrade, what you heard of her voice above the din careened away from the beat in a different and more frightening way than it had before, the looseness of it no longer suggesting her great confidence and skill but instead revealing her exhaustion. She had finally kicked the dope, but it had already taken the aforementioned liberties, and drink was doing the rest. At last it was time for the long, slow way to do its work, and from the outside it did not look slow at all.

II. AND ALWAYS, IN THE DEEPEST SENSE, A LADY

I said that I imagined hearing Billie Holiday sing for the first time might have prompted 'an undoing, a rewiring, a sense that something fundamentally new and significant had happened' in the listener. Here is proof: in the early thirties, Benny Carter, the iconic bandleader and saxophonist, saw Holiday perform at a small club in Harlem, and the way he described it suggested a profound spiritual change. 'I don't know that I ever heard anything prior to hearing her sing for the first time,' he said. 'Or indeed since.' Because this is reported speech, it is possible that there is an implied or omitted 'like that' or 'like her' in Carter's statement, and that what he was describing was the singularity of her sound – its euphonious, bewitching strangeness. This is plausible enough, and it is certainly high praise. It is more interesting, though, to take him at his word, and to believe that he is saying that the beauty of her adenoidal warble left him deaf to everything but her. We here in the present day can hear exactly how she sounded then, as well as seeing how she looked, by watching her brief appearance in the 1935 short *Symphony in Black: A Rhapsody of Negro Life*, made as a showcase for Duke Ellington, but featuring Holiday as a heartbroken woman who is unlucky in love. First glimpsed in profile, what is striking about her is that even though she is barely five foot five, she looks imposing, almost statuesque: she has a terrific face, with a high forehead and smooth, vaulting cheekbones that make her resemble, from the side, an antiquarian bust. Her voice is just as instantly memorable and lovely; just as obviously hers. 'A large, fleshy, but beautiful-boned woman,' her great friend the trumpeter Max Kaminsky called her, lovingly. 'And always, in the deepest sense, a lady.'

By 1937, everyone had begun to call her Lady Day, a nickname that was half mocking, half sincere. It was above all else a tribute to her manner, which was always cool and poised, always suggestive of the dignity that she would not relinquish under any circumstances, even when she was heartbroken or high, or being punished for the fact of having committed a triple sin at birth: being poor, being Black, and being a woman. When one night before a show she burned her hair with a too-hot curling iron, she grabbed a white gardenia and covered up the ruined spot in such a way that it looked like a deliberate affectation. From that moment on, gardenias – previously seen as an old-fashioned flower for a rich man's boutonnière – became newly fashionable, newly sexy. This transmutation of a bit of bad luck into something beautiful and stylish was a perfect example of how brilliant Holiday, née Eleanora Fagan, was at finessing her persona, and at disguising her damage with glamour. (In 1949, under arrest for heroin possession, she famously swept into the police station wearing big movie-star shades, and what a contemporary newspaper described as 'high heels', a 'perky hat', and 'a black dress underneath a $7,000 mink coat'.) To say that she was a lady, though, was not to say that she was always lady*like*. Her hauteur and regal bearing were accompanied, in a blend whose contradictoriness served only to underscore her total singularity, by a feral sexiness: an appetite for fucking that her peers and lovers – just as Winehouse's peers and lovers would regarding her appetite numerous decades later – likened to that of a man.

'Her nickname among the men,' a former roommate says, 'was Mister Billie Holiday.' 'She was a sex machine,' adds an ex. 'She was like a man,' her bandmate Harry 'Sweets' Edison once claimed, 'only she was feminine.' To be like a man only feminine, in this context, meant being beautiful but also having swagger; it meant having poise, but also being something of a merciless erotic tyrant. 'If you're looking at Lady Day you've gotta think about her sex life,' the pianist Jimmy Rowles once observed, 'or you're not looking at her.' The first time Rowles had seen her in the flesh, it had been when he was twenty, and the 'flesh' part had been literal: she was standing in her dressing room, fully naked other than her heels, imperiously commanding him to write down some piano chords that had suddenly burst into her head. She referred to sex itself, airily, as 'a little light housekeeping', a delicious shrug of a phrase that illustrated perfectly how casual she was about it. 'She sang from her crotch,' Rowles said, suggesting that sex had 'an awful lot to do with the way she was and everything she did'. This revelation, as well as those of her former roommate and 'Sweets' Edison, comes from a 2019 documentary called *Billie*, which is based around a series of audio interviews conducted in the seventies by a journalist named Linda Lipnack Kuehl. As with *Amy* versus *Back to Black*, *Billie* offers a less sentimental view of its subject's life than the Diana-Ross-starring *Lady Sings the Blues*, whose tone is elegiac – light on sensuality, heavy on tears.

'[In the media] she's been cast as a kind of saint,' the biographer John Szwed observed of Holiday, in an interview with *TIME* in 2015, 'but she never put herself in that role. She both mythified herself, if that's a word, and had to deal with the [myth] that was put around her.' Szwed is presumably thinking of the word 'mythologised', although it hardly matters – he has neatly summarised the tension at the heart of being famous, which is that the celebrity in question will inevitably end up being streamlined into a simpler, broader cartoon of themselves in the press, and that it is up to them whether they play up to this crude outline, or resist it. This easily categorised version of the star is, very often, the one that ends up being the centre of one of those melodramatic biopics later on. Occasionally, a film about an icon comes along that deviates a little from the form. *The United States vs. Billie Holiday*, a 2021 film by Lee Daniels, begins with a title card that refers to the decision, by the US senate, not to criminalise lynching in 1937; underneath that title card is a real photograph of the body of a lynching victim, flanked by a crowd of white, smiling men. Immediately, it announces its intention to present Holiday not merely as an entertainer, but as a historical figure, and as a victim of relentless, white-supremacist state surveillance. If the film still sometimes lapses into music biopic cliché – opening, for instance, with the framing device of a late-career interview in order to facilitate a flashback – it is also refreshingly frank in its depiction of American law enforcement as a deeply flawed institution of which Black Americans were (and are) right to be suspicious. It, too, turns its subject into a symbol, but it dodges some of the typical failures of the genre by making that symbol a political one, rather than one that is only sexual, or romantic, or starry.

The United States vs. Billie Holiday is also well served by its star, the singer and actress Andra Day, who skilfully conjures Holiday's warm rasp, and her habit of turning her face towards the heavens, or the stage lights, when she sings; she has the stern jaw, the resilient grace, and the air that Holiday's friend Sylvia Syms once described, when attempting to pin down the appeal of the woman herself, as 'pantherlike'. Her singing scenes, unsurprisingly, still stop short of capturing Holiday's transcendence – as ever, imitation cannot equal an original work of art. Where Marisa Abela's attempts at recreating familiar Winehouse performances were hindered in part by contemporary audiences' familiarity with the real thing, however, there is far less footage of Holiday to draw on, leaving space for Day to exercise a little more spontaneity. Her status as a real jazz singer, as opposed to being an actress who has trained for the part, is evident onscreen. In 2015, in a review of her first album, an NPR critic described Day as having 'Amy Winehouse's effortless grasp of classic jazz' and 'Billie Holiday's access to raw emotion'. She has sometimes been called 'the Black Amy Winehouse', a comparison she professes to enjoy because '[Amy Winehouse] loved jazz music', and she once performed a cover of one of Winehouse's songs, 'He Can Only Hold Her', in a mash-up with Lauryn Hill's 'Doo Wop (That Thing)'. As for Holiday herself, Day has described her as one of her earliest musical influences, having begun to listen to her music at the age of twelve. If the comparisons drawn between Day and her forebears in the piece for NPR are hyperbolic, à la most music PR, there is also something touching about the implication of a trickling down of voices – woman (or, perhaps, diva) to girl – through the decades, with each new incarnation of the sound both reshaping itself for the present, and containing within it a reminder of the past: a vintage-styled matryoshka doll of multi-generational, multi-racial feminine experience.

'Winehouse may seem like such a dedicated tearaway because the lens recording her movements is wider than anything a sixties celebrity would have encountered, doesn't switch off, and continually feeds a twenty-four-hour newsstand,' the music critic Sasha Frere-Jones wrote, in a piece for *The New Yorker* in 2007 – wider, too, in media terms, than Holiday would have encountered during her career, and yet for her there were far larger forces than the media to contend with. Aside from the papers, who did cover her drug use with prurient interest, Holiday was being trailed by the Federal Bureau of Narcotics, who tricked her again and again in order to repeatedly arrest her for possession. This is the particular period covered by *The United States vs. Billie Holiday*, as its title suggests, and while the film does deviate from the truth for the sake of the plot in some aspects, many of the facts it contains are startling enough that they need no further embellishment to shock and, in the perverse fashion of a more traditional biopic, 'entertain'. If a white girl doing heroin is 'hunted through the village', as Nick Cave said of Amy Winehouse, a Black one is more likely to be chased all the way into a prison, or some other institution. In 1947, Holiday was jailed for a year; she later said that she did not sing a note through her entire incarceration, as if she were punishing the world right back. On her release, she was prevented for some time from renewing the cabaret card that allowed her to legally perform in a club. In 1949, she was arrested again, albeit without successfully being charged, in a bust coordinated by her second husband John Levy. In 1959, she was hospitalised with cirrhosis of the liver. 'Some damnbody is always trying to embalm me,' she reportedly said as she lay there, lighting cigarette after cigarette. 'They are going to arrest me in this damn bed.' Her prediction was correct: bone-thin, marked with ulcers from her drug habit, and having trouble with her heart, she was placed under arrest there a month before her death, with guards stationed outside her room. She was taken suddenly off methadone at the request of Harry Anslinger, the FBN Commissioner, and the loss made swift work of her fragile body. She died handcuffed to the bed.

A minor but telling detail in *Billie* emerges as interviewees disagree with each other as to why Holiday departed Count Basie's band around 1938. John Hammond, the historically significant critic, talent scout and producer who 'discovered' her in 1933, tells Kuehl that she simply left because she wanted more money. The drummer Philly Joe Jones maintains, on the other hand, that Holiday resented the idea of being classified as a blues singer, and that Hammond fired her as a result. As when Winehouse refused to be cast as a pop star, having integrity was recategorised as 'being difficult'. Based on every detail that we know about her personal and professional life, it would have been understandable enough if she had only ever sung the blues. In *Billie*, as in Daniels' fictionalised account of her dealings with the law, the indignities rack up. We learn that at a show in Kentucky, the town's sheriff demanded to know when 'that Black bitch' was going to sing; that, routinely, segregated hotels would require her to sleep in a car parked outside when the band went on tour; that she got into the habit of ordering two hamburgers at once at every diner on the road, shoving one into her purse in case the next place she stopped refused her service. If her white listeners knew about these strictures and humiliations, many of them, given the prevailing attitudes of the time, might have seen them as a normal part of the Black American experience. (In the forties, public opinion polls still suggested that, for instance, two in three white Americans wholeheartedly supported the segregation of schools.) Perhaps they were capable of separating Holiday's voice from the reality of her three-dimensional Black self to some degree, like a version of the eerie disconnection of sound and body that occurs when a performer mimes to a tape – or, perhaps, when an actor mouths along to a recording in a biopic. In any case, both her ghost-written memoir and her final album were called *Lady Sings the Blues*, as if she were at last giving the people what they wanted: an admission of how hard it had all been. How could Billie Holiday, who had suffered so completely for her art, ever have rejected the blues?

The answer is that she did not, exactly; she embraced them carefully and discriminately, wanting to decide for herself what she had the blues about. What Holiday needed her white audience to understand, her selectiveness implied, was that there was nothing inherently sad about being Black – that what was sad about her experience of it sprang only from the way that the white world reacted to her Blackness. Jones tells Kuehl on tape that Hammond, a white man, wanted Holiday to stick to the blues because 'he wanted her to be a coloured mammy! . . . He wanted her to just be "Yassir, boss!"' This was not, needless to say, a role that Billie Holiday would ever have agreed to play. Many of the blues songs that we do associate with her are about failed love affairs, but there is no track more heartbreaking or personal in her repertoire than 1939's 'Strange Fruit', a protest poem by the Communist writer Abel Meeropol set to music. Its lyrics, which describe a lynching, are explicit to the point of being nauseating: 'The bulging eyes and the twisted mouth ... here is a fruit for the crows to pluck.' Holiday's repeated performance of the song was controversial; Columbia refused to allow her to record it, giving her a one-track pass from her exclusivity contract so that she could cut the track with Vocalion Records. She first performed it in 1939 at the Café Society, New York's first integrated nightclub, and from then on, every time she sang it, the house lights were cut and a spotlight was focused on her face, as if she meant to say: you are about to *really hear* something for the very first time. 'The things that I sing,' she once said, 'have to have something to do with me, and with my life.'

'The only words she could speak,' the jazz guitarist Al Avola observed, echoing this sentiment, 'were those in the song.' What he meant was not that Holiday could not, or would not, speak for herself about racial injustice in America, but that the power of 'Strange Fruit' was enough to get the message across by itself. *The United States vs. Billie Holiday* positions her performances of 'Strange Fruit' as the catalyst for the government's obsession with bringing her to heel, and such reasoning makes perfect, awful sense. Eventually, her recording of it sold a million copies; 'if the anger of the exploited ever mounts high enough in the South,' a journalist wrote in the *New York Post* in 1939, 'it now has its Marseillaise.' If it made certain audiences – certain white audiences – furious, it also connected with people, Black and white, who were sane enough to recognise that what was happening to Black Americans was madness, sickness, cruelty without meaning or purpose. The screenplay for Daniels' film, which was written by the

Pulitzer-Prize-winning playwright Suzan-Lori Parks, sometimes lapses into simplified statements about racial injustice and misogyny, and one presumes that this is because Parks is writing for a generalised, commercial and partially white audience. One of these simple statements, however, sums up with a pleasing clarity the reason why the government hated 'Strange Fruit', and it also makes it easier than ever to understand why a thing as beautiful as Billie Holiday's voice might have been treated like a weapon of mass destruction: 'It reminds them that they're killing us,' Day's Holiday says matter-of-factly, her eyes glittering with defiance.

'A little tune written especially for me,' Holiday calls 'Strange Fruit', in a clip that was recorded the year that she died. While the truth of this statement has long been contested, it makes perfect conceptual sense: no other singer is as inextricably linked with the song, and her decision to refer to it as 'a little tune' is a cool bit of mockery that only serves to enhance the sudden wham of its gory opening lines about bloodied roots, and bodies hanging limply from the trees. She looks thin, a little older than her years, but there is nothing diminished in the glorious foghorn blast of her voice. She is not singing from her crotch, but from the pit of her stomach, and on certain words – 'drop', for instance, near the end of the third verse – she almost wails. I wondered at first whether this televised recording might be recreated for *The United States vs. Billie Holiday*, but instead, Daniels chooses to depict the younger Holiday performing 'Strange Fruit' in the context of a nightclub. Most of the action is presented in a medium shot, a smart decision when it comes to evoking

Holiday's isolation on the stage: a tight close-up would be wrenching, overwhelming, and would place us almost literally in Holiday's head, running the risk of feeling like a bit of mawkish directorial manipulation.

Because the scene is not a one-to-one re-creation of real footage, as ever in Daniels' film, we are not required to compare Day and Holiday one-to-one as far as skill or passion is concerned; nobody will ever sing 'Strange Fruit' like Billie Holiday, either way. It is bizarre, to my mind, when a white singer even makes the attempt, and I have to admit to being relieved to discover that there is no evidence of Amy Winehouse ever having done so. As Day herself once said: *Amy Winehouse loved jazz music*, and that love would, I think, have prevented her from trying to inhabit a song she could not feel in her bones. Holiday and Winehouse had so many things in common, and when they sang about love and sex, they might as well have been spiritual twins. Both of them knew what it was like to be watched far too closely, and what it was like to be set up for a fall, and yet still there remains this one undeniable difference between their respective experiences of life, and accordingly of fame. In *The United States vs. Billie Holiday*, when an interviewer asks Holiday what it's like to be a 'coloured woman', she fires back that he would never say the same thing to Doris Day. 'Well, Doris Day's not coloured, silly!' he replies offhandedly. It is a grim exchange, and both of them are right.

III. ALL OF THE BEAUTY AND ALL OF THE MISERY

In 2013, the American author Sam Wasson published a biography of the choreographer and film director Bob Fosse. In it, he described the vocal stylings of a young Liza Minnelli, pre-*Cabaret*, in vivid, visceral language. 'Liza had a big voice,' he wrote, 'one that conveyed the punishing truth about making entertainment: It was mean. It was messy. It was a C-section and she was both mother and baby.' Wasson's use of a caesarean rather than a 'natural' birth for his metaphor is notable, suggesting as it does an additional level of violent intervention – a requirement that the mother be cut open, her insides exposed. The idea of Minnelli being both mother and child, too, is fraught in a fascinating way: does Wasson mean that the *voice* is the infant, being painfully yanked from the body, or is the mysterious thing being extracted a facet of the *self*, brought into the world through the scarifying ritual of performance? (Minnelli, in real life, was genuinely the baby of a suffering mother-genius, and her own struggles were her birthright – the inheritance of being a woman in entertainment, yes, but also the inheritance of being the very famous, very drug-addicted Judy Garland's* daughter.) Either way, it is a gorgeous observation for the way

---

* The Federal Bureau of Narcotics' Harry Anslinger was just as aware of Judy Garland's problems with drugs in the fifties as he was of Billie Holiday's, but chose to characterise Garland as 'a fine woman caught in a situation that could only destroy her'. One has to assume that the modifier 'white', although missing from this sentence, is implied.

that it gets at what is surely the confounding, bloody terror of possessing, and expressing, true artistic genius, which can rarely be extracted cleanly, and without some damage to the host.

In its closing scenes, *Back to Black* implies that the impetus for Amy Winehouse's fatal return to drink had nothing to do with the punishing figurative birth of producing her art, and everything to do with her discovery that her ex-husband's new wife was pregnant. In fact, the music journalist Laura Snapes pointed out in the *Guardian* around the time of the film's release, in a furious piece about *Back to Black*'s oddly sexist obsession with Winehouse's thwarted motherhood, a single statement that she made to *Rolling Stone* in 2007 about wanting to be a wife and mother is 'the sum total of those desires [available to us] in her own words'. What really happened the night before her death has been reported by her former bodyguard, Andrew Morris, who describes sitting with her watching, by her own request, footage of her old performances on YouTube: 'She said, "Boy, I can sing",' he told the *Mirror* in 2021, 'and I said, "Damn right, you can sing".' Morris' account is echoed by a similar comment made by Winehouse's father in an interview with Fox News in 2023. 'I remember a year before she passed away,' he claimed, 'we were looking at one of her early shows together. She said to me, "I was good, wasn't I, Dad?" I said, "You're still good."' The similarity between these two stories is striking, and if both of these exchanges did take place in exactly this way, it suggests that this visitation of past performances was a habit or a ritual for Winehouse, proving just how much she cared about her work. It also calls to mind what Benny Carter said about first hearing Billie Holiday's voice – the way it made him feel as though he had never heard another sound before or since. It is as if Winehouse, near the end of her career, was continually encountering her own work for the first time, and then being bowled over by it. Perhaps this is another way in which expressing an innate skill like this is like producing a child from your body: that the thing which emerges can feel new every time.

When I described *Back to Black*'s re-creation of that scene in the recording booth as precise, this was mostly accurate: the clothes, the pose, the vocal beats *et cetera* are all the same. One difference, though, is that the film has her cry while she is singing, and that rather than making an offhand comment once she's done, she wails about Blake. 'He's killed me,' she sobs. Aside from the fact that Taylor-Johnson's film does not seem to agree with this assessment, it's an odd alteration. It makes this demonstration of her art about him, and not her, and it suggests that there would be no art in the first place if it weren't for her heartbreak, as if she would not have been able to write or perform so brilliantly if she had not met – let us be honest with each other for a moment – this apparently unremarkable man. Yes, *Back to Black* was an album figuratively written in the blood she had spilt in those fights with her ex-husband, but she was above all else a woman of intensity and of great, blustering strength, and she would have found a way to make it flow whatever happened. It was always near the surface of her skin. She was a dedicated, fatalistic lover, but she was a musician first.

What the original footage shows is not merely a woman in deep mourning for a failed relationship, but a woman so enmeshed with her art that it is only after she's created it that she is able to observe to herself, *boy, can I sing.* The instant where she seems to break a trance, re-entering the room as if by force or surprise, is the cathecting moment in the clip, demonstrating as it does that talent, a thing half demonic and half holy, is a force far greater than the individual who possesses it, for good as well as ill. It is a birth, and it is also an exorcism; perhaps even a miracle if you squint.

Part of what makes the footage fascinating is its relative air of privacy and calm, a world away from the footage of her large-scale misfires on stage later on in her career. This performance, originally recorded for posterity rather than for inclusion in a documentary, is not about Winehouse's relationship with her audience, but about her relationship with her instrument, which is to say herself. Its Hollywood reproduction, made with the multiplex in mind, could not possibly fake something this real. 'The essential dilemma' of the biopic, the critic Lidija Haas wrote in *The New Republic* in 2021, reviewing both *Billie* and *The United States vs. Billie Holiday*, 'is how to milk the life for drama while also accommodating what was singular enough to merit biopic treatment in the first place: the work.' As a biopic, *Back to Black* focuses on the familiar experience of doomed love, but it seems frightened of addressing actual mortality, and it bows out several months before the real end of the story, shunting Winehouse's death to a stark intertitle card. Even the blood-spatters on her ballet pumps, an image as synonymous with her final years as any, are excised. To be scared of death and blood is to be scared of life, and of its mad, scatting pulse, and flattening Winehouse's tale into an agreeable romantic melodrama also flattens – civilises, one might say – her appeal. We are talking, after all, about a woman whose 2007 music video for 'Back to Black' shows her heading up a funeral procession to a gravestone that reads, with wonderfully gothic hysteria, 'THE HEART OF AMY WINEHOUSE'. In conflating her with a fox or a canary, as Taylor-Johnson does with all that thunderously obvious symbolism, the film tries extremely hard to convince us of her wildness, but Winehouse was not wild like an animal, exactly. She was wild like an artist, and watching Abela nail her mannerisms and yet somehow not quite reach her heights, you're reminded of her just enough to remember how *big* she was – the way she lit your screen up just by shooting off that huge, luscious mouth.

Given that stardom is so often seen as a blessing, the decision of some stars to waste themselves remains a source of fascination for both fans and detractors. Now and then, even other famous people voice their curiosity about what it is, exactly, that can drive their peers to self-destruction. The jazz and soul vocalist Tony Bennett makes an appearance, either in person or being interviewed on tape, in both *Billie* and *Amy*, and because the events of both documentaries stretch across generations, he is introduced in two very different roles – as a boy-fan of Holiday's, and as a mentor and hero for Winehouse. In *Amy*, he is shown coaxing the latter through a duet of 'Body and Soul'; although her nerves get the better of her at first, soon his gentle encouragement helps her find her voice. (Incidentally, according to Holiday, 'Body and Soul' was one of the first songs she ever sang in front of an audience, and its lyrics are about self-immolating sacrifice in the name of desire: 'My life, a wreck you're making.') 'If [Amy] had lived [past twenty-seven],' Bennett went on to tell *Entertainment Weekly* in 2011, 'she would've been right up there with Billie Holiday and Dinah Washington. It's just a tragedy.' Notice that although he says her death was a 'tragedy', he does not suggest that it came as a surprise. 'I want to know why all girl singers crack up,' he tells Kuehl in *Billie*, on a 1973 recording. 'When they hit the top, something tragic happens. I want to know what causes that.' Obviously, it is not only 'girl singers' who crack up, and in fact there are far more examples of male idols whose reckless behaviour has both killed them and canonised them in a single swoop, although as previously discussed, they do not tend to be met with quite the same level of judgement for their actions. In the shock expressed when a famous and prodigiously talented woman who is also an addict dies too young, there is a vague implication, perhaps, that she ought to have been more grateful not only for her fame, but for having been legitimately recognised as a great artist – that, accordingly, she should have treated her gift with more respect.

'Billie Holiday sang only truth,' Sylvia Syms says in *Billie*. 'She knew nothing false. I saw the whole world in that face. All of the beauty, and all of the misery.' Of these two things, the misery was sometimes the most arresting, as when she sang 'Strange Fruit' with such aching torment and at such great personal risk, but it also sometimes implicated the listener in her pain – so, too, with Amy Winehouse singing 'Rehab', drily insisting that she did not need our help even when she could barely stand on the stage. *My life, a wreck you're making.* That our need to see such complicated artists perform might be compounding their hurt, keeping them as it does in the eye of a swirling media storm, is a bitter pill to swallow, and its bitterness might explain why general audiences tend to prefer their music biopics sanitised and sweeping, rendering all that beauty and misery only in the broadest, most conventional strokes. When a woman who is famous, and especially a woman who is famous for excess, dies, the biopic's tendency to reimagine her as an archetype often becomes a tendency to reimagine her more specifically as a secular saint – to 'mythify' her, as Szwed put it, so that the version of her we see onscreen finds its equivalence in, say, someone standing in for Mary Magdalene in a Passion Play. What in life the media might have treated as grotesque or inexcusable – Winehouse and Holiday's respective, genuine love of drugs, for instance, or of great sex; of crass humour and loud laughter; of hard liquor; of being, sometimes, maddeningly impulsive – is in fiction neutered and made poignant by the addict-genius' slow and accidental martyrdom, whether by drink or heroin or, in Holiday's case, both these things plus institutionalisation. Abela, Ross and Day, all undeniably beautiful women, still look undeniably beautiful while suffering in their movies, and all three biopics' final scenes are sad, but also curiously rapturous: Abela, as Winehouse, padding phantom-like through her North London home and singing to herself, either going mad or transported to some elysian place in her head; Ross on-stage, as Holiday, clinquant and beaming in a long white gown, even as the headline BILLIE HOLIDAY DEAD AT 44 goes floating by; Day, as Holiday again, dying in hospital but doing it bravely, *politically*, as if she did so for our white supremacist sins.

It is often suggested that figures like Holiday and Winehouse simply have some inborn inclination towards chaos: that a 'girl singer' who can sing so convincingly about bad romance and danger, sex and junk, being hit and being an adulteress, must always have been rushing headlong towards 'something tragic'. This is certainly part of the story, and that rush may have something to do with both women's conviction that experiencing everything gave them permission to express it all with total clarity, transmogrifying the good and the bad into something audibly honest – Holiday herself, for instance, claimed that the best jazz singers are characterised by the desire to 'try to live a hundred days in [every] day'. (A relief, in a sense, to think of both hers and Winehouse's too-short lives at least feeling longer from within than they looked from the outside.) Two things can be true simultaneously: that Holiday and Winehouse were both larger-than-life consumers of everything pleasurable and decadent and hot – and, often, dangerous – and that the exposing fishbowl of fame helped to hasten their races to oblivion. Frankly, it is fun to get fucked-up, and it is also sometimes perverse fun to be fucked by a person whom you know will break your heart, and it seems likely that Holiday and Winehouse needed or deserved all that fun to counteract the seriousness of their work, and of their lives as public figures. 'There's no damn business like show business,' Holiday once famously said. 'You have to laugh to keep from throwing up.' If now and then you had to shoot up to keep from throwing up, too, well, that was that. In that piece in the *Mirror*, Winehouse's security guard mentions another thing she said to him the night before she died, just after being newly stunned by the sound of her own voice. 'If I could give it back just to walk down the street with no hassle, I would.' One has to assume that when she said 'it' she did not mean her ability to sing, or her unpredictable artistic streak, but all the hoopla that came with it: the money and the fame and the Grammys and the crowds.

Two months before she died, Holiday gave an interview to a journalist named Mary Sampras, in which she revealed that her doctor had begged her to stop singing. 'He thinks I'm too ill,' she added, with what Sampras characterises as a 'brief, impervious laugh'. 'But what else am I made for?' Sampras did not answer, since the question was so obviously rhetorical. 'So long as I have breath to sing, and someone still to listen . . .' Holiday concluded, trailing off because the end of this thought was obvious, too. Needing somebody to listen was the hard part – harder even, arguably, than needing somebody to love. Such a talent could not thrive in a vacuum. At the beginning of *Amy*, there is a home video of a teenage Amy Winehouse at a friend's birthday party, showing her and a small group of other girls singing 'Happy Birthday'; one by one, as they notice the unusual power of Amy's voice, they fall silent and permit her to take centre stage. 'The whole joint quietened down,' Billie Holiday says in *Lady Sings the Blues*, describing the first time she sang in a nightclub at fifteen. 'If somebody had dropped a pin, it would have sounded like a bomb.' Here, in front of those first audiences, was where the trouble started, and yet what else were they made for? There would always be in both of them that holy demon, genius, demanding to be heard, and this negotiation with the work would eventually prove itself to be the most important relationship of their respective lives – perhaps even the most romantic, in the gravest, saddest, best and most ridiculous sense of that worn-out word.

Acknowledgements

Sincere thanks to my mother, who passed away while I was in the final stages of finessing this book – you remain the best film critic I have ever met in my life, in spite of your never having committed a word of it to the page. Thanks, also, to my father, who is endlessly supportive in spite of not really knowing what the hell I'm writing about most of the time. Thank you to my editor, Anna, who saw the potential in this project, and to my agent, Imogen, who is skilled at doing so many of the practical things I'm hopeless at when it comes to shepherding a book into the world. Thank you to everyone else at Virago who worked so diligently on this project, and to all of the editors elsewhere who have ever allowed me to write seriously – and if I'm completely honest, often quite eccentrically – about famous women. Thank you to the writers who blurbed me. Thank you to my wonderful, clever, sometimes maddening partner, Thogdin, and to God's most perfect creation, our cat Dora. Thank you to my pseudo-sisters, Chloe, Erin and Stephanie, and to the glorious Amy for talking me out of many black moods. Thank you to every other wonderful person in my life who has encouraged me, cheered me up and supported me through grief. And finally, thank you, whoever you are, if you've read this all the way to the end despite not being a friend of mine or a member of my immediate family. Believe me, I appreciate it.

Credits

p.ix 'I used to ...' *L.A. Woman*, Eve Babitz, 1982, Canongate

p.30 'You could have ...' *Don't Bother to Knock*, dir. Roy Ward Baker, 1952 (Screenplay: Daniel Taradash)

p.48 'Hit me, baby ...' '... Baby One More Time', Max Martin, 1998, Jive Records

p.54 'notice me ... ' 'Everytime', Britney Spears and Annet Artani, 2003, Jive Records

p.68 'succeed ...' 'Try Again', Timothy Mosley and Stephen Garrett, 2000, Virgin

p.78 'I'm Miss American ...' 'Piece of Me', Christian Karlsson, Pontus Winnberg and Klas Åhlund, 2007, Jive Records

p.250 'regret ...' 'Back to Black', Amy Winehouse and Mark Ronson, 2006, Island Records

p.269 'No, no, no ...' 'Rehab', Amy Winehouse, 2006, Island Records

p.277-8 'The bulging eyes ...' 'Strange Fruit', Abel Meeropol (as Lewis Allan), 1937

p.286 'My life, a ...' 'Body and Soul', Edward Heyman, Frank Eyton, Johnny Green and Robert Sour, 1930